For the Soul of France

FOR THE
SOUL
OF
FRANCE

Culture Wars in the Age of Dreyfus

F R E D E R I C K   B R O W N

ALFRED A. KNOPF
NEW YORK
2010

THIS IS A BORZOI BOOK
PUBLISHED BY ALFRED A. KNOPF

Copyright © 2010 by Frederick Brown

Portions of this work originally appeared in slightly different
form in *The Hudson Review* and *The New England Review*.
Chapter 7 is adapted from a chapter of *Zola: A Life* by
Frederick Brown (New York: Farrar, Straus & Giroux, 1995).

Library of Congress Cataloging-in-Publication Data
Brown, Frederick, [date]
For the soul of France : culture wars in the age of Dreyfus / by
Frederick Brown.—1st ed.
p.   cm.
Includes bibliographical references and index.
ISBN 978-0-307-26631-6 (alk. paper)
1. France—History—Third Republic, 1870–1940.
2. France—Civilization—19th century.
3. Nationalism—France—History—19th century.
4. Secularism—France—History—19th century.   5. Church
and state—France—History—19th century.   6. National
characteristics, French.   I. Title.
DC337.B68   2010
944.081—dc22   2009030912

Manufactured in the United States of America
First Edition

For Ruth, Aggie, Peter, and Chris

Contents

ILLUSTRATIONS

Chronology

1848

· FEBRUARY: Paris revolts against the constitutional monarchy established after the Revolution of 1830. King Louis-Philippe flees and the Second Republic is proclaimed.

· JUNE: In a second uprising, the Parisian populace, goaded by economic hardship, threatens the republican government and is crushed.

· DECEMBER: Louis-Napoléon, Napoléon Bonaparte's nephew, captures 75 percent of the vote in an election for the presidency.

1851

· DECEMBER: Louis-Napoléon carries out a coup d'état. One year later, he will emerge from a plebiscite as Napoléon III and establish the Second Empire.

1853–1856

· The Crimean War, fought between Imperial Russia on one side and an alliance of France, the United Kingdom, Sardinia, and the Ottoman Empire on the other.

1857

· Lieutenant Georges Boulanger, in North Africa, fights in his first campaign, against Kabyles.

1859

· APRIL: France, in alliance with Piedmont-Sardinia, declares war against Austria. Two major battles take place in Northern Italy, at Magenta and Solferino. Lieutenant Boulanger serves under General MacMahon. Fighting on another front is Gustave Eiffel's father.

1863

· Michel Lévy publishes Ernest Renan's *Vie de Jésus,* stirring enormous controversy. It will be one of the two or three best-selling books published in France in the nineteenth century.

· Georges Boulanger serves with the French colonial army in Southeast Asia.

1864

· Pius IX issues the encyclical *Quanta Cura,* containing *The Syllabus of Errors.*

1867

· APRIL: The Exposition Universelle opens.

1869

· A Vatican Council is convoked to condemn "modern errors deriving from rationalism." It affirms the doctrine of papal infallibility. It concluded in October 1870.

1870

· JULY: France declares war against Prussia and her German allies.

· SEPTEMBER 1: Defeated at the battle of Sedan, Napoléon III abdicates. Three days later, on September 4, the Empire gives way to a Government of National Defense, whose animating spirit is Léon Gambetta.

· SEPTEMBER 19: The German Army besieges Paris.

1871
· JANUARY: An armistice is declared; the siege is lifted.

· FEBRUARY: Nationwide elections of a National Assembly are held, to form a government with which Germany can treat.

· MARCH: The government moves from Bordeaux to Versailles, but is not recognized by Paris, where National Guard regiments proclaim a Commune and organize elections. (Paris is again besieged, this time by a French army.)

· MAY: France cedes Alsace and part of Lorraine to Germany in the Treaty of Frankfurt.

· JUNE 21–29: Adolphe Thiers unleashes the Versailles army on Paris, under Marshal MacMahon, in a bloody campaign known as *"la semaine sanglante."*

· SEPTEMBER: The National Assembly confers the title of president of the Republic on Thiers, but, paradoxically, the conservative majority refuses to confer the title of Republic on the State.

1872
· MAY: The first group of Communards condemned to transportation departs for New Caledonia. Trials of Communards, resulting in imprisonment or execution, take place throughout the year.

· SEPTEMBER: Religious fervor swells the ranks of pilgrims to sites consecrated by mystical visitations: Lourdes, La Salette, and elsewhere.

1873
· JANUARY: Napoléon III dies in England.

· MAY: Thiers is forced to resign the presidency by a conservative coalition, which elects Marshal Patrice de MacMahon for a term of seven years, inaugurating a reactionary regime known as the Septennate, or, more often, l'Ordre Moral. Forbidden thenceforth is the celebration of Revolutionary events such as the capture of the Bastille (July 14) and establishment of the First Republic (September 21).

· JUNE: A pilgrimage to the Cluniac basilica of the Sacred Heart at Paray-le-Monial attracts tens of thousands. The National Assembly

authorizes expropriations for the construction of a basilica in
Montmartre.

· AUGUST: Pretenders representing the two branches of the French royal
family establish a line of succession, the Comte d'Orléans agreeing to
follow the Comte de Chambord; in October, however, Chambord will
effectively withdraw from any future in French politics by announcing
that he will never consent to reign under the tricolor flag.

1874
· Frémiet's statue of Joan of Arc is unveiled at the place des Pyramides.

1875
· JANUARY: The universal jubilee of the Catholic Church commences.
With passage of the Wallon amendment, the government is
officially designated a Republic.

· JUNE: The archbishop of Paris presides at the laying of the
cornerstone of the Sacré-Coeur de Montmartre.

1876
· FEBRUARY: In legislative elections, republicans emerge with a decisive
majority.

1877
· MARCH: Pius IX protests against anticlerical laws passed by Italian
legislators. In France, Catholics petition the government to intervene.

· In the Chamber of Deputies, Gambetta, reacting to "ultramontane"
agitation, makes his famous pronouncement "*Le cléricalisme, voilà
l'ennemi!*"

· MAY 16: MacMahon attempts to establish an autocratic presidency
by dissolving parliament. Three hundred sixty-three Republican
deputies issue a manifesto of protest.

· SEPTEMBER: Adolphe Thiers dies. Hundreds of thousands in Paris
witness his funeral cortege.

· OCTOBER: In legislative elections, the republican Left increases its
majority.

1878
· The Chamber of Deputies passes a law severely curtailing the power
of the president to adjourn or dissolve the Assembly.

- FEBRUARY: Pius IX dies and is succeeded by Leo XIII.

- MAY–NOVEMBER: The first Exposition Universelle of the Third Republic takes place.

- MAY: Eugène Bontoux is appointed director of the Union Générale investment bank.

- JUNE–JULY: The Congress of Berlin, hosted by Bismarck, reorganizes the Balkan states following the Russo-Turkish war.

- NOVEMBER: Leo XIII promulgates his encyclical *De inscrutabili dei consilio* ("On the Evils of Society"). "Now the source of these evils, we are convinced, lies chiefly in this, that the holy and venerable authority of the Church, which in God's name rules mankind, upholding and defending all lawful authority, has been despised and set aside."

1879

- JANUARY: MacMahon resigns the presidency and is replaced by Jules Grévy. Léon Gambetta is overwhelmingly elected president of the Chamber. These events signal the beginning of an era of liberal reform, under the leadership of Gambetta and Jules Ferry.

- JULY: The first "republican" military review takes places at Longchamps.
  The government moves to Paris after eight years at Versailles.

- AUGUST: Leo XIII issues the encyclical *Aeterni patris* ("On the Restoration of Christian Philosophy") in defense of Thomist teaching.

- Ferdinand de Lesseps announces plans to build a canal across the isthmus of Panama.
  The Assembly passes a law requiring the establishment of normal schools for both men and women, to train teachers, in every prefectural district.
  The first bond for the construction of a canal in Panama is issued.

1880

- JUNE: The Jesuits are expelled from their houses and schools. Other "nonauthorized" teaching orders are under threat of expulsion.

- JULY: July 14 is decreed a national holiday.

· SEPTEMBER: Jules Ferry becomes prime minister but retains his portfolio at the ministry of education.

1881
· JUNE: A law is passed abolishing tuition in public primary schools. It will be followed in March 1882 by laws making primary school education compulsory and secular.

· MARCH: Bontoux wins a contract to build a trans-Serbian railroad.

· OCTOBER: Boulanger attends the centennial celebration of the Revolutionary battle of Yorktown in Virginia as France's military representative and spends the following months touring the United States.

1882
· JANUARY: The Union Générale crashes; many publicly traded establishments follow suit, triggering a general economic slide.

· The public is offered the first of six Panama Canal Company bond issues.

· DECEMBER: Léon Gambetta dies of septicemia, following appendicitis, at the age of forty-four.

1883
· Assumptionists found the daily newspaper *La Croix,* whose regional satellites will bear the same name. It will eclipse *L'Univers* as the most influential Catholic newspaper in France.

· AUGUST: The Pretender, Henri, Comte de Chambord, whom Charles Maurras will describe as "the priest and pope of royalty rather than a king," dies at his castle in Austria.

1884
· FEBRUARY: Boulanger is appointed commander of the army of occupation in Tunisia.

· Divorce is legalized and public prayer abolished.

1885
· MAY: Victor Hugo dies. Three million people witness the funeral procession across Paris. In June, he is the first "grand homme" to be buried in the pantheonized Église Sainte-Geneviève.

1886
- JANUARY: Charles de Freycinet appoints Boulanger minister of war in his cabinet.

- Édouard Drumont's *La France juive* and *La France juive devant l'opinion* appear, months apart. The former will run through one hundred fifty editions by year's end.

- JULY 14: Boulanger emerges from the annual military review at Longchamps the idol of the crowd.

1887
- Ground is broken for construction of the "one-thousand-foot tower."

- APRIL: The Schnaebelé incident earns Boulanger the enthusiastic support of warmongering nationalists.

- MAY: With the fall of the Goblet government, Boulanger loses his ministerial portfolio and is assigned to a lackluster command in central France.

- JULY: Boulanger's departure from Paris provokes a tumultuous demonstration of hero worship.

- DECEMBER: Two prominent royalists confer secretly with Boulanger, hoping to bring about a restoration of the monarchy through him.

1888
- MARCH: Boulanger is discharged from the army. The Boulangist newspaper *La Cocarde: Organe Boulangiste* begins publication. Maurice Barrès will serve briefly as editor-in-chief.

- APRIL: Boulanger is elected to the Chamber of Deputies from the industrial north.

- AUGUST: Boulanger is the victor in three by-elections, affirming his national stature.

1889
- JANUARY: Boulanger trounces the moderate Left candidate in his first bid for election from a Parisian district. Urged to march upon the Élysée, he demurs.

- MARCH 31: Inauguration of the Eiffel Tower.

- APRIL 1: Boulanger flees to Belgium.

- MAY–NOVEMBER: The Exposition Universelle. It draws twenty-eight million visitors.

- JUNE: With government authorization, the Panama Canal Company offers a "lottery bond."

1890

- An outbreak of influenza in Paris claims hundreds of lives. Cholera claims more lives in the course of the year.

- FEBRUARY: The Panama Canal Company is liquidated by order of a civil tribunal.

- OCTOBER: Boulanger and Marguerite de Bonnemains leave London for the island of Jersey.

1891

- SPRING: France's economic problems are widespread. The price of bread soars in Paris. Workers throughout the country demonstrate for an eight-hour workday, with several such demonstrations leading to violent confrontations.

- MAY: Leo XIII issues the encyclical *Rerum Novarum,* defining the Church's view of the relationship between capital and labor, and refuting the basic premises of socialism.

- SEPTEMBER: A production of *Lohengrin* at the Paris Opera provokes anti-Wagnerian demonstrations. They are broken up by mounted police. In Brussels, Boulanger shoots himself.

1892

- JANUARY: Drumont and Paul Déroulède, leader of the Ligue des Patriotes, speak at an anti-Semitic rally in Neuilly.

- FEBRUARY: Leo XIII promulgates the encyclical *Au Milieu des Sollicitudes,* addressed to French bishops, clergy, and "faithful," urging all concerned to accept the legitimate authority of the Republic but to resist the onslaught of anticlerical legislation.

- Édouard Drumont founds *La Libre parole.* Its early issues feature an exposé of fraud perpetrated by executives and financiers of the defunct Panama Canal Company.

  The Prince de Sagan's mansion is dynamited. This is the first of half a dozen anarchist bombings in Paris in 1892. Tried, convicted, and executed (on July 11) for at least one of them is Ravachol.

· Baron Jacques de Reinach is found dead in his mansion, allegedly a suicide. Cornelius Herz flees the country.

· AUGUST: France negotiates an entente cordiale with Russia, thwarting Germany's attempt to isolate her.

1893

· De Lesseps father and son and Eiffel are tried on various charges, including breach of fiduciary responsibility. Trials related to the Panama bond issues will continue intermittently in subsequent years, until 1898.

· DECEMBER: A bomb hurled from the galleries by a professed anarchist, Auguste Vaillant, explodes in the Chamber of Deputies. It caused only slight injuries; Vaillant was nevertheless sentenced to death and executed in February 1894.

1894

· France and Russia sign a secret military convention.

· FEBRUARY: The first in another series of anarchist bombings takes place in the café of the Hotel Terminus, at the Gare Saint-Lazare.

· JUNE: Sadi Carnot, president of the Republic, is assassinated in Lyon by an Italian anarchist, Caserio.

· NOVEMBER: Czar Alexander III dies and is succeeded by Nicholas II.

· DECEMBER: Captain Alfred Dreyfus is court-martialed and convicted of treason.

1895

· JANUARY: Dreyfus is transported to Devil's Island.
　　Félix Faure is elected president of the Republic.

· APRIL: Zola, Raymond Poincaré, and others honor Marcelin Berthelot at a "Banquet de la Science."

· OCTOBER: Louis Pasteur is buried with national commemorative rites.

1896

· MARCH: Discovery and analysis of the *petit-bleu* persuade Commandant Georges Picquart of Dreyfus's innocence.

· AUGUST: Picquart becomes aware of Esterhazy's culpability and early in September informs the army chief of staff, Boisdeffre.

· NOVEMBER: Picquart is forced out of the intelligence service and posted to Tunisia.

1897
· MAY: The Bazar de la Charité burns to the ground.

· JULY: Picquart's lawyer communicates Picquart's evidence to Scheurer-Kestner, vice president of the Senate.

· NOVEMBER: Scheurer-Kestner, Mathieu Dreyfus, and others agree to wage a publicity campaign and solicit Émile Zola's collaboration.

1898
· JANUARY: *J'Accuse* is published on the front page of *L'Aurore*. Rioting against Jews erupts throughout France and in the Maghreb, with particular ferocity in Algiers.

· FEBRUARY: Zola is found guilty of libel. The conviction will be upheld on appeal in July, whereupon Zola will seek asylum in England.

· AUGUST: Colonel Hubert Henry commits suicide in his jail cell at the Mont-Valérien military fortress.

1899
· JUNE: The High Court annuls Dreyfus's conviction. A new court-martial is ordered and Dreyfus is released from prison. René Waldeck-Rousseau becomes prime minister.

· AUGUST: Dreyfus's second court-martial commences on the seventh in the city of Rennes, in Brittany.

· SEPTEMBER: Dreyfus's conviction is upheld. Upon appeal, he is pardoned by the president of the Republic, Émile Loubet, and set free.

1900
· APRIL: The Exposition of 1900 opens.

· JUNE: The *Appel au Soldat* banquet honoring Maurice Barrès is held at the Trocadéro.

1901
· Government measures are taken against religious teaching orders.

1902
· SEPTEMBER: Émile Zola dies.

1905
· DECEMBER: The Assembly passes a law decreeing the separation of Church and State, called "the Separation."

1906
· JULY: The High Court reverses Dreyfus's conviction and reinstates him in the army.

1908
· JUNE: Zola's remains are interred in the Panthéon.

Preface

In March 1871, Versailles, once the seat of the Sun King, became the capital of a defeated nation. France had declared war against Prussia on July 19, 1870. Six weeks later, Napoléon III had abdicated the imperial throne after surrendering his battered army to General von Moltke at Sedan. In January, with trumpets blaring, Otto von Bismarck, the Prussian prime minister, proclaimed King Wilhelm of Prussia emperor of Germany during armistice negotiations in the Hall of Mirrors. A treaty signed on February 26 in the same grandly baroque setting forced France to cede Alsace, the border province Louis XIV had annexed in 1697, and Lorraine, formerly known as Lothringen.

It was there at Versailles that France's provisional government established itself. A newly elected legislature, dominated by conservative gentry and provincial notables, had no sooner convened than the Parisian populace, led by two hundred armed National Guard battalions, rose up against it, disputing its legitimacy and creating a rival government, in the Paris Commune. Civil war followed. Troops who had recently fought against Germany were now mustered against their countrymen, and ordered to besiege Paris only two months after the Germans had withdrawn their own batteries. They would reconquer the city for Versailles during a week of slaughter—May 21 through 28, 1871—commemorated as *la semaine sanglante*. By late May the Tuileries Palace was a smoldering ruin. Retreating across Paris, the Communards, who had toppled Napoléon's victory column on the place Vendôme, set fire to City Hall—the Hôtel de Ville—and all the civil records contained therein.

Had France's defeat been a fortunate fall? Men prominent in the ranks of Napoléon III's left-wing opposition felt that the country had indeed been brought to its senses when brought to its knees. They beheld the future as an opportunity for France, freed from the shackles of Bonapartism, to leap forward, secularize civic institutions, and confer upon science the prestige it enjoyed across the Rhine. Germany's military success, according to Ernest Renan, an eminence at the Collège de France, was the product of "Germanic science, Germanic virtue, protestantism, philosophy, Luther, Kant." Higher educational institutions in France, he wrote, "have been too influenced by the Jesuits, their latin verse, and stale orations . . . France's malady is its need to speechify." Renan's *Moral and Intellectual Reform* validated the agenda of politicians who went on to found the Third Republic and, at eleven-year intervals—in 1878, 1889, 1900—organize universal expositions that presented France as the champion of liberty, the impresario of science and technology, the genial host clasping nations in a spirit of exuberant cosmopolitanism. Those republicans known as "opportunists" who made policy in the late nineteenth century set their sights beyond Alsace-Lorraine. Their aim was to regain French stature on a world stage.

In other quarters, cosmopolitanism, far from reflecting well upon the State, was seen as tantamount to profanity or treason. The many for whom military defeat followed by civil war had opened an abyss found safe purchase in ideas of transcendence or innateness: in fervent celebration of Christ's bleeding heart, miracles, and saints' relics (which multiplied), or in race. Pilgrims who assembled at sites sanctified by visitations from Mary heard bishop after bishop insist that France wanted salvation, not enlightenment. She had lost the war for having strayed from godliness and would find her way home again only as a penitent determined to right wrongs that descended from the original sin of eighteenth-century regicides. Salvation was also the cry and promise of nationalists, whose most eloquent voices argued the sacredness of soil, the virtue of roots, the infallibility of instinct, and the subversiveness of intellect. To them, "fin de siècle" in most of its cultural manifestations signified decadence.

Although nativist gospel and a religion proclaiming its universality did not always occupy common ground, both the politics of bereavement embraced by the Church and the reverence for ancestral Frenchness exemplified by the writers Maurice Barrès and Charles Maurras oriented believers of one kind and the other toward the past. The past was, above all, a refuge from the dangerous mobility of people and things. It was stillness, order, containment. "The qualities I love in the past are its sadness, its silence, and most especially its fixity. Everything that moves disconcerts me," wrote Barrès (who must have reconciled his aversion to movement with his cult of "national energy").

The ideal of a guarded, self-referential nation schooled in the imperative of war flourished outside the pale of universal expositions. Among subscribers to that ideal, revanchism was synonymous with patriotism and Germany was an indispensable threat. But no less indispensable than the ogre next door was the alien within. Like Catholicism, nationalism had its ritual Judas. And these two forces converged as never before during the tumultuous nineties, in the Dreyfus Affair.

For the Soul of France

CHAPTER I

From *The Life of Jesus* to the Sacré-Coeur

If I place myself in 1900, and then look forward thirty-six years, and backward for as many, I feel doubtful whether the changes made in the earlier time were not greater than anything I have seen since. I am speaking of changes in men's minds, and I cannot in my own time [1936] observe anything of greater consequence than the dethronement of ancient faith by natural science and historical criticism, and the transition from oligarchic to democratic representation.

—G. M. Young, *Portrait of an Age*

After observing the pilgrims thronging Lourdes in 1891, Émile Zola noted that the time and setting were right for a novel about the intractability of mankind's dependence upon the miraculous. "Study and dramatize the endless duel between science and the longing for supernatural intervention," he instructed himself. The theme pervades his great fictional cycle, *Les Rougon-Macquart,* in which modernity is dogged by the pious and the primitive. Rural folk who aspire to a higher level of awareness are weighed down by the archaic baggage they carry with them; bourgeois women surrender to a priest's erotico-mystical predation. Everywhere, the Church casts a long shadow.

"Science" and "supernatural intervention" were indeed the competing prescriptions for France's recovery after the Franco-Prussian debacle of 1870–71, which toppled Napoléon III from his imperial throne. These alternatives informed her social, political, and cultural life in the last third of the century, framing a bitter debate over the country's heart and soul. It's as if a nation divided needed only humiliation at the hands of a foreigner to turn upon itself and wage without restraint the civil war that had long excited its most implacable hatred.

For everyone, 1789 was the inevitable reference point.

There were those on the one hand who held that France would betray the best of herself if she did not remain loyal to the eighteenth-century thinkers who had fathered the Republic. On the other hand, "*intransigeants*" committed to the ideal of a Catholic monarchy anathematized the Enlightenment. In their view, divine grace was needed, and France could receive it only as a penitent mindful of the sins she had accumulated over the course of eighty years.

How this impasse was reached is worth examining. The battle line was first boldly drawn during the Revolution—when clergy who would not pledge allegiance to the republican constitution risked exile or death, when saints' days were expunged from the calendar and Church property amounting to a fifth of France was seized by the State to be auctioned off. Men contemptuous of the Scriptures staged a service honoring Reason at Notre-Dame cathedral. By 1801 Napoléon Bonaparte had gained power as First Consul. Mistrustful of anything clandestine, he negotiated with Pope Pius VII a treaty, or Concordat, that granted permission to worship "openly" and "freely" while reserving for himself the right to map dioceses and appoint prelates: Gallican bishops. The Church was visible, but only as an emaciated shadow of itself, with far fewer parishes than before 1789, and no priests to serve many of them. Young men who at one time might have taken vows were instead fighting and dying all over

Europe. Clerical black enjoyed little prestige in a military state that treated the curate as a minor agent of social order.

The downfall of Napoléon at Waterloo in 1815 was thus an occasion for celebratory masses. Repatriated nobles and clerics went about setting things right. In 1797, Louis XVI's brother, the exiled Comte de Provence, had instructed exiled French bishops never to forswear the marriage of throne and altar. "How indispensable it is that they support each other! May ecclesiastics imbue my subjects with this truth. . . . The marvelous order that is the Catholic Church will not long survive unless it remain bound to the Monarchy." Eighteen years later, as King Louis XVIII, he restored the Church to its eminence, replacing Napoleonic functionaries with an episcopate of high-ranking aristocrats. Catholicism became once again the state religion. Religious orders reestablished themselves. Writing disrespectfully about the Church or insulting a priest constituted grounds for imprisonment; destroying liturgical objects was punishable as a capital crime; dolor and ecclesiastical pomp informed civil life; and a secret society called Knights of the Faith ("Chevaliers de la Foi") controlled patronage. To those émigrés in whom loss had fostered humility, what often mattered most was the consolation they found in religion for their immense reversals of fortune. Not unlike the thousands who flocked to pilgrimage sites after the Franco-Prussian War half a century later, they prayed with fervor. But the war-torn nation, throughout which new church spires rose, also bred the kind of priest Julien Sorel encounters at his seminary in Stendhal's *Le Rouge et le noir* and Emma finds at Yonville in Flaubert's *Madame Bovary*—country boys unable to do much more than administer the sacraments. "All told, the clergy has never been as ignorant as it is today, yet never has true science been so necessary," wrote Father Félicité de Lamennais, France's great Catholic philosopher.

The Revolution of 1830, which enthroned Louis-Philippe, the Duc d'Orléans—a constitutional monarch descended from the cadet branch of the House of Bourbon, on whom Bourbon loyalists heaped obloquy—exposed the rift between Frenchmen greeting the new century and those fending it off. Knights of the Faith had subscribed to the orthodox precept that society must be a hierarchical edifice in which authority descends from God to sovereign to paterfamilias. But most of the bourgeois notables entitled to vote and run for office—those constituting *le pays légal* under Louis-Philippe—set up as Voltaireans.* Piety was unfashionable, if not subversive. And where piety was unfashionable, militant Catholics made themselves scarce.

Militants there were all the same, most prominently those who had associated themselves with a liberal movement founded by Lamennais in 1830 and known by the name of its journal, *L'Avenir.* United in the belief that religion was doomed to irrelevance so long as the government subsidized religious institutions, they called for the separation of Church and State. A disaffected populace—the same that had recently pillaged, among other ecclesiastical mansions of note, the archbishop's palace outside Notre-Dame cathedral—would find spiritual meaning in an independent Church. By the same token, a Church no longer hostage to the powers that be would find strength in the converted masses. After forty years of republics and despotisms and monarchies eliminating one another in blind succession, what was left intact? "Only two things," Lamennais declared in the first issue of *L'Avenir.* "God and liberty. Unite them and all the intimate and permanent needs of human nature are met. Calm prevails only where it can do so on earth, in the domain of human intelligence. They are no sooner separated than turmoil resumes and intensifies." The providential laws that govern the "moral world" shone forth never more brilliantly, he declared, than during periods of transition, when "everything is being reborn, when everything is changing, when everything is transforming, when breezes of the future waft home scents of a new earth." Having just launched a regime conspicuously disinclined to make preservation of the faith its first order of business, France might be ready at last to let religion walk free. Was a free Catholic Church not thriving across the ocean, in America? Reports to that effect would be confirmed by Alexis de Tocqueville, traveling abroad.

L'Avenir made its mark. Several thousand younger priests, many of

---

Le pays légal described the several hundred thousand citizens in a population of over thirty million whose status as taxpayers entitled them to vote and run for office.

whom served poor urban parishes, joined the movement. Threatened from below, French bishops condemned it. Lamennais and two close collaborators—Father Lacordaire and Charles de Montalembert—then set out for Rome to win the pope's support. What they elicited instead was an Apostolic Letter that sealed the fate of *L'Avenir.* Loath to alienate the Gallican episcopate, to risk a quarrel that might imperil the Concordat, and to encourage liberals abroad while calling upon Austria to help him repress red-shirted republicans at home, a beleaguered Gregory XVI stood behind the bishops. "[We cannot] predict happier times for religion and government, from the plans of those who desire vehemently to separate the Church from the State, and to break the mutual concord between temporal authority and the priesthood. It is certain that that concord which always was favorable and beneficial for the sacred and the civil order is feared by the shameless lovers of liberty," he declared in the encyclical *Mirari vos. L'Avenir* ceased publication. Lamennais kept faith with himself by abandoning the priesthood and writing a testament, *Paroles d'un croyant* ("Words of a Believer"), that earned him special condemnation in yet another encyclical. It became one of the great best sellers of its day.

Equally obstinate was Montalembert, the half-Scottish son of an émigré count, whose rhetorical brilliance matched his missionary zeal. Unable to influence policy from outside parliament, he resolved after 1837 to work from within it, as a member of the Chamber of Peers. Declaring that "those who profess or defend the Catholic faith must expect marked unpopularity," he ruffled not only anticlerical colleagues but prelates resentful of a layman bold enough to fight for religious advantage with secular weapons in hostile territory. One of those weapons was the word on every progressive's lips during the Louis-Philippian era—"*liberté.*" Liberal-minded Frenchmen were rallying behind Poles tyrannized by the czar, Italians living under a feudal regime in papal territories, German states ruled by a Lutheran Prussian squirearchy. Why then should Montalembert's own country not afford its citizens freedom of conscience, freedom of the press, freedom of association? Above all, why should France compel parents to have their children earn baccalaureates in state institutions?

Relentlessly, year after year, he championed *"la liberté de l'enseigne-ment"*—meaning by "freedom" the full accreditation of schools run by religious orders. *"La liberté de culte"* (freedom of worship) was its corollary. In the Committee for the Defense of Religious Freedom, Montalembert fashioned a modern-day instrument of political action, supporting candidates who vowed to defend the faith. It proved itself in elections held midway through 1846, a year and a half before the revolution that would bring down Louis-Philippe.

By then, Catholic interests had gained some ground in the court of public opinion. Responsible for this shift were the dynamism of several Catholic luminaries, the social consciousness of clergy loyal to Lamennais, the pastoral work of provincial missions, and a wedge of daylight in bourgeois perception between the Church and the Bourbon monarchy. "For us French, who are slaves of words, a great thing has taken place," Frédéric Ozanam observed in 1838, "the separation of two big words that seemed perfectly inseparable hitherto: throne and altar."* But of paramount importance for unorthodox Catholics was the enthronement in 1846 of a new pope, Giovanni Mastai-Ferretti, who took the name Pius IX. Succeeding the archconservative Gregory XVI, Pius comported himself, until 1848, as the liberal he was thought to be by the bare majority of cardinals who had elected him. He began with a reform of civic life in the Papal States. Political criminals were amnestied, and residents were granted such unheard-of privileges as freedom of the press. Pius's behavior astonished Europe. Count Metternich, Europe's staunchest advocate of monarchical absolutism, fumed over it. Among progressives, clerical and secular alike, there was jubilation. France's Protestant prime minister, François Guizot, predicted that the Church would now reconcile with modern society. In its annual address to the king, parliament praised Pius for inaugurating "an era of civilization and freedom." Frédéric Ozanam, a well-known Catholic intellectual associated with the ideal of Christian democracy, wrote that Heaven had put on Saint Peter's

---

*To be sure, there were regions intransigeantly hostile to the Church. During the Revolution of 1848, villagers in the Auvergne expelled priests known to have royalist sympathies.

throne "a saint the likes of whom we have perhaps not seen since the pontificate of Pius V"—in the sixteenth century. The pope's firmest supporter, he declared, was the common man.

Economic depression accounted for some of the common man's support. Half-starved workers who rose up against Louis-Philippe on February 24, 1848, were indeed more disposed than a later generation of Parisian insurrectionists to befriend the Church, even if many of the countless immigrants from the countryside could not have identified the parish to which they nominally belonged. On February 29, the provisional government asked all clergy to bless "the people's achievement" by chanting *Domine, salvam fac rempublicam* after Sunday mass. And "God save the Republic" was taken seriously. "The principles whose triumph will introduce a completely new era are principles the Church has always proclaimed, and has just proclaimed again, to the entire world, through the mouth of its august leader, the immortal Pius IX," Cardinal du Pont, archbishop of Bourges, told his congregation.* Prelates hastened to affirm that liberty, equality, and fraternity were Christian truths (although not truly Christian, Lacordaire reminded his audience at Notre-Dame cathedral, unless broadly enough conceived to include obedience, hierarchy, and veneration). Many of them blessed the young "liberty trees" planted on city and village squares all over France in the spring of 1848, bringing holy water and incense to a ritual celebration of republican values. The archbishop of Paris, Monsignor Denis Affre, remarked upon the "Christian courage" and "virile demeanor" of street fighters with rifles in shoulder belts who attended a mass for their slain comrades.†

This general enthusiasm did not survive a second, failed insurrec-

---

*When Ozanam launched a newspaper called *The New Era* (*L'Ère nouvelle*) in April 1848 with Jean-Baptiste Henri Lacordaire, a Dominican priest who was among the greatest pulpit orators of the nineteenth century, the prospectus included this: "There are two forces in France: the people and Jesus Christ. If they separate, we are lost; if they join, we are saved."

†Monsignor Affre's warm embrace had a precedent in the so-called *baiser Lamourette* of 1792. Responding to the exhortation of a revolutionary bishop aptly named Lamourette that they "form themselves into one and the same body of free men," other-

tion in June. The Constituent Assembly elected nationwide in April was a conservative body. When radical leaders demanded strong measures to alleviate the suffering of destitute Parisians, the Assembly demurred. The bourgeoisie saw socialism in the offing, and among churchmen who had recently trumpeted liberty, equality, and fraternity, equality no longer passed muster as a Christian truth. "All my political beliefs are shaken, not to say destroyed," Montalembert wrote on the day a firebrand named Armand Barbès proposed extracting five billion francs in taxes from the rich. "I have devoted the twenty best years of my life to a chimera, to a transaction between the Church and the modern principle. . . . My ideas are not yet completely settled on this score, however. I am waiting. Pius IX's example will guide me." He would be guided more immediately by the death of Archbishop Affre, who along with two vicars presented himself at a barricade in the Faubourg Saint-Antoine during the June insurrection, hoping to mediate between combatants, and received a bullet in the back for his trouble. Thousands died.

As for the pope, in November 1848 his trusted minister of justice, Pellegrino Rossi, was killed by insurgents who besieged the Quirinal Palace, forcing Pius to seek refuge in the city of Gaeta and creating a Roman republic. Pius reestablished himself in Rome fourteen months later, with the help of a French expeditionary force. His politics had meanwhile changed: the former liberal had become even more unbendingly authoritarian than his predecessor. And in the newly elected president of the Republic, Napoléon's nephew Louis-Napoléon, who was praised by the Catholic paper *L'Ami de la religion* as "the genius of strength and order . . . come to France's rescue," the pope's worldview found an open ear. Parliament, largely a collection of conservatives horrified by the events of June 1848, might have scuttled the Republic right away had they not been divided among themselves—some wanting a constitutional monarchy to replace it, others a Bourbon restoration, and others still a Napoleonic empire.

---

wise factious legislators leaped to their feet, in Louis XVI's presence, and kissed one another.

In his memoirs, Alexis de Tocqueville observed that those deputies with whom he sat in the Assembly might have been spared their grief if, earlier on, they had been mindful of historical precedent. When aristocratic émigrés who had been libertines in their youth regained power twenty years after the Terror, they made sure to enthrone devoutness. In the same way, the irreligious middle classes of Louis-Philippe's day discovered the social usefulness of ecclesiastical authority during the upheavals of 1848. With the ground quaking under them they looked for stability to the Church's sacraments, hierarchy, and mores—and its pedagogical precepts. The philosopher Ernest Renan might scoff at the exercises in classical rhetoric devised by Jesuit masters, but for Tocqueville eloquence was a guarantor of civilization. It performed the function that ancient Roman custom assigned to *oratio*. It was political wisdom's first defense against tyrannical wrath. Nothing distressed him more in the Constituent Assembly of 1848 than the crude language of revolutionary delegates, the so-called Montagnards. "For me it was like the discovery of a new world," he wrote.

> One consoles oneself for not knowing foreign lands by supposing that one knows one's own country at least, and one is wrong; for there are always areas of one's own land that one has not visited, and races of men who are new to one. I experienced this fully then. I felt that I was seeing these Montagnards for the first time, so greatly did their mores and way of speaking surprise me. They spoke a jargon that was not quite the language of the people, nor was it that of the literate, but that had the defects of both; it was full of coarse words and ambitious expressions. A constant jet of insulting or jocular interruptions poured down from the benches of the Mountain; they were continually making jokes or sententious comments; and they shifted from a very ribald tone of voice to one of great haughtiness. Obviously these people belonged neither in a tavern or in a drawing room; I think they must have polished their manners in the cafés and fed their minds on no literature but the newspapers.

The café invaded other European parliaments at a later date, to the chagrin of other statesmen. During the 1880s, Ernst von Plener, the leader of Austria's Liberal Party, would have recognized in Tocqueville's predicament a foreshadowing of his own exposure to vehement demagoguery. Appalled by Georg von Schönerer and Karl Lueger (Hitler's political models), who filled the Reichsrat with coarse invective, he lamented "the barbarization of the parliamentary tone in our House of Representatives."

As Tocqueville saw it, demagoguery would be the ultimate political expression of a society bereft—of family pride, manners, grammar, local custom, hierarchical structure, religious principles, and sacred space. "What now remains of those barriers which formerly arrested tyranny?" he asked in *Democracy in America* thirteen years before the 1848 Revolution. "Since religion has lost its dominion over the souls of men, the most prominent boundary that divided good from evil is overthrown, everything seems doubtful and indeterminate in the moral world; kings and nations are guided by chance, and none can say where are the natural limits of despotism and the bounds of license. Revolutions have forever destroyed the respect which surrounded the rulers of the state; and since they have been relieved from the burden of public esteem, princes may henceforward surrender themselves without fear to the intoxication of arbitrary power."*

Tocqueville could not have failed to appreciate that the prodigious reconstruction of Paris during the 1850s and '60s intensified feelings of "indeterminacy" by destroying neighborhoods, abolishing familiar

---

*Another threat to those moral barriers that formerly arrested tyranny made itself known to Tocqueville in *Essay on the Inequality of Human Races,* a pseudo-scientific thesis written by Arthur de Gobineau, who had served as his principal private secretary in the Foreign Office in 1849. Published between 1853 and 1855, *Essay* became the locus classicus of racial nationalism in fin-de-siècle France and twentieth-century Germany. Tocqueville told Gobineau, with whom he corresponded prolifically, that the doctrine of Aryan superiority erased all moral boundaries and paved the way to social hell. "Do you not see that your doctrine leads naturally to all the ills to which permanent inequality gives rise: pride, violence, contempt for one's fellow man, tyranny, and abjection in all its forms?" he declared in November 1853. "Your doctrine and mine are intellectually worlds apart." Gobineau's was, he wrote, false and pernicious. It was the theory of a horse trader rather than a statesman.

vistas, and estranging Parisians from their past. But it was the Communards' secession that conformed most closely to his prophecy. Theirs was the "intoxication of arbitrary power." Or so it seemed to conservatives for whom, during the 1870s, in the bloody wake of the Paris Commune, "moral order" became a motto. As much as the Franco-Prussian War of 1870–71, the Commune, short-lived though it was, demonstrated the fragility of venerable institutions.

Tocqueville was interned at Vincennes Prison in December 1851, when President Louis-Napoléon ended the Second Republic with a coup d'état. Other noncompliant legislators, Victor Hugo among them, fled the country. After having himself dubbed Napoléon III by plebiscite one year later, the usurper ruled very much to the advantage of the Church, which pledged fealty to him, as it had at first to the Republic. The Church grew richer and stronger during the Second Empire. Teaching orders thrived. Jesuits banished from France under Louis-Philippe now slipped back into the corridors of power. Intellectuals known for their positivist convictions were purged from the school system. Louis-Napoléon's first minister of education abolished programs in history and philosophy but required high school students to be examined in religion. Lycées and universities scraped along on science. Necessity mothering invention may best explain the accomplishments of Louis Pasteur, the chemist Marcelin Berthelot, the physiologist Claude Bernard, and other great scientists who made their mark at this time. In 1858 Pasteur complained that not one farthing had been budgeted for the advancement of science through laboratory work. Bernard grimly observed that laboratories were the tombs of scientists.

This situation improved somewhat after 1859. When Louis-Napoléon defeated Austria at Solferino in that year—driving it out of the northern Italian territories it had controlled since Napoléon I's downfall and leveling a formidable obstacle to the movement of national unification—his relations with Pius IX, whose temporal authority extended over one-third of the peninsula, deteriorated. Less reliant upon ecclesiastical support than at the time of his coup d'état, he seemed to rediscover the young exile who thirty years earlier had joined the Carbonari in Rome fighting against papal rule. Certainly, the Italian campaign announced a general liberalization of the Empire. While pious appearances were maintained, the spirit of scientific inquiry, like the language of political opposition, was given greater play. Thought that would have invited censorship before 1860 now dared to speak aloud, though still not always with complete impunity.

The battle line between champions and foes of the Enlightenment formed once again in bitter controversy over a book titled *La Vie de Jésus,* by Ernest Renan. Its publication, in 1863, four years after Darwin's *Origin of Species,* was a momentous event.

Renan, who had come to Paris from Brittany destined for the priesthood, might have made a learned cleric had he not studied Semitic languages at the Saint-Sulpice seminary. There, his voracious intellect found nourishment in philology, and this disciplined study of texts, when applied to biblical exegesis, raised doubts that ultimately convinced him to defrock himself before his ordination. "I took the measure of which concessions the Church can make and those that must not be demanded of it," he later wrote in his memoirs. "If the Church admitted that *The Book of Daniel* is an apocryphal text of the Maccabean era, it would be admitting error; if it had erred there, it might have erred elsewhere. It would no longer be divinely inspired." The Catholicism bred in his bone—of Scripture, of the Councils and dogma—no longer sat right in his mind, and he began life anew, charting a secular course. "I thought it disrespectful of the faith to fiddle with it."

Letters that attest to Renan's loss of belief in divine revelation also document his precocious acquisition of mastery in the languages of biblical antiquity. On May 2, 1847, when he was twenty-four, the Institute of France (a cluster of learned societies including the French Academy) awarded Renan the Volney Prize for his *Historical and Theoretical Essay on the Semitic Languages in General and the Hebrew Language in Particular.* In 1848, amid revolutionary havoc, he earned an advanced degree in philosophy and completed a long essay called "L'Avenir de la science" ("The Future of Science"), which enunciated the intellectual creed by which he proposed to live. *Devenir*—historical development or flow, implying evolution—was now the conceptual basis of his scholarship, and he argued against obscurantists sworn to social and cultural absolutes. "The science of the human mind must above all be the history of the human mind, and only through patient, philological study of the works it has brought forth in different ages does that history become possible."

Ernest Renan at the time of the publication of La Vie de Jésus.

Philological study fully occupied him during the 1850s, the first decade of Louis-Napoléon's Second Empire. His contributions to learned journals ranged in subject from the religions of antiquity to the origins of Islamism. Before long Renan stood tall enough to be remarked by the Académie des Inscriptions et Belles-Lettres, which made him a member, and to be targeted by the Vatican, which put his critical study of the Book of Job on the papal index of prohibited publications. There was also ambivalent recognition from Napoléon III's entourage. Empress Eugénie, a devout Catholic, did not welcome apostates, but he was admired by a small coterie to whom intellectual distinction meant something, and all the more so when it expressed itself with literary flair. A member of this coterie who wielded considerable influence at court arranged an archaeological tour of Palestine and Syria for Renan at state expense in 1860. It was during his sabbatical that he embarked upon *La Vie de Jésus*.

Since the 1830s, the life of Jesus had inspired a substantial body of erudite opinion across the Rhine at Tübingen University, most famously David Friedrich Strauss's *Das Leben Jesu* (1835), which George Eliot translated into English and Émile Littré into French. In

1849 Renan, having thoroughly familiarized himself with German scholarship, published an essay titled "Les Historiens critiques de *La Vie de Jésus.*" His debt to Strauss, the Hegelian, is obvious—but so is his divergence from him, for while Strauss held that Jesus Christ was largely a mythical creation tailored to Old Testament figurations of the Messiah, Renan insisted upon his historical reality. Jesus the man required chronicling, and at twenty Renan may already have known that this would be his mission in life. At Saint-Sulpice he recorded a dream that seems to signal the future biographer. A sentence of death had been passed upon Jesus, he wrote. "No one present said anything, except me. I sprang forward and pleaded his cause. Some witnesses laughed, others were serious. I remember several phrases from my speech. I spoke about his youth, about his sweet, pure demeanor. I wanted him to love me. . . . Oh, Jesus, could I have denied you? The mere thought of it is painful. I must absolutely believe that you lived. . . . If I am to love you, you had to have been flesh and blood."

The man pictured in *La Vie de Jésus* is a charismatic leader, a paragon of virtue, a Romantic hero scornful of the patriarchate, a prophet who believes himself to be the son of God. But he is no divinity. The new order he promises is a fullness of being that vanquishes death. But he dies. Renan shaped his work around the cultural rift, as he saw it, between Judea and Galilee. Among Judeans, an obsession with pedantic disputation had stifled communion with God and enslaved the spirit to ritual. Their leaders, the earthbound Pharisees, favored polished architectural vistas over God's Creation. "[Jesus] called such showy architecture 'realms of the world and all their glory,' " Renan wrote of Herod's city, Sebaste (but thinking as well, perhaps, of Napoléon III's new capital, rising over the rubble of medieval Paris). "This administrative and official art displeased him. What he loved were his Galilean villages, a jumble of huts, of basins and presses carved into the rock, of wells, tombs, fig and olive trees. He always remained near nature."

Jesus, the village illuminato, descended upon Judea with no more regard for its hierarchies, laws, and mores than the wind of the wilderness. Renan infers from the Gospels and Saint Jerome's commentary in *Dialogi contra Pelagionos* that blood relations meant little to a man, the "Son of God," unloved by his family.* Like all messianic ideologues, he recognized as kin only followers pledged to his Word. "We see him trampling underfoot everything human: blood, love, fatherland, and reserving heart and soul for precepts that embodied the good and the true." In common with French revolutionaries who celebrated the birth of the Republic as Year 1, Jesus stood for fatherless dispensations. "Nowadays, man risks little and wins little," wrote Renan, in language reminiscent of Pascal's wager. "During the heroic ages of human activity, man risked everything and won everything. The good and the wicked, which is to say those who believe themselves good or wicked and are believed to be such by others, form enemy camps. Apotheosis is achieved on the scaffold; characters have features so sharp that they get etched into men's memories as eternal types. Except for the French Revolution, no historical circumstance was more propitious than Jesus's to the development of those hidden strengths that humanity deploys only in days of fever and peril."

In short, Jesus was a man, but an incomparable man, with something of the *magister ludi,* whose one true miracle was the revolution he fostered.

Renan had portrayed Jesus this way a year before the publication of *La Vie de Jésus,* in his inaugural lecture as professor of Hebrew at the Collège de France, France's most prestigious academic institution. His course was suspended immediately. The uproar that followed gave wings to his book. By 1865, one hundred thousand copies had been sold (this in an age of small editions, when the sale of five thousand would have been reckoned a success). No religious work had enjoyed such popularity since Luther's day, asserted Renan's friend Hippolyte Taine. The critic Sainte-Beuve blessed it. Writers of the Romantic generation, notably the great historian Jules Michelet, were

---

*Among other citations, Renan refers to Mark 6:4 ("But Jesus said unto them: A prophet is not without honor, but in his own country, and among his own kin, and in his own house.") and to John's account of the marriage in Cana, 2:3–4 ("And when they wanted wine, the mother of Jesus saith unto him, They have no wine. Jesus saith unto her, Woman, what have I to do with thee? Mine hour is not yet come").

lyrical in their praise. George Sand—who, in 1848, had joined the revolutionaries extolling Jesus the "democrat"—read Renan's work as the trump of doom for Christianity. "Let's accept the plain truth, even when it surprises us and changes our point of view," she wrote to Prince Jérôme Bonaparte. "Jesus has been thoroughly demolished! So much the better for us perhaps." In her opinion Christianity could no longer do anything but harm, and the book served an eminently useful purpose.*

On the other side, tracts and articles abounded, with *La Vie de Jésus* making rich pasture for theologians galled by its argument. Hate mail also rained upon Renan, much of it from parishioners who had heard his book damned at Sunday service. He was called a fool, a madman, a public poisoner, a mountebank, the scourge of the earth, Baron de Rothschild's hired hand. "You great imposter!" one letter-writer exclaimed, with mandatory allusions to Judas Iscariot. "Lie down with your head in the dust; you who are nothing but ashes and dust, retract this impious work and confess your error. For it is known by everyone . . . that you wrote your infamous book to enrich yourself, like the traitor Judas who sold our Saviour to the Jews." Enraged that he had turned his God-given gift of intellect against his divine benefactor, a countess declared that "the corruption flowing from your soul is even more hideous than its fleshly envelope, revoltingly ugly though that is." Canon Lambert of Saint-Sulpice, whom Renan had known at seminary, threw *La Vie de Jésus* in the fire but assured him that there was still time to save himself from the flames. "Poor errant soul. Fallen angel, it isn't too late, go back home to yourself. Should you sincerely re-enter the fold, you will be pardoned." There was strong support in the conservative Senate for a bill banning Renan's works, along with Voltaire's, Rousseau's, Sand's, and Michelet's, inter alios, from public libraries.

What abounded, besides vituperation, were miracles, many of them credulously reported by the ultraorthodox Catholic newspaper

---

*Renan himself felt, at that point in his life, that France was well served by religious principles inculcated in "the mass of the people"; that the latter would otherwise show a disinclination to subordinate the "will of the individual" to the order and welfare of society.

L'Univers. Pius IX's pronouncement in 1854 that the Immaculate Conception was thenceforth to be official dogma had reinforced a cult of the Blessed Virgin, and *La Vie de Jésus* did nothing to arrest an outbreak of Mariophanies. In provincial France, apparitions were rampant, as was idol worship. On July 30, 1864, the archbishop of Avignon crowned a statue of the Virgin at a Vauclusian sanctuary called Notre-Dame de Lumières. The crowd of twenty thousand who gathered to witness the coronation acclaimed it with chants of "Long live Mary," "Long live Notre-Dame de Lumières," "Long live the Queen of Heaven and earth," "Long live our Lord Bishops," "Long live Pius IX." Similar demonstrations took place not far away, at La Salette, where the Virgin, speaking in patois, had presented herself some years earlier to two young shepherds, and at Lourdes, where She had appeared to the illiterate daughter of poor millers.

An encyclical promulgated in 1864 by Pius IX, *Quanta Cura,* while making no special mention of *La Vie de Jésus,* was a global condemnation of the "depraved fictions of innovators" afflicting the modern world. It came with a list, or syllabus, of eighty "errors." The last error of thought, epitomizing all eighty, was that "the Roman Pontiff can, and should, reconcile with progress, liberalism and modern civilization." Pius ratified his predecessor's contention that to regard freedom of conscience and worship as the inalienable right of every man was insanity (*deliramentum*). Only those who possessed the truth enjoyed freedom (a doctrine that recalls Robespierre's invocation of the Supreme Being to legitimize "the despotism of liberty"). And what spelled insanity for individuals unanswerable to the moral authority of the only true church spelled revolution or unbridled materialism for society at large. "At this time there are found not a few who, applying to civil intercourse the impious and absurd principles of what they call Naturalism, dare teach 'that the best form of Society, and the exigencies of civil progress, absolutely require human society to be constituted and governed without any regard whatsoever to Religion, as if this [Religion] did not even exist, or at least without making any distinction between true and false religions.' " Was it not plain, he asked, "that the society of man, freed from the bonds of Religion and of true justice, has no other purpose than the effort to obtain and accumulate wealth, and that in its actions the only law it follows is that of unrestrained cupidity, which seeks to secure its own pleasures and comforts?"

Deploring every change wrought by the scientific revolution, Pius chased from the temple not only money changers but also rationalists. Warped, he declared, is the notion that human reason, without any reference whatsoever to God, can be the sole arbiter of truth and falsehood, or of good and evil. Misguided are all who believe that divine revelation contributes nothing to the perfection of man. Radically in error is the contrarian brought before Pius's inquisition who declares: "The prophecies and miracles set forth and recorded in the Holy Scriptures are the contrivance of poets, and the mysteries of the Christian faith are the result of philosophical investigations. In the books of the Old and the New Testament there are contained mythical inventions, and Jesus Christ is Himself a myth." What follows is the dangerous belief (Error no. 47) that public schools intended for instruction in letters and "philosophical sciences" should function without ecclesiastical interference.

Pius's bulls became more vehement as the territories over which popes had exercised temporal authority since Charlemagne's day—the whole midsection of Italy, from Ravenna to Rome—began to shrink. We have seen how France was implicated in this contraction. By expelling Austria from Lombardy-Venetia in 1859, it removed a major obstacle to the unification of Italy under the Piedmontese prince Victor Emmanuel II. What is more, French troops garrisoned in Rome since 1849 to protect Pius against republican insurgents did not intervene when rebels in Romagna, a papal state, overturned the pope's feudal government. Pamphlets justifying the emperor's quiescence with the argument that the pope's temporal loss had only increased his spiritual stature offended militants in France. Quiescent he remained while two more papal states, the Marches and Umbria, joined the Risorgimento. "Your emperor is a deceitful rogue," Pius told the French ambassador, an opinion seconded by ultramontane loyalists such as Louis Veuillot, who edited *L'Univers*. A convert, Veuillot took pride in being *plus catholique que le pape* and even more pugnacious.

The Syllabus of Errors was the roar of a beleaguered Vatican.* Witnesses describe Pius in his private chapel, praying for hours on end. At war with a world whose rulers he could no longer best, he came increasingly to believe that his decisions were divinely inspired, or had to be understood as such. In *Quanta Cura* he had claimed plenary power "conferred on the Sovereign Pontiff by Jesus Christ" to guide and supervise "the Universal Church." Five years later, in 1869, a Vatican Council elaborately staged by his prefect of propaganda collaborated in the ultimate exaltation of pontifical power. Bishops who had come from as far away as India, China, and the South Sea Islands (rather like the heads of state who had recently assembled in Paris for a universal exposition) spent seven months together and at last, in July 1870, after much lucubrating over less significant matters, proclaimed the infallibility of the pope. The supernatural privilege of never erring in *ex cathedra* pronouncements about the faith and morals had been accorded Jesus' surrogate.

Not every French bishop at the Council voted *placet,* or yea. But "anti-infallibilists," as they were known, often found themselves snubbed when they returned to their flock. Given a choice between the Roman and French ("Gallican") liturgies, eighty of ninety-one dioceses chose the former. In much of Catholic France, Pius IX wore a martyr's halo for having been divested of the Papal States, and his theological Luddism burnished his image. *L'Univers* described the pope as Christ on earth. One high-ranking clergyman preached that the Son of God was incarnate in the Virgin's womb, in the Eucharist, and in Pius. With few exceptions, parish priests followed him obediently. Charles de Montalembert, who no longer took his cues from Rome, complained that the pope had become an idol, and reason and history, truth and justice were being immolated in his name. "The history of the Church presents mysteries in great profusion," he wrote, "but I

---

*E. E. Y. Hales, in a biography sympathetic to Pius, explains him as follows: "In his experience, the claim for liberties, not necessarily in themselves harmful, led in fact to Mazzini's Religion of Humanity and to the persecutions of Turin [Victor Emmanuel's realm]. 'Liberty, Progress, and Recent Civilisation,' in their Italian guise—the guise in which the Pope had met them—meant something which the Church could not tolerate."

don't know any that equals or surpasses the extraordinarily sudden transformation of Catholic France into a farmyard of the Vatican." Reacting to this groundswell of religious zeal, Gustave Flaubert declared that the really decisive issue for France was neither the prospect of war with Prussia nor the enfeeblement of Napoléon III. The only important thing, he wrote, was religion, or clericalism (meaning the role of the Church in political life). "We must no longer dream about the best form of government . . . but of seeing to it that Science rules." It seemed to him entirely possible that France, like Belgium, might end up divided into two parts, with Catholics here and the secular-minded there.

FRANCE'S INTERNAL DIVISIONS found a new theater in which to speak when, only days after the proclamation of papal infallibility, war broke out with Germany. Since 1866 Otto von Bismarck, the Prussian prime minister, whose grand design was to forge a German Empire in the heat of war, with Wilhelm of Prussia as its sovereign, had been carefully devising a casus belli against France. History abetted him when the Spanish throne fell vacant. Bismarck persuaded King Wilhelm's relative Prince Leopold of Hohenzollern to present his candidacy, knowing full well that France could not allow itself to be pinned between two of that family. Leopold subsequently withdrew his bid at Wilhelm's urging, but his gesture did not mollify France's foreign minister, the Duc de Gramont, who insisted that Leopold should never again be allowed to come forward. Wilhelm refused, and the matter might have rested there had Bismarck not made the refusal sound contemptuous by mischievously editing a telegram from Wilhelm to Louis-Napoléon. Inflamed by the press, which geneally denounced Prussia's "slap in the face," Frenchmen mobbed the streets of Paris. On July 14, 1870, an order to mobilize was issued. Two days later, deputies voted funds for war, with only 10 of 255 in parliament dissenting. The huge crowd outside the Palais Bourbon was jubilant. One witness thought that the scene might have been not much different at the Colosseum in Rome when frenzied spectators climbed the

Vestals' tribune to demand the execution of a gladiator, little realizing that France herself was the doomed combatant.

Gramont, a militant Catholic, may have been animated by hatred of Protestant Prussia. In any case, war had no sooner erupted than it spilled into the realm of religious politics. French pontifical troops garrisoned in Rome, the last enclave of papal power, were immediately pulled from the city to join battle with Germany. As a result nothing impeded the triumphal entry of Victor Emmanuel's army. Although Gramont declared that France could not lose its honor on the Tiber (by leaving the pope undefended) and preserve it on the Rhine, his well-turned phrase rang hollow, for it quickly became evident that Louis-Napoléon's army was outnumbered, outgeneraled, and outgunned. On September 1, some six weeks after hostilities began, the emperor, under relentless German shell fire, hoisted a white flag over the river town of Sedan. On September 20 the pope, also under shell fire, hoisted a white flag over the Castel Sant' Angelo. While Louis-Napoléon was abdicating in the Ardennes, Pius IX was declaring himself a prisoner in the Vatican. To French no less distressed by the fall of Rome than by the prospect of enemy troops besieging Paris, it was the consummation of the pope's martyrdom. "Let us pray that God hasten the moment when France, delivered from the Prussians, but above all from itself, shall deliver Rome from the Italian slough and restore to degraded humankind a God-given benefaction it cannot forsake without perishing," wrote Louis Veuillot. The "Government of National Defense" formed by republicans on September 4 deepened his gloom.

God was in no rush to deliver France from the foreign enemy or from the enemy within, though it seemed for a moment that Veuillot's prayers had been answered. There would be far more killing, of French by Germans, and of French by one another.

HAVING QUICKLY FOUGHT through the Vosges mountains and occupied the belt of country between Alsace-Lorraine and the Île-de-France, General Helmuth von Moltke felt certain that his men could safely camp around Paris until the besieged city surrendered to hunger. Neither he nor Bismarck anticipated one of the more valiant second efforts in the history of warfare. On October 7, 1870, Léon Gambetta, a dynamic orator serving as minister of the interior in the Government of National Defense, escaped from Paris by balloon. He joined fellow ministers at Tours, and improvised a whole new army, the Army of the Loire, which proceeded to drive German troops out of Orléans. Alarm spread all along the enemy line. The Loire valley now became a war theater, forcing France's extramural government to relocate farther south, in Bordeaux.

But victory along the Loire was a small candle in the gathering night. For many, it flickered out on October 27 when a French army trapped inside the fortress-city of Metz surrendered, freeing large German divisions to serve elsewhere. The ill-trained French often acquitted themselves well, but theirs were campaigns of heroic futility. The siege had reduced Parisians to starvation. Krupp cannons kept lofting shells into the capital from miles away, and German forces marched inexorably down the Seine valley. On January 17, 1871, the last army corps patched together under Gambetta's provincial administration was defeated near Belfort, between the rivers Rhine and Rhône. Over 150,000 Frenchmen had given their lives since July, in what the historian Michael Howard has called the world's first total war. On January 28, after several weeks of secret shuttling between Paris and Versailles, where Bismarck had established German headquarters, Jules Favre, minister of foreign affairs (one of those ministers who had not escaped from Paris), negotiated an armistice. Its central provision was that France, in free elections, should form a government with which Germany could treat. By then, implacable resistance to the Germans was the position of only isolated groups: notably, working-class Parisians. Most French wanted peace. Gambetta, honoring, *à contre coeur*, what he acknowledged to be the general will, resigned his ministry. Up north, wagons laden with food entered Paris, which surrendered the perimeter forts.

Early in February, Paris invaded Bordeaux, or so it seemed when journalists, power brokers, actresses, and boulevardiers flocked south, some to observe the newly elected Assembly, others to convalesce. Bordeaux's population grew hourly, and almost all the deputies arrived before the inaugural session. One who didn't was Victor Hugo. Hailed en route from Paris by crowds shouting, "Vive Victor Hugo! Vive la République!," Hugo met even larger crowds in Bordeaux, where, he, Gambetta, and the future prime minister Georges Clemenceau, among others, joined against conservatives eager to buy peace at any price. They were a minority within parliament, but these republican stalwarts found support outside it among Bordelais whose demonstrations became so boisterous that light infantry and horse guards were summoned to patrol the streets. The horse guards closed ranks on February 28, when Adolphe Thiers—elected chief executive ten days earlier with a mandate to negotiate a peace treaty at Versailles—set forth Bismarck's draconian terms. By evening it was common knowledge that Germany wanted most of Alsace and part of Lorraine. Furthermore, German troops would occupy French territory until France had paid reparations in the amount of five billion francs. On March 1, after hearing eloquent protests, the legislature yielded. "Today a tragic session," Hugo wrote in his diary. "First the Empire was executed, then, alas, France herself!"

At its penultimate meeting in Bordeaux, the Asssembly, led by a conservative majority who feared Paris—where three revolutions had taken place sinced 1789—voted to reconvene on March 20 at the palace of Versailles.

Governing from Versailles conveyed a political message distasteful to republicans. But of greater immediate consequence was the Assembly's decision to end two moratoria that had eased the pain of Parisians trapped and unemployed since September 1870: one suspending payment due on promissory notes, the other deferring house rent. The measures restoring their obligations promised further hardship to several hundred thousand inhabitants of an economic wasteland and alienated the capital en masse. Debt-encumbered shopkeepers, idle workers, and artisans whose tools were in hock made common cause against an enemy all the more vengeful for being French. Indeed, the German soldiers camped outside Paris became mere spectators, as hatred of the foreigner turned inward.

The legislature might not have been so obdurate had Paris not previously challenged its authority. After the elections of February 8, republicans in Paris had presumed that the Assembly's conservative majority—provincial deputies for the most part—were determined to restore throne and altar, and their anger voiced itself through the National Guard, a democratized version of the bourgeois militia founded in 1789. It became a quasi-political organism, and on February 24 delegates from two hundred battalions ratified a proposal to replace the centralized state of France with separate autonomous entities—confederated "collectivities."

For Thiers, reports of troops breaking ranks all over town brought back memories of February 1848. At that time he had urged Louis-Philippe to leave Paris and recapture it from without, but the king had rejected his advice. This time, God alone stood above him. As soon as he had left the city, he issued general evacuation orders. Forty thousand army regulars were thus marched out of Paris, never to serve again. Up from the provinces came fresh conscripts "uncontaminated" by the capital, and before long one hundred thousand men occupied camps around Versailles. The day of reckoning was imminent, Thiers proclaimed on March 20. Forty-eight hours later, Versailles accepted the role Germany had played several months earlier. It declared Paris under siege once again.

In the city, forsaken ministries were staffed by tyros who somehow improvised essential services. The National Guard's Central Committee served, perforce, as an alternative government, though its avowed program was to organize elections for a Communal Council, then dissolve itself. Elections took place on March 26 and produced a council with very few moderate members, most of whom resigned straightaway. This left the high ground to extremists, whose abhorrence of a government that had in their judgment traded honor for peace intensified their visions of a new political and social order. On March 28, in front of City Hall, Paris proclaimed itself a Commune. Newly elected councillors all wore red sashes. They stood under a canopy surmounted by a bust of the Republic, draped in red. A red flag flew overhead. Forming up to music first heard during the 1789 Revolution, National Guard battalions played the "Marseillaise" as people sang and cannon fired salvos.

In Versailles it was clear that a policy of conciliation with the Communards would find few friends right of center. Given a choice between force and pragmatism, legislators chose inaction. "Meeting follows meeting, and emptiness yawns ever wider," Émile Zola despaired. "The majority will brook no mention of Paris. . . . This is a firm resolve: Paris doesn't exist for them, and its nonexistence sums up their political agenda." Zola, a parliamentary reporter for *La Cloche,* a Parisian newspaper, regretfully informed readers that in Versailles Paris seeemed very far away. "People there imagine our poor metropolis swarming with bandits, all indiscriminately fit to gun down."

Paris needed no instruction from Versailles in the art of gross political caricature, and neutral parties had reason to observe that Communards were spoiling for Armageddon as fervently as right-wing deputies. A movement whose initial goal had been municipal independence soon consecrated the schism between the ancien régime and the new order. "The communal revolution . . . inaugurates a new era of scientific, positive, experimental politics," the Commune proclaimed on April 19 (in a manifesto fraught with terms used elsewhere by writers seeking to legitimize "naturalist" fiction).

It is doomsday for the old governmental and clerical world, for militarism, bureaucracy, exploitation, speculation, monopolies, privileges to which the proletariat owes its servitude and the nation its disasters. May this great, beloved country deceived by lies and calumnies reassure itself! The struggle between Paris and Versailles is of a kind that cannot end in illusory compromises.

Throughout April, decrees rained thick and fast in Paris. Rent unpaid since October 1870 was canceled. The grace period on overdue bills was extended three years. Newspapers hostile to the Commune, including Veuillot's *L'Univers,* were suppressed. Church was separated from State and mortmain property nationalized. The corridors and wards of the largest city hospital, the Hôtel-Dieu, were "debaptized." And anticlericalism demanded the secularizing of education. A petition from "The New Education Society," whose advice was not ignored, besought the Commune to "immediately and radically" suppress religious instruction, for both sexes, in schools supported by the taxpayer. "Liturgical objects and religious images should be removed from public view. Neither prayers, nor dogma, nor anything that pertains to the individual conscience should be taught or practiced in common." (As priests and nuns were religious images incarnate, most removed themselves from the classroom.) Only one educational method should hold sway, "the experimental or scientific, which is based upon the observation of facts, whatever their nature— physical, moral, intellectual."

Aggrieved Catholics wondered whether France would ever be "delivered from itself," as Veuillot put it, or whether Pius IX's banishment from Rome had only augured a kindred fate for them. All over Paris, churches were converted into political clubhouses, arsenals, or military posts. Some resisted. The congregation at one large church fended off the National Guard as best it could, opposing the "Marseillaise" with a rendition of the "Magnificat." But resistance was hopeless. In festivities at the Panthéon, a large wooden cross with its arms sawed off became a mast for the red flag.* In the verbal scrum of club meetings, participants won attention by proclaiming their atheism. Sacrilege served as popular entertainment. In Saint-Sulpice, the crowd applauded a speaker holding an icon who defied God to stay his hand when he plunged a knife into Christ's sacred heart. At Saint-Germain l'Auxerrois, which housed a revered statue of the Virgin and Child, a militiaman punched open the Virgin's mouth, inserted a pipe, detached the infant Jesus, and marched him around on the end of his bayonet—all to frenzied cheers from the crowd. A woman at Saint-Nicolas des Champs proposed that the Commune reinforce Paris's defensive wall with gunnysacks containing the bodies of the sixty thousand priests (by her delirious count) still present in the city.

---

*The Panthéon had been built as a church during the ancien régime—the Église Sainte-Geneviève—but was deconsecrated during the Revolution. Thereafter its name and status changed with successive regimes. It was the Église Sainte-Geneviève during the Restoration of 1814–30 and the reign of Napoléon III (1852–70) but the Panthéon under Louis-Philippe (1830–48). It became the Panthéon again in 1885, to receive the mortal remains of Victor Hugo.

Another woman urged that nuns accused of poisoning hospitalized Communards be drowned in the Seine. Some sisters were forced to wear red sashes over their black habits.

In Louis Veuillot's view, the demon possessing his compatriots could be exorcized only by fasting and prayer, and the French wanted a man of God to cure their ills, not a politician or a man of war. "We all know it, and we all exclaim: *Perimus!* But such is the depth of our illness that no one dares to say: *Domine, salva nos!* And the storm will toss our poor, foundering bark as it will. How sad, this people without God!" One might have expected more muscular sentiments from a writer who several months earlier had hailed King Wilhelm of Prussia as a divinely ordained instrument punishing "France the courtesan" for her dissoluteness.

But to subdue the Communards, Versailles called upon a man of war, not a man of God. It marshaled its battalions—as announced by Thiers on March 20—under General Patrice de MacMahon, whose army had surrendered at Sedan. What followed was a week of slaughter and arson commemorated in historical accounts as *la semaine sanglante,* "bloody week." On May 21, government troops poured through five gates and swept across western Paris in pincer columns. Had MacMahon, who set up headquarters on the heights of Passy, known that the Commune's only serious preparation for urban warfare was an immense barricade on the place de la Concorde, his army might have taken City Hall by dusk. Instead it regrouped after its headlong advance, giving the populous quarters time to fortify themselves. Several hundred barricades rose overnight, and the Versaillais fought their way eastward, street by street, as fires set to impede them or to gut abhorrent monuments raged out of control. The Tuileries Palace was soon ablaze, then the entire rue de Rivoli, the Ministry of Finance, the Palais de Justice, the Prefecture of Police, the three-hundred-year-old Hôtel de Ville. Paul Verlaine, who lived on the quai de la Tournelle, across the Seine from City Hall, witnessed this conflagration.

[I saw] a thin column of black smoke come out of the campanile of the Hôtel de Ville, and after two or three minutes at most, all the windows of the monument exploded, releasing enormous flames, and the roof fell in with an immense fountain of sparks. This fire lasted until the evening, and then assumed the form of a colossal brazier; this in turn became, for days after, a gigantic smoldering ember. And the spectacle, horribly beautiful, was continued at night by the cannonade from the hills of Montmartre, which from nine that night to three in the morning provided a fireworks display such as had never been seen.

Before long spectators saw the July Column, which had been festooned with wreaths and flags, burning like a torch over the doomed Faubourg Saint-Antoine.* By Saturday, May 27, all that remained unconquered of Paris was its northeast corner. Caught between implacable Versaillais and German troops camped on the city's perimeter, many National Guards drew their last breath during a skirmish in Père Lachaise Cemetery. Those who didn't fall among the mausolea were lined up against a wall known ever since as "the wall of federals," shot, and thrown into a common pit. Outside Père Lachaise, evidence was flagrant of a much greater hecatomb. Corpses lay strewn behind ruined barricades, against walls, on the riverbanks. Thousands had been given summary justice and brought before execution squads. Blood ran down gutters, coloring the Seine red.

Fifty-six hostages held by the Commune died between May 21 and May 29. They included Jesuits, Dominicans, and, most prominently, Georges Darboy, archbishop of Paris. Darboy might have survived if Versailles had agreed to exchange him for a prisoner the Communards lionized, the radical thinker Auguste Blanqui. Darboy himself petitioned Thiers, arguing that the exchange would involve "only people, not principles." But Thiers stood on principle, and Darboy, a Gallican anti-infallibilist who had once been reprimanded for blessing the coffin of the Grand Master of the Freemasons, enjoyed little sympathy from right-wing deputies in a conservative parliament. Representations made by the American ambassador, Elihu Washburne,

---

*The July Column had been erected on the place de la Bastille to commemorate the Revolution of 1830. The remains of more than five hundred revolutionaries lay in its base.

went unheeded. On May 24, Darboy was taken from La Roquette Prison and shot dead. On his chest he wore the cross of Denis Affre, the archbishop who had died during the Revolution of 1848 while trying to mediate at a barricade. On the hand that blessed his executioners he wore the ring of Monsignor Sibour, an archbishop assassinated in 1857.

Ten days after the conquest of Paris, Darboy's coffin, preceded by a standard-bearer and followed by a delegation from the National Assembly—which had not saved him when it could have—was carried to Notre-Dame cathedral. In Louis Veuillot's eyes, the funeral was a triumphal march. "The cross, banished for nine months . . . demands and reclaims its right through martyrdom," he asserted. "It is summoned by the voice of blood and of testimony. One must yield, God wills it. The barricades are coming down; the savage's passion is under control; and the cross is borne aloft. . . . Tomorrow you will do as you please, you will understand or you won't, you will follow a new path or resume your evil ways. But here is a martyr, and you will let the cross pass by."*

Even more hortatory was Pius IX's foremost episcopal advocate, Bishop Louis-Édouard-Désiré Pie of Poitiers, who wanted Paris to throw off its mourning clothes and greet an era of national regeneration. The myriad dead had been a "sacrifice." The civil war was likened to the Great Flood inflicted on sinful humanity. Arising from it was a "sweet savor" agreeable to the Lord, who would now, he hoped, establish his covenant with France. "Above the bloody scenes of la Roquette one saw a rainbow portending better days." To be sure, Monsignor Darboy had not been above reproach, Pie wrote in a pastoral letter, but the "bloody scythe" of death had pruned him of unseemly growth. His death was impeccable.

The nation that emerged from civil war put few people in mind of Noah's Ark securely perched on Mount Ararat. It remained a house divided: equivocating over its political identity, either vilifying or glo-

---

*At the same time, in Berlin, Bismarck, the German generals, and Kaiser Wilhelm—all on horseback—led a victory parade of forty-two thousand troops, replete with triumphal arches.

rifying its past, and finding devils under its own roof. "Regeneration" was everyone's slogan, but pinned to it were very different meanings. For some it meant the embrace of science. For others it entailed rituals of purging and contrition. When a prominent republican consoled himself with the thought that such ordeals as society had endured might have "transfigured" it, Bishop Pie noted that change would be for the better only if it brought a change of "doctrine." France, the revolutionary "tool of Satan," had once more to become "the soldier of Christ." Possessed by an imposter since 1789, it had to recover its true self.

AN OBSERVANT TOURIST would have found ample evidence to support the view that God seemed happier in France during the early 1870s than He had been for some time. Many young people took holy orders after the war, much as they had after Waterloo during the Bourbon Restoration. Though money was scarce, hard-up congregants still paid Peter's pence—a voluntary contribution made annually to the pope. In 1872, the Assumptionists (or Augustinians of the Assumption) organized a league—the Association Notre-Dame du Salut—whose mission was the salvation of France through prayer. And a weekly magazine they launched on July 12, 1873, became the vade mecum of French pilgrims. Vendors of religious statuary drove a thriving trade. Dom Guéranger's efforts to revive plainsong at the abbey of Solesmes yielded *Les Mélodies grégoriennes* in 1880. Choral societies flourished. Country churches and presbyteries multiplied. Saintly patronage spread. Having been proclaimed "a patron of the Catholic Church" by Pius IX in 1870, Saint Joseph, Mary's humble consort, became the tutelary spirit of family men, carpenters, Christian spouses, primary school teachers, the exiled and deported, missionaries, and "people given to the inner life." Saint Philomena, Saint Anthony of Padua, Saint Roch, Saint Germaine Cousin sat on prayerful lips. Queen Radegund, a Merovingian saint better known in England than in France, acquired national celebrity when train passengers bound for Lourdes began to make a point of invoking her aid during their stopover at Poitiers.* At Tours, flanked by soldiers, they ritually paraded down the main street under a banner of Saint Martin chanting *"Sauvez Rome et la France au nom du Sacré-Coeur."* On a twenty-hour voyage to Lourdes from Avignon in 1874, pilgrims took turns reciting the rosary around the clock, their ecclesiastical travel agent having assigned each train compartment a precise timetable of recitation before departure.

This postwar revival, whose intense emotionalism harked back to the Counter-Reformation, benefited from the industrial age. Notwithstanding Pius IX's indictment of all things modern in *The Syllabus of Errors,* rapid transportation enabled the devout to make their presence felt en masse. There were spectacular assemblies, and 1873 was a notable year for them. The faithful gathered in their thousands to hear apocalyptic homilies at Lourdes, at Mont Saint-Michel, at La Salette, at Sainte-Anne d'Auray. National salvation was the issue, Monsignor Pie declared on May 28 at Chartres, where his huge audience, spilling beyond the cathedral, included forty bishops, one hundred forty legislators, and military officers of every rank. "To what state of prostration and impotence has public society been reduced among us? By what means can we wrest ourselves free from this despondency?" he asked. With "the rights of God" subverted by idolators extolling natural law, no wonder parliament couldn't decide whether France was fish or fowl, a republic or a monarchy. Nations that spurned the principle of Christian authority always lost their way. "We go in circles, we flail about at an impasse: *In circuitu ambulant, effusa est contemptio super principes, et errare fecit eos in invio et non in via."†*
One month later, many of these same pilgrims, heeding Pie's exhortation, gathered at Paray-le-Monial, in the great Cluniac basilica of the Sacred Heart, to hear another bishop deliver much the same message. "Since you have reconvened at Versailles," he said, addressing the

---

*Aristocratic ladies organized a welcome committee to demonstrate "the traditions of chivalric devotion."

†The quotation, beginning with *"effusa est,"* is from Psalm 107: "He brings princes into contempt and leaves them to wander in a trackless waste."

politicians present, "you have often asked God to forgive France her crimes. You have often made honorable amends to the Sacred Heart of Jesus for the ingratitude we have repeatedly shown, especially during the past eighty years" (in 1793 the royal family was guillotined). In an unopposed proclamation, assurances were given to Pius IX that the French stood foursquare behind "the courageous *Syllabus.*"

Responsible for killing a king and deserting a pope, the French were thus reminded that they had sins of parricide to expiate. Mea culpas had begun ringing out even before the execution of Archbishop Darboy. On May 14, 1871, when Communards still held Paris, the National Assembly in Versailles agreed by majority vote that the public should pray for divine leniency. "Long have we been oblivious of God," it declared. "It behooves this truly French Assembly to repair our lapse and show the world that France at last recognizes the only hand able to cure and save her." The words "Lord, we are a guilty, woeful country" echoed through every parish, voicing the conviction that moral deliquency and military unsuccess went hand in hand. Countless articles exploited this penitential axiom after the war. The conservative newspaper *Le Figaro* pointed out that the first defeats inflicted by Prussia, at Wissembourg and Reischoffen, had coincided with the removal of French Zouaves from Rome.

The zeal that raised money for chapels throughout France also inspired plans for a national shrine in Paris. Under Bishop Pie's aegis, this idea was promoted during the winter of 1870 and '71 and found favor with Catholics everywhere. When Pius IX blessed the project, Monsignor Guibert, archbishop of Paris, lost no time formulating its raison d'être, mobilizing support, and raising money. At stake was the re-Christianization of his godforsaken country, and the shrine—a grandiose monument as Guibert envisioned it—would display France's magnificent humility. It would be called the basilica of the Sacred Heart, in honor of a special devotion founded in the seventeenth century by the ascetic French nun Marguerite Marie Alacoque, whose visions of Christ's heart burning with divine love had commanded her to establish "a feast of reparation" on the Friday after the octave of Corpus Christi.

This cult had provided more martyrs to the eighteenth-century

Revolution than almost any other. "It was from France that the evil that has caused us such anguish spread across Europe," Guibert declared privately, "[and] from France, birthplace of special devotion to the Sacred Heart, will come the prayers that lift us up and save us." But no less symbolic than its name was its site. In October 1872, Archbishop Guibert reconnoitered Montmartre—the Mount of Martyrs in Catholic etymology—for some lofty real estate. Like Balzac's Eugène de Rastignac, the hero of *Père Goriot,* shouting "À nous deux!" from the nearby hill of Père Lachaise Cemetery, Guibert was bent on lording it over Paris. Unlike Rastignac, a consummate arriviste who rushed downhill to duel high society on its own ground in the Faubourg Saint-Germain, the archbishop made his stand up above. The Sacré-Coeur would be a sanctuary for refugees from Babylon, a Parisian home for a devotion of specifically French origin, a monument embodying allegiance to the pope cruelly separated from his seat in Rome, a majestic response to such pleasure domes as Charles Garnier's neo-baroque opera house, and insurance against further punishment by a wrathful god. It would be, said Guibert, "a lightning-rod on the highest point of the capital."

Still, the Church could not stake its claim and begin construction until the powers that be at Versailles deliberated, for expropriating landowners required legislative approval. Whether the project benefited the general public was the question, and because "benefit" lent itself to partisan judgment, Guibert couched his proposal in conciliatory terms, raising the flag somewhat higher than the cross. Who did not want France to knit together again? Portrayed as a patriotic omphalos, the basilica was deemed "publicly useful" by parliament, but not without clashes that might have been avoided if zealous members of the conservative majority had imitated the archbishop's tact. Most zealous of all were Émile Keller and Gabriel de Belcastel, two deputies who passionately conflated Church and State. After noting the almost unanimous acceptance of a statement that the construction of the proposed church served a public need, Belcastel went on, "But our committee, endorsing the patriotism and faith that inspired the project's sponsors, considers itself entitled and obliged to . . . add these words: ' . . . its purpose being to draw divine mercy and protec-

"Le Cantique," by Jean Béraud, at the building site of the Sacré-Coeur, 1887, twelve years after the laying of the first stone. Marguerite Marie Alacoque, who inspired the devotion to the Sacred Heart in its modern form, wrote many "canticles," or songs of praise. They were collected and published in 1867.

tion upon France and upon the capital.' " While private faith is the wellspring of great virtues, he declared, the honor and mainstay of a civilized nation reside in the public profession of faith. "Must one drum these things into French ears, into Christian ears? Gentlemen, France was born on a battlefield, by an act of faith."

One rebuttal came from Edmond de Pressensé, a well-known Protestant divine and scholar of Church history, whose son, Francis de Pressensé, would, two decades later, figure prominently in the passage of legislation separating Church and State. He contended that while France might have been born on a battlefield by an act of faith, the National Assembly was born to debate political issues, not matters of conscience, which one sorted out alone with one's God. Invoking divine mercy exasperated him most of all because it concealed, in his view, an attempt to establish the Sacred Heart as a state cult.*

---

*Before national elections in 1873, the Church had called for "a crusade of prayers" in the name of the Sacred Heart, to guarantee "good results," meaning a parliament of legitimists pledged to restore the monarchy.

Another deputy put it even more bluntly. "What I object to is the confusion of two very distinct orders, the temporal and the spiritual, the State's jurisdiction and the Church's, the duties of civil society and those of religious society. I object to a bill that confers upon the State what belongs to the Church and upon the Church what belongs to the State."

In the end, parliament compromised. It passed a safely bland proposal. But Pastor Pressensé's suspicions had been well founded. Shortly before the vote was taken, Belcastel rescued his deleted rhetoric at Paray-le-Monial (where Marguerite Marie Alacoque had made her home, in the Convent of the Visitation), addressing some twenty thousand pilgrims. In a statement hailed by one hundred fifty or more like-minded legislators, he consecrated France to the Sacré-Coeur.

The Sacred Heart, in Saint Marguerite Marie Alacoque's vision, asked her to build a chapel. Archbishop Guibert's dream of Catholicism sponsoring a revival of the national soul demanded something much larger. All seventy or more structures proposed in an open competition were very large indeed, and especially the winning design. Surmounted by ovoid domes and cupolas of Romano-Byzantine inspiration, and striped from base to lanterns with dark stone ribs, it looked like a giant Turkish folly. Or so said its critics.* Criticism left the archbishop unfazed, however. What did trouble him was the discovery that tunnels for mining plaster riddled Montmartre. Engineers explained that a massively heavy edifice would collapse sooner rather than later. After much anguished deliberation, they hit upon the idea of seating the church on eighty stone pilings driven deep into the bedrock. The indomitable Guibert approved, and soon, with its underground stilts in place, the Sacré-Coeur began rising over Paris. Few who saw the foundation stone placed would be alive to celebrate the consecration of the basilica forty-four years later.

The laying of the first stone took place on June 16, 1875, in a cere-

*By the end of the century it had been called many worse things: "A monument of provocation," "an insult to freedom of conscience," "an idolatrous temple built for the glorification of the absurd" (Émile Zola), "a repugnant temple built for a cannibalistic cult."

mony witnessed by the papal nuncio, a contingent of papal Zouaves, nine bishops, and two hundred members of the National Assembly. Although Guibert had wanted every French bishop at his side, prudence called for less pomp. Several days earlier, the speaker at a gathering of Catholic charitable societies was reported to have prophesied that the foundation stone would mark the grave of "the principles of 1789."

A funeral for those principles was the recurrent dream of hard-core monarchists among the many deputies in attendance. They had already tried and failed to bury the Republic, as we shall see, but hope sprang eternal.

CHAPTER II

BIRTH PANGS OF A SECULAR REPUBLIC

WITH THE YOUNG Republic struggling to emerge, birth and death pervaded the rhetoric of political discourse. Its most zealous partisans often waxed evangelical, as when the politician Jules Ferry, addressing fellow masons at the Grand Orient lodge on the rue Cadet in 1876, spoke of a new dispensation. The future prime minister, who would soon be sponsoring laws that made primary school education free, compulsory, and secular, panegyrized human progress. "Only when one begins to see Humanity not as an accursed race slouching decadently through a valley of tears, but as an endless cortege proceeding toward the light, does one feel part of an imperishable Being, of a humankind whose salvation, aggrandizement, and improvement are unceasing; only then has one truly conquered one's freedom, for one has liberated oneself from death."

Several years later and across the parliamentary aisle, much the same language was used to opposite effect. Maurice Barrès entered the Assembly in 1889, the year Ferry lost his seat for good. Elected from the portion of Lorraine not ceded to Germany, he commanded attention as the apostle of doctrinaire nationalism and a novelist many of whose devotees would have been content to see the Republic abolished by another coup d'état. On March 10, 1899, in a lecture sponsored by the Ligue de la Patrie Française, Barrès declared that he, nonpracticing but instinct with Catholicism, had found a home for his religiosity in the earth below. "I have brought piety down to the earth in which my dead are buried." Beneath his "restless" intellect lay an "immoveable" self, a collective unconscious, an impersonal being, a Barrès rooted in French soil. "The sensations that surge through me are not those of a transient individual." If identity was racial, did freedom of thought exist? Or was it a fantasy of the deracinated? He neither enjoyed it nor desired it. "I live only in accordance with my dead. They command me to act as I do."

Had Ferry and Barrès been cast as Aeschylean litigants facing off on an epic stage, Ferry would properly have recited Athena's line "Time in his forward flood shall grow ever more dignified," while Barrès, the younger man, argued for those older deities dwelling underground, who keep the dead alive. But there was no one to adjudicate their claims. The Palais Bourbon was not the hill of Areopagus; Republican France had no divine arbiter; and so the debate would rage, until the Furies won, in the bloodshed of another war with Germany.

IN JUNE 1871, several weeks after the horror of *la semaine sanglante,* Pius warned French visitors to the Vatican that an evil worse than the Commune still afflicted France. "What I fear is the wretched politics of Catholic liberalism: that's the real scourge," he said, anticipating Pius X's famous encyclical of 1907, *Pascendi Dominici Gregis.* Overt enemies were less intolerable than coreligionists propagating revolution while striving to reconcile Catholicism with freedom.

Provincial notables, who constituted a majority in the legislature elected on February 8, 1871, did not strive mightily to reconcile Catholicism with freedom. The prevailing sentiment among them was that France would run amuck if not bridled by religious principles, and the quasi-official term for the government to which they lent their support between 1871 and 1876, "l'Ordre Moral," bespoke a dour agenda. Though some paid lip service to "the principles of 1789," even they regarded the Church as society's frontline defense against havoc wrought in the name of liberty, fraternity, and equality. Most did not desire a restoration of the Bourbon monarchy, but neither were they prepared to evacuate Versailles and institute a republic. The mere mention of Paris made them furious, according to Émile Zola, who attended sessions as a legislative reporter. "The Right, on hearing [a deputy propose that the Assembly reestablish itself in Paris], stood up with the wrathful air of a prude who had heard a dirty word. M. de Marnier, in his anguish, couldn't help shouting: 'Would you have us run the risk of invasion?' "*

Any assumption that the Commune had fatally tarred the entire Left was soon to be proven wrong. By-elections held on July 2, 1871, saw republicans carry the day, notably Léon Gambetta, who found his voice again after months in limbo. Convinced that only a republic built along conservative lines stood some reasonable chance of surviving opposition from monarchist ranks, he made common cause with the adroit strategist of conservative republicanism Adolphe Thiers. These two formed a tenuous marriage of convenience, with Gambetta watching his words in parliamentary debate but hoisting petards during his stumps through provincial France. "Have we not seen laborers in the cities and fields win the vote?" he asked a sympathetic crowd at Grenoble. "Do all signs not suggest that our land, which has tried every other alternative, intends at last to risk a republic and call upon new social reserves?"

Lest those "new social reserves" emerge straightaway, the heterogeneous Right sought to act in concert. At daggers drawn since 1830, Legitimists (supporting the Bourbon pretender Henri, Comte de Chambord) and Orléanists (supporting Louis-Philippe's grandson the Comte de Paris) now agreed, in an arrangement called "fusion," that Chambord, after reigning as a constitutional monarch, should be succeeded by the Comte de Paris.† What their plan did not consider

---

*On more than one occasion in 1848, mobs had invaded the Palais Bourbon, where the legislature met.

†Chambord's grandfather, who reigned between 1824 and 1830 as Charles X, was a brother of Louis XVI. Louis-Philippe descended from Louis XIV's brother, Philippe I,

was the obduracy of Chambord, who lived in a castle near Vienna, as cut off from the world as Pirandello's Henry IV. For Chambord, the alternatives were either the faithful restoration of the kingdom France had overturned in 1830 or the enthronement of someone other than himself. His proviso was that the country raise the white lily-spangled flag of French monarchs, and rational heads could not prevail upon him to bend when he came home after four decades abroad. "[That flag] has always been for me inseparable from the absent fatherland; it flew over my cradle, I want it to shade my tomb," he declared in a statement published on July 6 by the royalist paper *L'Union*. "[Under that flag] the unification of the nation was achieved; with it your fathers, led by mine, conquered Alsace-Lorraine [in 1697]. . . . In the glorious folds of this unblemished standard I shall bring you order and liberty!" While eighty die-hard legitimists stood firm behind Chambord, a majority of conservative deputies dissociated themselves from his manifesto. Finding revolution and anachronism almost equally objectionable, they pledged allegiance to the Republican tricolor but yearned for a polity of ambiguous complexion— something neither lily white nor true blue.

For lack of a suitable king, the conservative majority or coalition of centrist factions improvised a government under the redoutable Adolphe Thiers. Having caught his second wind at the age of seventy-four, Thiers energetically tackled the monumental problems that beset France. Repairing war damage, inventing an economy, negotiating new frontiers, building up the army, and calming restless cities, this plump, high-strung little man, who looked more like a ninepin than a pillar of state, manipulated the contentious legislature by flattering all hopes with bland courtesy.

Thiers triumphed nominally on August 31, 1871, when fellow deputies, in a semantic tour de force, baptised him president of the

---

or Philippe d'Orléans. Much of the historical antagonism between the branches stemmed from the fact that Louis-Philippe's father accepted the title "Citoyen Égalité" (Citizen Equality) bestowed upon him by the Commune in 1792, and, as a member of the Revolutionary Convention, voted for Louis XVI's execution. Nevertheless, he, too, was guillotined.

Republic while implying that France might yet become a monarchy. "Until the country's definitive institutions are established," it read, "our provisional institutions must . . . assume in everyone's eyes, if not such stability as only time can vouchsafe them, stability enough to harmonize conflicting wills and end party strife." As deputy, prime minister, and president all together, Thiers would have liked a free hand, but the majority insisted upon controlling him through ministerial accountability.

For eighteen months these adversaries fought over everything from trade policy to military law. Important though they were, their skirmishes postponed the main battle, and on November 13, 1872, Thiers joined it. In a "Report to the Nation," he declared:

[A republic] is the government of the country; to resolve anything else would mean a new revolution, and the one most to be feared. Let us not waste time in proclaiming it, but instead let us use time to stamp it with the character we desire and require. A committee selected by you [the Assembly] . . . gave it the title of Conservative Republic. Let us seize this title and make sure it is deserved. . . . The Republic will be conservative or it will not be.

The public ratified the message in by-elections held through 1872 and 1873. Of thirty-eight legislative seats contested nationwide, republicans won thirty-one.

One such by-election led to Thiers's fall. On April 27, 1873, when Monsignor Pie was preparing the homily he would deliver to pilgrims at Chartres, the radical candidate defeated Thiers's minister of foreign affairs. Among right-wing conservatives, this event sharpened regrets of the kind that the novelist Edmond de Goncourt voiced in his journal: "Society is dying of universal suffrage. Everyone admits that it is the fatal instrument of society's imminent ruin. Through it, the ignorance of the vile multitude governs. Through it, the army is robbed of obedience, discipline, duty. . . . Monsieur Thiers is . . . a very short-term savior. He fancies that he can save present-day France with dilatory tactics, temporization, finagling, political legerdemain: small means cut to the measure of his small frame."

Having outlived his position as the irreplaceable negotiator by raising five billion francs in short order and liberating French territory, Thiers could not rely on Bismarck to save him from the consequences of his foreign minister's defeat. Conservative deputies blamed him for it. They excoriated a government hospitable to "new barbarians [who] threaten society's very foundations" and, flouting national sentiment, demanded that the cabinet be reconstituted without republican ministers. Thiers stood his ground, but Duc Albert de Broglie, the conservative leader, drafted a resolution expressing regret that recent ministerial modifications had not given conservative interests their due. It carried narrowly. An enraged Thiers felt compelled to resign, and on May 21 the Assembly named Patrice de MacMahon president. Just two years after "bloody week," MacMahon took office with a program of "moral order," foreshadowing another marshal, Philippe Pétain, who was to govern Vichy France during the 1940s under the motto "Work, Family, Fatherland." In his first presidential message, MacMahon declared: "With God's help and the devotion of our army, which will always be an army of the law, with the support of all loyal men, we shall together continue the work of liberating the country and reestablishing moral order in our land." Broglie, the grandson of Madame de Staël and Benjamin Constant and the son of Victor de Broglie, who had sided with Louis-Philippe in 1830, became the prime minister of what was soon to be dubbed "the Republic of Dukes."

At sixty-five, Marshal MacMahon assumed, not unhappily, that he was warming the seat for someone else, and that the parliamentary royalists who renewed their overtures to the Comte de Chambord in August 1873 would return from Austria with a king in tow.

Aside from old-line aristocrats and clergy of every rank, few people outside Versailles wanted Chambord enthroned, least of all the Right Wing's own peasant constituents, who, practicing Catholics though many of them were, feared that a Bourbon monarch would restore the ancien régime under which their forefathers had groaned. Such, at any rate, was the impression of the scientist and future minister Marcelin Berthelot. "The return of Henri V is the greatest chimera that could possibly have entered the heads of intriguing politicans," he wrote to Ernest Renan from his country retreat. "Anything is possible except that. The peasant will rise, note this well, in thirty or forty counties, because he really fears . . . that the common lands which he acquired in 1793 will be taken away from him. . . . One must distinguish pilgrimages and popular superstitions—which represent art and ideality for all poor people—from acquiescence in the clergy's will to dominate. . . . Not one in ten of people who throng to pilgrimage sites would countenance Henri V."* More apprehensive was George Sand, who, on October 3, wrote to Gustave

Marshal Patrice de MacMahon, president of the Third Republic (1873 to 1879) and guardian of l'Ordre Moral. He was ennobled by Napoléon III as Duc de Magenta after the French-Sardinian victory over Austria during the second Italian War of Independence.

Flaubert from her estate in rural Berry how much she feared that another Henri would soon be crowned. "People say I'm taking a gloomy view of things, but it's not what I view, it's what I smell, and I smell an odor of sacristy spreading over the land."

*Berthelot would have been cognizant of a violent incident that had taken place in the Dordogne on August 16, 1870, when news of Prussia's early victories was reaching remote villages. During a fair at Hautefaye, peasants fiercely loyal to Napoléon III, under whom they had enjoyed virtual exemption from taxes, set upon a young nobleman accused (falsely) of having proclaimed the advent of a republic. An aristocratic republican was, for them, a mortal enemy on two counts. The crowd beat him to a pulp, and burned his corpse. It was rumored that several of the tormentors then engaged in acts of cannibalism.

Chambord's suitors persisted. Once again they visited the portly old dauphin, whom one reporter described as having "all the blubber and divinely stupid ponderousness of an idol." On October 29, he dashed their hopes by vowing publicly never to become the "legitimate king of the revolution" and "inaugurate a restorative regime with an act of weakness." Any shackles placed upon his will were intolerable. "My person is nothing, my principle is everything. . . . When God has resolved to save a people, he takes care that the scepter of justice be placed in hands strong enough to grasp it." On this sanctimonious note Chambord exited from French history, leaving his acolytes behind. Several months later they commemorated their dream at the place des Pyramides with the inauguration of Emmanuel Frémiet's equestrian statue of Joan of Arc (which would become a yearly ritual). Was there not always a king to be restored? *"Le roi est mort. Vive le roi!"* However grave the defects of this crowned head or that one, declared Count Arthur de Gobineau (whose *Essay on the Inequality of Human Races* argues the principle of Aryan superiority), France could not be separated from royalism itself. It was her essence. It informed the country's racial being.* "There, deep down, revolutions don't mean anything," he wrote. Charles Maurras, Léon Daudet, and others—all future anti-Dreyfusards—would march that conviction into the twentieth century.

No longer bound by "fusion," moderate conservatives regrouped. Their strategy was to prop up MacMahon for the long haul and to invest his office with such power that a republic, if formalized, would be a constitutional monarchy in disguise. Broglie, the prime minister, achieved one goal by getting MacMahon's term extended: the marshal would serve for seven years. Embittered legitimists, who had meanwhile agreed to blame the collapse of plans for a Bourbon

---

*Another spokesman for the conjunction of kingship and racial identity was Marshal Hubert Lyautey, the future resident-general of Morocco and minister of war. After visiting Chambord (who died in 1883), he wrote: "I've just left [Chambord]. I was so moved, so powerfully gripped by his presence that I haven't yet been able to regain possession of myself. I merged into him during those hours of grace. I saw the King of France, I touched him, I heard him. The son of the Race which, province by province, made my country."

restoration on the Orléanist Broglie, found this so-called Septennate parodic. From then on they regularly attacked their former ally, doing damage by any means. To foul relations with Bismarck, they encouraged pastoral denunciations of Germany's Kulturkampf against the Catholic Church. When France recognized Victor Emmanuel as king of Italy, rallies were held to denounce the impious French diplomacy. At last the extreme Right joined the extreme Left to expel Broglie from office in a vote of no confidence. Another Orléanist (whom Broglie would in fact control) replaced him.

The law that promulgated the Septennate called upon the National Assembly to organize a constitutional commission, which was duly elected, and throughout 1874 thirty disputatious Frenchmen did nothing but quarrel. While France waited for its official identity, they wrangled over nomenclature, with right-wing deputies vetoing all formulae that incorporated the word "republic" or overtly legitimized republicanism. They might have spent another year quarreling had not one sensible deputy, during a debate over the law for election of the president, proposed an amendment that matter-of-factly read: "The president of the Republic is elected by the plurality of votes cast by the Senate and Chamber of Deputies united in a National Assembly." Somehow the amendment passed.

It passed by only one vote, but it sparked a common purpose, and with every subsequent item the majority grew larger. After several months, France's Third Republic was laboriously knocked together. Monarchical in design, it featured many of the safeguards against popular rule for which Broglie had lobbied, above all a bicameral legislature whose upper house, or Senate, could, at the president's request, dissolve the lower house, or Chamber of Deputies. Although universal (male) suffrage applied to the latter, election to the former was based on a system that gave disproportionate influence to rural, traditionally Catholic, sparsely populated districts.

Leftists with serious misgivings had had good reason to set them aside and take up residence in this eclectic structure. Deferring to Gambetta's political wisdom, they recognized that if ever they should gain control of the entire legislature they could disarm a hostile executive or anyway fight him at equal odds. But they also saw how government improvised without a constitution was serving those who argued the need for another Napoléon to restore order. Bismarck had been forging a European alliance against France while France lay paralyzed by domestic conflict, and Bonapartists were exploiting the public's thirst for revenge. Several had become deputies; and to the chagrin of monarchists and republicans alike, Napoléon III's former equerry won a by-election in March 1874. Was there any political ghost that, given the proper nourishment, might not spring to life again? "Fear! That is their political means. They engender it, they inoculate it, and, once they've frightened a certain class of citizens, they present themselves as saviors," Gambetta declared at a public rally, inveighing against what he called "Caesarian democracy, this order obtained by force, this brutal power, this clerical connivance, this patronage accorded to representatives of old aristocratic clans." More than any other factor, the knowledge that "Caesarian democracy" had not lost ground in the countryside, in the army, in the administration, or in the magistrature impelled Gambetta to make his peace with the sober Orléanists. However hastily contrived, a body of law offered some protection against despotism, he thought. And so it did. It saved France then, and it would save her again fourteen years later, when General Georges Boulanger very nearly became Napoleon IV.

THE SETTLEMENT THAT created a hybrid polity did not appease anti-Republicans or weaken the resolve of their spokesmen to defend Church and army against subversion. MacMahon considered social order his sacred trust. Having succeeded Thiers reluctantly, this soldier famous for his exploits during the Crimean War occupied the Élysée Palace as if it were the Malakhov fortress, from whose mined rampart he had declared, twenty years earlier: "Here I am; here I stay."

By law MacMahon could stay put until 1880, but legislators were obliged to go home when the National Assembly dissolved itself on December 31, 1875, and in elections held soon afterward, on February 20, 1876, conservatism suffered a heavy blow. Ignoring Mac-

Mahon's advice to reject all who might disturb the security of lawful interests or threaten it with the propagation of antisocial doctrines, voters returned republican candidates en masse. For every deputy seated Right of center three sat Left of it, and in the Chamber of Deputies Léon Gambetta's voice rang triumphant. Three years earlier, before another election, he had sounded this alarm.

> Opposing us is only one enemy, but it is well organized, well disciplined, with an effective instrument in passive obedience, with a powerful lever in the money it worms out of every kind of foolishness and superstition, overcoming all obstacles because it has no scruples, and hating modern society, not only in France, but throughout the world. There is the enemy! Henceforth, I repeat, only two parties will be facing off: the republican democrats and the clericals.

Now he exulted. Frenchmen had just given proof of their aversion to the hidden hand that guided every move made by the previous Assembly. Along with all of Europe, he told an audience at Lyon, the country had come to realize that the "clerical spirit," exploiting national disasters and sorrows, had been working its will under color of monarchism or restoration.

> A league, an association inspired by our religious quarrels of the fifteenth century, was formed in the heart of France, and we witnessed the creation of special associations, pilgrimages, missions, the confection of miracles, the organized migration of pilgrims to the Vatican, or the creation of circles for indoctrinating workers and youths, for propagandizing the development of primary and secondary education. And what was said in these associations, at these congresses, in these circles? That we should simply proceed to bury civilly the principles of '89.

It angered him that so many religious orders—hundreds of them unauthorized—continued to catechize the young. He was confident that with science as its guide, France, restored to its "glorious role," would be primus inter pares in advocating "modern truth" and "contemporary progress."

Incapable of focusing on objects left of Left Center (especially large objects like Gambetta) without seeing red, MacMahon appointed as prime minister a seventy-eight-year-old whose republicanism, like his frock coat and rhetoric, evoked the fashion of 1830. Jules Dufaure had no sooner taken office than troubles beset him. Damned by the Right for having dismissed conservative functionaries, Dufaure found himself damned by the Left for not having made the purge complete. Caught between Catholics, who insisted that his government deplore the omission of religious ceremony from funerals, and anticlericals, who held that the State must remain neutral, he proposed a compromise obnoxious to both. The Chamber of Deputies and the Senate, ignoring him, clashed time and time again over religious matters. When the Chamber fought to disqualify ecclesiastics from the juries that granted university degrees, the Senate, whose conservatives enjoyed a majority, gave no ground. It stood firm when the Chamber questioned the raison d'être of France's Vatican embassy. And when Gambetta persuaded the lower house to cut several items from the Public Worship budget, the upper house hastened to restore them.

Dufaure's diplomatic skill availed him even less in clashes provoked by left-wing deputies demanding exoneration for convicted insurgents. After all, Dufaure had been the minister of justice who, under Thiers, organized the machinery of prosecution that tried Communards, and this deed left him stranded between hostile allies and kindred foes. The leftist Chamber passed an amnesty bill over his protests; the rightist Senate then rejected it with a complicitous wink in his direction. Frustrated by the ambiguity of his position, he resigned on December 12, 1876, after nine months in office.

To succeed Dufaure, MacMahon appointed Jules Simon, a gifted intellectual whose occasional departures from leftist orthodoxy had earned him a reputation among conservatives as a *merle blanc*, or "white blackbird," with whom they could deal. "You know full well that I am both deeply republican and deeply conservative" is how he portrayed himself in his inaugural address to parliament, and proofs were furnished immediately. Simon might have stayed the course by tacking right and left had waves from abroad not capsized him. In January 1877, Pope Pius IX summoned good men everywhere to condemn Italy's leftist regime, specifically the Clerical Abuses Law with which that regime had armed itself for use against subversive priests. Crowds marched throughout France in sympathy. Simon vowed to maintain order. But republicans wanted something more. They wanted ultramontane politics suppressed, brutally if need be, and most of them backed a resolution to that effect after hearing Gambetta exclaim in one of his most celebrated speeches: *"Le cléricalisme, voilà l'ennemi!"*

Léon Gambetta, protagonist of the Government of National Defense during the Franco-Prussian War and a towering figure in republican ranks during the 1870s and early 1880s. He was elected prime minister in 1881.

A leader without followers, Simon the white blackbird now found himself shunned as a mutant by every political species. MacMahon accepted his resignation.

It would have taken supreme arrogance or desperation or both for MacMahon to flout the republican majority at this juncture, but flout it he did on May 16, 1877—a famous date in French political annals. Proclaiming himself responsible to "France" rather than to parliament, he named Albert de Broglie prime minister, and informed the Chamber through an envoy that he would not suffer "radical modifications of all our great administrative, judicial, financial, and military institutions." Three hundred sixty-three republican deputies thereupon issued a declaration stating that France was not a mere figment of MacMahon's sovereign will. This challenge was no sooner made public than MacMahon adjourned the Assembly. When it reconvened a month later (republican provincial governors, or prefects, having meanwhile been fired), the so-called "363" reprimanded Broglie's right-wing cabinet. "Considering that the government formed on May 17 by the president of the Republic . . . was summoned to power in violation of majority rule," they declared, "considering also . . . that it represents the coalition of parties hostile to the Republic—a coalition whose leaders fomented clerical riots, . . . we say that this government does not enjoy the confidence of representatives of the nation." Had custom prevailed, a vote of no confidence would have brought down the government. Instead, MacMahon, facing another Hobson's choice, arranged to dissolve the Chamber. With vivid memories of December 2, 1851, when Louis-Napoléon seized power, Victor Hugo and several other left-wing senators assembled at Hugo's apartment, half expecting a coup d'état.

There would be no coup d'état, but an event of signal importance did take place several weeks before the scheduled election to form a new Chamber. On September 3, 1877, Adolphe Thiers died. Having won a parliamentary seat in 1876 and joined the "363" who declared Broglie unacceptable as prime minister, this astonishingly resilient Provençal had been, at eighty, buoyed by great expectations. If France returned a republican majority, he hoped—with Gambetta's assistance—to evict his nemesis MacMahon from the presidential palace. Thiers and Gambetta had indeed already sealed a partnership that made the latter's agenda for social change less ominous to conservatives and the former's moderation less unpalatable to social reformers. For Gambetta, Thiers was a valuable ally who through his influence over fence-sitters could thwart any attempt by MacMahon to counter Broglie's defeat with a centrist coalition.

Although Thiers was gone, his vengeance survived him. In his grave he posed an even more serious threat to MacMahon than in parliament, for radical republicans who had shunned the live politician rallied around the dead statesman. Posthumously absolved of sins committed against the working class, Thiers (whose widow would not authorize a state funeral) received tribute from multitudes as his flower-laden hearse clattered across eastern Paris to the cemetery where Communards had made their last stand during *la semaine sanglante*. This demonstration presaged a united republican front.

"For me, the idolatry that attended Thiers's funeral stands testimony to France's monarchical temperament," Goncourt noted, anticipating Arthur de Gobineau's dictum in his book on the Third Republic: "In its president it will always want a monarch, a dominator, and not a servant of elected assemblies." Republican deputies concurred, which may be why, after winning the national elections, they lost no time neutering the presidency. Dissolution was MacMahon's chief weapon against an unruly Chamber, and this they made him surrender. "We must, in our national interest, resolve the present crisis once for all," he affirmed against his will, in a dictated message that was to shape France's political course until 1939. "The exercise of the right of dissolution is nothing more than recourse to a tribunal from whose judgment there is no appeal: it cannot serve as a system of government." With MacMahon stripped of effective power, the republican majority went about unseating seventy-two deputies in whose electoral campaigns priests and notables were alleged to have exerted undue influence. What became axiomatic thereafter was the principle that corrupt behavior manifested itself only in conservative ranks. No republican legislator would ever face expulsion because a Masonic lodge, an anticlerical schoolmaster, or a like-minded prefect had endorsed his candidacy.

The World's Fair of 1878 imposed decorum upon the Chamber. And deputies of the republican Left had additional reasons to temper their reformist zeal: too much impatience might alarm those cautiously progressive elements Gambetta described as *"les nouvelles couches"* (the new strata), whose support would be indispensable in forthcoming Senate elections. It behooved republicans, Gambetta declared, to table some reforms until they had won a Senate majority. Until then, he warned, "no imprudence, no dissidence, no mistakes." Although he himself, on one occasion, could not refrain from proclaiming that education should be laicized, that "wherever the Jesuit spirit finds a crack, clericals slip in and take over," he generally practiced what he preached.

This entente cordiale ended as soon as republicans gained control of both houses. Administrative, diplomatic, and judicial officers appointed by Broglie knew that the Senate victory would cost them their posts. The purge began straightaway, on January 25, 1879, with ministers submitting long lists of candidates for dismissal. Mac-Mahon did not bother to fight, or rather fought only to make certain that army chums retained high commands. On January 30, the marshal tendered his resignation and walked into private life, after congratulating his successor—a drab, cautious, tightfisted lawyer even older than he, with impeccable republican credentials, named Jules Grévy.

There were many who supported Grévy in order to keep the flamboyant Gambetta from occupying the Élysée Palace. Gambetta would not do as chief executive, they felt. He sucked up too much oxygen, he hogged center stage, he loomed too large, he lived too high, he schemed too fast. History had taught republicans to distrust luminaries. But on January 31, the same deputies who refused him the presidency of the Republic elected him president of the Chamber, or house speaker. In that role, he helped several prime ministers steer a course toward separation of Church and State.

Leftists had repeatedly declared that unless the school system was secularized, the clergy would continue to hold France hostage, poisoning young minds against the Republic. Its secularization became a priority of government after MacMahon stepped down, and the republican principally associated with this enterprise, along with Gambetta, was Jules Ferry, who served as minister of education during the late 1870s. Earlier in the decade, Ferry had earned the enmity of the Church by declaring in the Chamber of Deputies:

> I believe in the lay State, lay in its essence, lay in all its organs. . . . The conflict between the rights of the State and those of the individual is as old as society itself, but conflicts between the rights of the Catholic Church and the rights of the State I simply do not recognize. I will not agree to discuss them.

The proper functioning of the Republic hinged, in his view, on the expression of individual wills, and for individuals to be well-informed benefited France collectively. "Instruction and education are at once the Republic's goal and its vehicle: its goal because they alone allow each person to be fully a citizen; its vehicle because citizens alone make it work." Women's suffrage had not yet become a republican mandate. To be "fully a citizen" remained a male prerogative (women would not obtain the vote until 1944). But Ferry, confronting the episcopate, insisted that women be permitted, indeed encouraged, to attend secular schools. "Bishops know perfectly well that whoever controls a wife controls her husband. That is why the Church wants to hold her fast, and why democracy must make her its own. Citizens, democracy must choose, under pain of death. Woman must belong either to Science or to the Church."

When the Senate closed ranks against an aggressive reform bill, Ferry, nothing daunted, issued decrees that required the Society of Jesus to leave France within three months and all other religious teaching orders to apply for legal residence. Right-wing journals wrung as much pathos as possible from the expulsion, with images of distinguished gentlemen in frock coats and top hats mournfully helping frail old Jesuits, their childhood mentors, into waiting coaches. Magistrates who resigned in protest had their names inscribed in a "Golden Book." Ferry, by then prime minister as well as minister of education, seized the opportunity to republicanize the legal system still further.

This conflict played out in towns and hamlets all over France, where teachers holding diplomas from normal schools locked horns with the local curate. How bitter it often was may be judged by the report of a schoolmaster in the mountainous Lozère region. Classes had already resumed after the summer holiday when the priest denounced a history text in which Joan of Arc was described as "believing" that she had heard voices. "He insisted that I use another text," wrote the teacher.

I replied that it was impossible to do so. "Well then, it's war between the Church and the School," he said. And war it was.

He attacked me all year long, every week, in a Catholic paper called *La Croix de la Lozère.* My personal and professional life offered endless pretexts to spit venom.*

At last a fraternal association came to his aid and brought charges against *La Croix,* compelling it to publish his rejoinders.

One morning, I found the door to our schoolhouse smeared with excrement. Our village paid for a woman to clean it up. Also at the priest's instigation, two families, a total of three children, refused to use the text and learn their lessons. I notified the regional Inspector, who had them expelled. The priest then took them in and tutored them. This didn't last long. The tribunal of Florac imposed a stiff fine on the curate for holding a class without authorization, and the three children ended their studies. . . . The priest was appointed chaplain of a convent in Mende and an editor of *La Croix de la Lozère.*

France's foremost Catholic newspaper, *L'Univers,* vilified republican schoolmasters as "professors of atheism," "masters of demagogy," "seasoned revolutionaries," "missionaries of the modern mind" intent upon corrupting *"la France profonde"*—rural France (where, in many regions, the Church had made its peace with sorcery and pagan superstition). "More than ever this glorious title of Catholic excites the hatred and scorn of men in power," it said. "Whoever bears it—be he soldier, magistrate, functionary—must henceforth expect only insult and persecution. The day is near when one will not enjoy the protection of common law unless the sign of the beast is stamped on one's brow. The spirit of Satan, embodied in the revolution, is successfully striving to obliterate what remains of centuries-old traditions and the religious institutions to which our country owes its past greatness." The plot of Émile Zola's late novel *La Vérité* features a schoolmaster and a curate at daggers drawn.

---

*The Assumptionist paper *La Croix* had many such regional satellites. All told, their circulation exceeded four hundred thousand.

While thus taking charge of future generations by expelling *manu militari* teachers pledged to a hostile doctrine, the new regime also took charge of its past, with gestures that validated or glorified republican history. In July 1879 the seat of government was returned to Paris, after eight years at Versailles. The "Marseillaise" became France's official anthem. One year later, on July 6, 1880, the Assembly made July 14 a national holiday, commemorating not only the fall of the Bastille but the Revolutionary festival called la Fête de la Réunion. And just before Bastille Day 1880, Communards who had rotted in prison fortresses and penal colonies, or lived abroad in penurious exile, learned that they had been amnestied, thanks largely to Gambetta's relentless campaign on their behalf. "You must close the book on these last ten years," he exhorted the Chamber. "You must consign to oblivion the crimes and vestiges of the Commune and say to all alike, to those whose absence one deplores as well as to those whose contradictions and discords one finds regrettable, that there is

"The Army Swearing Loyalty to the Young Republic," 1880, when July 14 became an official holiday celebrating the birth of the Republic.

but one France and but one Republic." Even as the black-robed soldiers of Jesus were bidding France farewell, the reds set foot on French soil again.

It was France's misfortune and originality, a journalist observed in 1861, that since the Revolution every form of government had been regarded as a usurpatory improvisation by one camp or another. Twenty years later, the remark still held true. Parties forgetful of their own sins found strength in remembering those of the enemy, and among royalists, Gambetta's entreaty fell on deaf ears. For them, "One France" meant the ancien régime. That would not change.

CHAPTER III

THE CRASH OF THE UNION GÉNÉRALE

IN 1878, WHEN the Sacré-Coeur had not yet risen much above its foundation, another ungainly Romano-Byzantine hulk materialized on the bluffs overlooking Paris's Right Bank. This one, named the Palais du Trocadéro, commanded a World's Fair grander than any of its predecessors, with international pavilions spread over sixty-six acres. The guidebook English visitors brought with them was titled *Paris Herself Again.* Across the Seine, on the Champ de Mars, where Eiffel was to build his tower a decade later, an immense hall displayed material evidence of France's postwar recovery. Side by side under transverse arches in a long gallery stood machines large and small. On the Esplanade of the Invalides, an agricultural show featured every breed of French goat, cow, and sheep. Several hundred "indigenous people" spent six months in a human zoo called the Negro Village. Model houses illustrating the domestic architecture of countries the world over (except Germany, where a more fateful congress of nations took place in June, to carve up the Balkan peninsula) lined a central avenue lit after dark by electric streetlamps. Each continent exhibited its dress, its food, its art, its wares, its tools. And America was well represented at the groaning board. Thomas Edison's phonograph and

Alexander Graham Bell's telephone drew large crowds. Crowds also swirled around the disembodied head of Bartholdi's statue of Liberty, which sat outside the Trocadéro Palace years before it crossed the Atlantic.

The newly triumphant Left, celebrating its ascendancy in conjunction with this kermis, declared June 30 a national holiday. The occasion was an unhappy one for antirepublicans. "I was surrounded all day long by the howling, hateful, stupid joy of the multitude demanding that Chinese lanterns and flags hang from all windows, and from mine in particular," Edmond de Goncourt complained. "Unbelievably, flags were draped on hearses transporting their dead to the cemetery." But Goncourt's progressive compatriots saw Paris as the impresario of a new, intellectually adventurous community. Should not this World's Fair dramatizing the victory of mind over matter enjoy even more prestige than the Olympic Games of antiquity? asked a newspaper columnist in *Le Temps*. "Every nation [wants] to relate its victories over the elements, to divulge the manner in which it has remade God's work, to exhibit the instruments it has invented to correct our planet, to channel rivers, to pierce isthmuses, to displace seas, to create continents, to render the transmission of thought swifter than lightning, to project the human voice over prodigious distances, . . . to govern water, air, fire. . . ." Why not dig a tunnel beneath the English Channel (plans for which were on display, along with those for other, more imminent, public works)? He confidently assured his readers that on the whirligig of modern life, visionaries born "before their time," who in slower times would have died unrecognized, could now expect to witness the accomplishment of their dreams.

Although Pius IX's denunciations of gross materialism were still ringing loudly when the fair opened, on May 1, three months after his death, Catholic France did not shun the event. The archbishop of Algiers joined Victor Hugo in sponsoring a lecture by the explorer Pierre Savorgnan de Brazza, who had recently returned from Senegal. Exhibitions attested to the Church's missionary work around the world. The faithful came in strength, for all the reasons that sixteen million people came: to revel, to learn, to buy. Above all, to buy.

The Palais du Trocadéro, built for the Exposition Universelle of 1878 (and demolished fifty-nine years later to make way for the Palais du Chaillot at the Exposition Internationale of 1937).

Like the Frenchmen who rejoiced in republican success, those who deplored it binged on exotic trophies. And their acquisitiveness was by no means limited to gala sprees at the fair. With their power waning in the National Assembly, the rich and the not-so-rich sought compensation outside parliament, in the financial world (just as many high-level administrations associated with MacMahon's regime of Moral Order left government service for commerce). Nothing illustrates this more vividly than the rise and fall of the Union Générale.

THE UNION GÉNÉRALE began as an investment fund launched during the summer of 1875 by two Parisian bankers in association with aristocratic sponsors and at least one deputy known for his allegiance to the Bourbon cause. A prospectus titled *Appel aux catholiques* announced that the founders had every intention of "consolidating the financial strength of Catholics, creating profitable returns for them, and thus enabling them to seize some of the power monopolized by opponents of their faith and of their interests." At stake was the very survival of "religion" and "Society." It behooved Catholics, the crusading prospectus went on, not to do business with Jewish and Protestant bankers. Should the fund prosper, its beneficiaries would be missions, convents, and parochial schools.

It did not really prosper until 1878, when an infusion of money from conservatives defeated in the recent elections gave it new life. Reorganized as a commercial bank, the Union Générale placed at its helm Eugène Bontoux, an entrepreneur with strong monarchist ties. Bontoux would one day acquire lasting fame outside high finance as the model for Zola's character Aristide Saccard in *L'Argent;* but while Saccard's dreams are all about a capitalist reconquest of the Holy Land, Bontoux's centered on Eastern Europe. The Eden ripe for industrial exploitation, as he saw it, was Austria-Hungary, where he had already made his personal fortune.

Bontoux came with a checkered past. Having studied civil engineering at France's élite technical institute, the École Polytechnique, he found himself in 1846, at age twenty-six, posted to Roanne as the director of public works in the upper Loire valley and, while there, published a pamphlet urging the construction of a railroad line between the Loire and the Rhône rivers. Written in the language of technocratic enthusiasm, his argument impressed Paulin Talabot, an older alumnus of Polytechnique, who had grasped the future of rail transportation years earlier, after watching George Stephenson's locomotive ply between Manchester and Liverpool. What Stephenson had done in the Midlands Talabot accomplished in the Midi, with a railroad that linked the coal fields near Alès to a Rhône River port at Beaucaire. Although rebuffed by government ministers, most of whom, like their counterparts in England, took a dim view of the new technology, he obtained financial backing from venturesome financiers, above all James de Rothschild, and during the 1840s proceeded to build the line that would ultimately connect Paris, Lyon, and Marseille: the PLM. It was well under way when Eugène Bontoux became his protégé.

By 1857 Bontoux had moved from Roanne to Vienna as a high-level employee of the Austrian State Railroad, or Staatsbahn (whose principal investors were French). What led to his expatriation remains unclear. It is thought that he launched an enterprise of his own upon leaving government service, that he failed, and would have suffered grievously if Talabot had not intervened. We know that Talabot himself played a decisive role in his subsequent career. In 1860, Bontoux left the Staatsbahn for the Südbahn (the Southern or Lombard Line), joining a company owned by the Rothschilds and directed by Talabot; he eventually succeeded Talabot as chief executive and stayed with the Südbahn until 1877.

Like his mentor, Bontoux—a stooped, gaunt, rumpled man—lived and breathed mines and railroads, and the thought of their proliferation generated inexhaustible energy in him. Space was there to be conquered: for the thrill of conquest, for the love of money, and for the sake of Christ. "Something of a promoter" is how the Crédit Lyonnais's informant pictured him. "Highly intelligent but feverishly imaginative." His showmanship propelled him beyond the Südbahn into a sphere of grand enterprise governed by his commitment to conservative ideals. Modern technology and the social order of yesteryear had equal claims upon Bontoux's imagination. In an article on the Carpathian basin he declared that Austria-Hungary, with what

The Gallery of French Machines at the Exposition Universelle of 1878.

strength it still retained, needed to develop its commerce and industry, this being "the only way open for empires in our day to achieve greater wealth and power." Empires included his own imperial ego.

Bontoux did not leave the Südbahn in 1877 of his own accord. His private ventures, undertaken with backing from financiers in Lyon, encroached upon the Rothschilds' sphere of influence. It is known, for example, that he curried favor with compatriots by attempting to have the Crédit Lyonnais replace the Rothschild bank as Hungary's principal loan contractor.

If such flagrant disloyalty offended his employer, so, no doubt, did his controversial participation in French politics. When still executive director of the Southern railroad, Bontoux had presented himself as a candidate for the Chamber of Deputies from his native town of Gap, near Lyon, in the elections that followed MacMahon's quasi–coup d'état. Republicans scored a decisive victory and afterward accused several elected conservatives of peddling influence. One of these was Bontoux, who had in fact donated liberally to Catholic charities. The right-wing newspaper *L'Union* declared that his munificence expressed the promptings of a conscience unacquainted with paltry political considerations. Bontoux, in defending himself before the Assembly, pleaded innocent of clericalism. "During the thirty years [it had been only twenty] I've lived outside France, the dictionary has undergone several modifications. . . . No one could define [the word clericalism] for me, so I have defined it as it applies to me, and it is this, gentlemen: I can't imagine human society doing without the faith that makes its unjustifiable sufferings and frightful inequities endurable. . . . I also can't imagine civil society functioning under church rule. To each its own domain." Neither his well-publicized advocacy of the pope's temporal power nor his overt courtship of Chambord, the would-be king in his castle near Vienna, signified hostility to the secular Republic, he protested. Rather, he "awaited" the restoration of the pope's temporal authority as Jews await the Messiah, without expecting it to occur in historical time. A liberal newspaper, *Le Rappel,* doubted that "clericals" less profitably employed than he were quite so "patient and platonic." In the end, Bontoux's self-defense did him no good anywhere. At Versailles his election was invalidated, and in Austria the government bridled at his insistence to the National Assembly that during his years abroad French interests had always been his foremost concern.

The man who took command of the Union Générale in 1878 brought with him a provision of anger that only nourished his grandiose dreams. Seventeen years earlier Bontoux had published an article in the influential monthly *La Revue des deux mondes* enumerating the benefits to be reaped from a rail connection between Trieste and Budapest. With an outlet to the sea, Hungary's Pannonian wheat fields would feed Europe, eclipsing Ukraine, and enrich the Hapsburg monarchy.* Since then his horizons had broadened. By 1878 he envisioned trains traversing southeastern Europe from Vienna and Budapest to Salonika and Constantinople. Nothing could then impede the industrialization of the Balkans. Capital would flow from France—through the Union Générale—and eventually yield huge dividends. To be sure, profit was not the whole of Bontoux's vision. Joined to a regenerated Austro-Hungarian Empire, the Balkans would fortify European Christendom against Russia. The whole Danube basin would serve as Europe's barbican, keeping Asia outside the continent.

Bontoux embraced the Union Générale's chartered goals—of pooling the financial resources of Catholics and challenging the power wielded by "opponents of their faith and their interests." The reconstituted joint-stock bank opened a branch in Rome, where high prelates (including Cardinal Jacobini, secretary to the pope) and rich princes invested substantial sums. Paris and Lyon attracted the same clientele. Bishops, archbishops, curates, aristocrats—among them, Henri, Comte de Chambord—crowded the list of shareholders. Surrounding Bontoux on the Union's board were Prince Bandini, Francesco Borghese, the Marquis de Ploeuc (a former director of the Imperial Ottoman Bank), the Vicomte Mayol de Luppé (four of whose six daughters were nuns), the Count Hennequin de Villermont, a dozen more active legitimists, and Eugène Veuillot—whose famous

---

*During the last decades of the century, Budapest did in fact become the largest milling center in the world and remained the second largest when overtaken by Minneapolis.

brother, Louis Veuillot, noted at this time, "In Italy, in Germany, in Austria, Jews are really leading the attack against Christianity. They take too much satisfaction in being 'kings of the age.' Never has a big Jew loomed as large as he does today."[*]

To strenuously apostolic colleagues, Bontoux did not seem enough of a crusader. His restraint, however, was no doubt calculated. Why flaunt the scepter and the cross when everyone knew what the Union Générale stood for? Emblems over the front door might needlessly scare away non-Catholic investors and depositors. With the accomplishment of his visions always in mind, Bontoux offered hospitality to anyone who could afford it.

Between 1878 and 1881, the Union Générale repaid its shareholders sixfold. Those three years were prosperous ones in France. Under prime minister Charles de Freycinet, the Republic initiated a program of public works aimed at revitalizing an economy laid waste by the Franco-Prussian War. Industrial production increased, foreign trade expanded, railway lines reached across the provinces, goods sped to their destinations. An age of plenty had dawned, and plenty begot an appetite for more, even among petit-bourgeois schooled in thrift. The result was a fever of speculation. Traders at the Paris Bourse made more noise than had been heard there since the get-rich-quick days of the Second Empire as stock issues multiplied and the value of shares soared.

The value of Union Générale shares soared higher than most, with a portfolio reflecting its president's aggressiveness and ubiquity. When insurance was all the rage, Bontoux launched half a dozen insurance companies. After gaining control of the Bank of Milan, he acquired real estate and water resources in Italy through affiliates of his own creation. He was instrumental in forming the company that built railroads in Brazil. He invested in Russian factories, in Roman tramways, in Romania's natural gas fields, in French breweries, in the Paris–New York Telegraph Society, in the French Electric Power company. To some extent, a wave of general prosperity was floating all boats; but

---

[*]*Les Juifs, rois de l'époque: Histoire de la féodalité financière* was the title of a book published in 1847 by Alphonse Toussenel.

when he addressed his shareholders, Bontoux credited divine providence with the Union's successful debut.

Divine providence smiled widest farther east, where Bontoux still situated his most tenacious dreams of entrepreneurial conquest. Having concluded that those dreams were not likely to be realized without a base in Vienna, he invented an Austrian sibling for the Union Générale: the Österreichische Länderbank. This new arrival could only be seen as an interloper in the territory of the credit bank established by Anselm von Rothschild in 1855, when Austria desperately needed capital to bail itself out of debt and regenerate industry. After twenty-five years, the Rothschild consortium was so well entrenched that Bontoux would have thought it impossible to find purchase in the Hapsburg Empire had political events not favored his intrusion. When the Liberal Party fell from power in 1879, the new prime minister, a half-Irish aristocrat named Eduard Graf Taaffe, formed a coalition government encompassing the court, the clergy, Czech and Polish militants demanding a federalist constitution, and Viennese burghers resentful of capitalism and Jews.* Taaffe wanted to oust German banking interests—particularly the Rothschilds, who had long been bedfellows of the Liberal Party. He found a natural ally in Bontoux, and thus the Länderbank enjoyed direct government patronage from the first, with clear results. No sooner had he assumed power than he set in motion a scheme for binding the newly independent kingdom of Serbia to Austria-Hungary economically and thus staving off Russia.† His Balkan policy hinged on a rail connection with the Ottoman port of Salonika, via Belgrade; building and controlling this Serbian link became Bontoux's mandate, and his prize.

---

*Their vituperation began in great earnest after the stock-market crash of 1873. More generally, anti-Semitism was fueled by economic problems that attended the institution of free enterprise. "Laissez-faire, devised to free the economy from the fetters of the past, called forth the Marxist revolutions of the future," Carl Schorske noted in his book *Fin-de-Siècle Vienna*. "Catholicism, routed from the school and the courthouse as the handmaiden of aristocratic oppression, returned as the ideology of the peasant and artisan, for whom liberalism meant capitalism and capitalism meant Jew."

†Serbia had been granted independence from the Ottoman Empire at the Congress of Berlin in 1878.

Claiming the prize meant groping through a labyrinth of peninsular politics. There were several proposals for a trans-Balkan railroad, the competition was fierce, and the players all had much to gain and something to skirt. Count Taaffe wanted a north-south line. Russia, which relied on its pan-Slavic lobby, sought independence of the Turkish straits with a line running west from Odessa to the Adriatic. Impoverished Serbia wanted any money it could borrow. And in Austria-Hungary, the Staatsbahn, Bontoux's original employer, proposed to loop around Serbia altogether by extending its track along the Danube east to Craiova in Romania, then south across Bulgaria to a junction with Baron de Hirsch's Constantinople line. The Staatsbahn fought Bontoux tooth and nail. Largely owned and administered by French banks, it put pressure on France's foreign minister, who immediately cautioned his ambassador in Constantinople about "the drawbacks of the monopoly that a powerful firm subservient to the Austro-Hungarian government may obtain." Turkey should communicate with the outside world by as many openings as possible, he believed, the better to hinder the "exclusive action" of any one power.

Within Serbia itself, Bontoux won out. Under military threat from Austria, Serbia signed customs and commercial treaties, one of which included a one-hundred-million-franc bond issue managed by the Bontoux group for construction of a trans-Serbian railroad extending 365 kilometers from Vranje near the country's southern border with the Ottoman Empire to Belgrade, near its northern border with Austria-Hungary. The terms of the concession, which was calculated to place Serbia squarely within Austria's sphere of influence, were more than favorable. Vienna offered to pay as much as 225,000 francs per kilometer, or 75,000 more than Bontoux's estimated costs. Bontoux would receive further subsidies (7 percent of the total value of materials used) and 2 percent of gross receipts. The Chemins de Fer de l'État Serbe would be Austrian- and Länderbank-owned in everything but name.

The French press played fanfares. Bontoux was seen not as a robber baron but as an agent of civilization. "Gathering over centuries the produce of their fields and livestock, Serbs have amassed veritable treasures, which awaited only the opportunity to emerge from the burrows in which they had been secreted," one publicist declaimed in *La Revue des deux mondes*. "Wrapped in their rustic goatskins, they rushed forward and, opening their valiant hands, hands full of gold, said to rich financial groups: 'Here, take this, and reattach our dear country to the most civilized nations.' " In truth, the valiant hands that dispensed contracts, then and after the accession of King Milan I in Serbia in 1882, held no gold but the bribes offered by predatory aspirants. One informed observer described French activity in Serbia as systematic despoliation.

Railroads and the coal mines that fueled them were kindred enterprises, and while negotiating the Serbian line Bontoux set about acquiring the region's mineral wealth. Beginning with Styrian coalfields south of Graz, he extended his reach around the Adriatic to fields near Trieste, and in 1881, presided over the creation of the Trifail-Carpano Society.

Bontoux had not forgotten the Church. He sent the pope an annual tithe of two hundred thousand francs. He gave the Jesuits of Lyon their headquarters. Under his sponsorship, all necessary arrangements were made to find the Dominicans a home in Austria. If divine providence had continued to smile upon him, how much more might have been accomplished? His original goal, he later wrote, had been to shelter the Church from political turmoil and render it impervious to the "covetous maneuvers of civil society." He lived in a world where "Catholics are threatened in the exercise of their rights by a foe who strives ever more relentlessly to starve their most essential institutions. They have suffered blows to head and heart: the Papacy has been despoiled; Catholic charity mutilated. The temporal realm of the former is no more; the patrimony of the latter diminishes day by day." Bontoux's endowment would let everyone know that the Holy See need never go begging. Plans for an impregnable shelter had been laid in the form of two funds—the Treasure of Saint Peter and the Treasure of Catholic Charities—but neither would ever come to fruition. Nor would Bontoux's plans to create a chain of newspapers combating Freemasonry in Italy and abroad.

The Union Générale lived only three hectic years. By mid-1881, playing the stock market in Lyon had become a collective delirium.

The arrest, in 1882, of the two principals
in the Crash of the Union Générale,
Bontoux and Feder.

Brokers invited all and sundry to open accounts. Purchases on credit were rampant. Outside the major banks, clerks chalked market quotations on blackboards every half hour, and large crowds gathered to watch. The Bourse was Grand Opera for ladies with lorgnettes perched in a gallery above the trading floor. Special trains brought speculators in from the suburbs on settlement dates. "All of Lyon," one journalist reported, "is at the Union Générale: silk merchants, textile manufacturers, grocers, concierges, shoemakers, pensioners, haberdashers." The Chamber of Commerce noted that money normally invested in the city's principal industry, silk manufacture, was being diverted to securities. "Many of our manufacturers curtailed their production and restricted their purchases of raw material to the bare minimum." Union Générale stock rose from 500 francs to 3,000. There were warnings that this overvalued, unregulated market would, like a fat man running harum-scarum on spindly legs, crash to earth once it stumbled. Léon Say, a distinguished economist who served several administrations as minister of finance, expressed grave concern. Nonetheless, in November Bontoux prevailed upon his colleagues at the Union to issue one hundred thousand new shares. His Balkan projects required more capital, he insisted, and, given the vastly enlarged scale of economic activity throughout Europe, it behooved the bank to enlarge itself accordingly.

The crash—which heralded an economic recession from which the country would not fully recover for years—came in January 1882. When, during that month, investors began to pull back, the market, lacking an appropriate clearinghouse and daily margin settlements, could not handle their withdrawal. As values plunged and money drained away, one calamity led to another. The turmoil at Lyon, France's most important financial center after Paris, had immediate repercussions on every French exchange. Suez shares trading at 3,440 francs on January 7 were down to 2,000 by the end of the month.

During that same interval the Union Générale fell from 3,040 back to 500 despite Bontoux's efforts to shore it up against market forces. On January 19, 1882, the firm suspended operations. In early February it was declared bankrupt.

The bank's books reflected badly on a director who fancied himself a knight pledged to king and Christ; the state-appointed auditor discovered pervasive malfeasance. Under examination, Bontoux blamed others. "I departed for Vienna at the beginning of January, leaving the bank in glowing health," he declared. "I returned to find a corpse. Irregular operations had been conducted during my absence." Company records were confiscated and Bontoux himself jailed in the Conciergerie (a suitable prison for a champion of the Bourbon pretender, as it was in this medieval fortress that Louis XVI and Marie Antoinette had spent their last hours). There he awaited trial on charges of fiduciary irresponsibility, violation of laws governing joint-stock companies, and fraud, until released on bail.

Investors were still reeling from news of Bontoux's imprisonment when his champions in the right-wing press declared irately that he had fallen victim to rival bankers. A malevolent syndicate, which Bontoux later dubbed "the Sanhedrin," had brought down the Union Générale by shouting fire and inciting a rush for the exit. Major shareholders planned to meet on February 3 and might have saved it at the eleventh hour, but minister of justice Gustave Humbert—portrayed as a Rothschild valet—delivered the fatal blow before they convened. *Le Salut public,* a Lyon newspaper, denounced the "maneuvers of a group of German Jews" on January 22. Four days later, another Lyon newspaper, the *Moniteur universel,* alluded darkly to a "plot hatched by German Jewish bankers." It asserted that "the Union Générale, stunned by an association of short sellers, faced death at its most vital moment. . . . Timely measures might have saved everything, and indeed, shareholders would have taken them. The abrupt intervention of the government destroyed all hopes." Arresting Bontoux two days before the shareholders met could have had only one motive.

Evidence did not support rumors of a conspiracy. To be sure, Albert Salomon von Rothschild, head of Austrian Rothschild interests, attempted to rein in a wildly exuberant horse by buying and dumping Union stock, but his maneuver was not what doomed the bank. Liberal newspapers agreed that Bontoux had only himself to blame. The Union Générale functioned as a "machine for speculating," one reporter observed. "The principle on which [it] rested is this: 'I buy all I can sell.' M. Bontoux never considered the real value of enterprises in which he invested, nor their probable revenue, but simply the prospect of being able to place their stock and create an immediate, necessarily factitious appreciation. He clearly excelled in such deals [and] had a numerous clientele . . . who regarded him as a financial messiah. They will now be ruined along with him." The false messiah was described as a true successor to John Law, the Scottish financial genius responsible for the eighteenth century's most notorious bubble, the Mississippi Scheme.*

At his trial in December 1882, Bontoux was found guilty of all charges (hiking the value of the Union Générale shares "by fraudulent ways and means," distributing fictitious dividends, falsifying stock subscriptions in a quarterly report) and sentenced to five years in prison. The following March an Appeals Court upheld the verdict but reduced the sentence to two years. In June, the High Court, or Cour de Cassation, decided not to quash previous rulings, whereupon Bontoux fled from France. He lived abroad until 1888, mostly in

---

*Comparisons were also made with the Belgian financier Langrand-Dumonceau, who proposed, during the 1850s and 1860s, to establish a Catholic banking power. He arranged a large loan to the Vatican, was made a papal count by Pius IX, and touted himself with much the same flair as Bontoux. He, too, cast a spell on conservatives. Like stockholders in the Union Générale, investors in Langrand's enterprise lost everything in a crash.

Édouard Drumont, author of La France juive *and founder of the daily* La Libre parole, *photographed by Nadar. Drumont railed obsessively against Jews during the Panama scandal and the Dreyfus Affair. He did not object to being called "the pope of anti-Semitism."*

Saragossa, Spain, making money from a silver mine, and returned only when the statute of limitations expired. Certain that the judgment against him had been dictated before the trial ever took place, he compared it to "the practice of law under arbitrary, tyrannical regimes."

As for the Church, an ecclesiastic from Lyon who taught theology at the community of Chartreux, Father Fleury Deville, offered Bontoux doctrinal absolution in a book written shortly after his well-publicized flight, *Stock Exchange Operations in the Court of Conscience: Moral and Juridical Studies*. While the court of conscience—that is, the voice of God—did not sanction *"agiotage,"* or gambling, it found *"spécula-tion"* entirely acceptable and, indeed, had nothing but praise for "laborious and intelligent financiers who study and work." A secular court might sometimes be harsher than the court of conscience, observed Deville, echoing John Calvin's justification of capitalist finance on the grounds that "if all usury is condemned, tighter fetters are imposed on the conscience than the Lord himself would wish." Should one always feel compelled, then, to respect a secular court's judgment? "We do not believe so. . . . One may in good conscience, by roundabout means, elude the often implacable decisions of tribunals," wrote Deville. In a preface, Cardinal Caverot, archbishop of Lyon, thanked Father Deville for guiding the reader so expertly through a minefield where "justice," presumably the justice Bontoux did not receive, "often comes out second best."

FOR TRUE BELIEVERS, the idea that one of their own had beguiled them proved intolerable. A scapegoat was needed, not only to pre-serve Bontoux's honor but to immunize his victims against the real-ization that their own greed had made them easy prey, and the scapegoat was found where it had always been sought: in the Jew. Bontoux, a Catholic financier, having providentially appeared to restore all that mattered most in public life—the pope's well-being, the Church's Italian estates, the king's crown, France's stature—had been crucified by Rothschild and his coreligionists. This legend, which the right-wing press lost no time in disseminating, soon established itself as fact in two books, *La France juive* and *La France juive devant l'opinion,* by Édouard Drumont, a journalist of modest attainments, who gained fame and fortune with a conspiratorial worldview that foreshadowed *The Protocols of the Elders of Zion.**

**La France juive devant l'opinion* appeared in 1886, several months after the more ambitious *La France juive*. Neither one discriminated between fact and fable in its

In every particular Drumont parroted Bontoux's trial testimony. He laid blame for all that had gone wrong at the doorstep of a colleague secretly beholden to "hostile interests," which encompassed the republican government as well as a fraternity of Jewish banks. Indeed, the two were held to be inseparable. "Today, the entire might of the State is placed at the service of the Jewish monopoly," he wrote. "The government, which supposedly represents everyone, uses the formidable resources conferred upon it by the collective citizenry to benefit a few at the expense of the many."

In Drumont's narrative, what had happened at the end of January 1882 proved that there was a conspiracy. The Union Générale scheduled a meeting of shareholders for February 3. The likelihood that enough money would be raised to save the bank alarmed Rothschild, who immediately conferred with his "lackeys," the ministers of finance and justice. Their hope, Drumont continued, was to build a case against Bontoux before February 3. On February 1 the public prosecutor investigating Bontoux's affairs, Louis Loew, was approached by a merchant named Lejeune, who alleged that the bank had pilfered 240,000 francs from his account in order to acquire its own stock through a straw man. Loew gave Lejeune a pen, dictated a deposition, and thus produced the document "that would cause the ruin of so many families and the suicide of so many unfortunates." Did this Jewish prosecutor (Loew was, in fact, an Alsatian Protestant) believe for a moment that he had behaved incorrectly? Not at all:

> Son of our innate enemy, he served his race and helped to crush ours. He has his own code and he applies it. Refer here to the passage in my *France juive* that contains Talmudic prescriptions governing trials between Jews and *Goyim*. Rabbi Ismael, in a chapter of the Baba-Kamina entitled "The Thief," declares that where no law supports a ruling in favor of the Jewish litigant, "fraud and guile are permissible." . . . Loew received his reward

---

account of Jews clandestinely conquering France. *La France juive,* an encyclopedic, pseudoscholarly harangue, became one of the four or five best-selling books of the nineteenth century, appearing in several hundred editions.

for services rendered to Israel. A simple prosecutor of the Republic at the time of the Union's crash, he was named attorney general in Paris on April 12, 1883, and appointed president of the High Court on May 16, 1886.

In this telling of the story, Loew effectively destroyed Bontoux: by February 3, 1882, when Bontoux's ship would have reached safe harbor, it was scuttled with all aboard, while Jews in Paris's *beaux quartiers* exulted. "That is how the Rothschilds understand war," wrote Drumont, "and no one should be astonished by the transports of joy with which *La France juive* has been received, a book that has afforded me the satisfaction of seeing victims dance in the street." Lejeune withdrew his deposition on February 7, six days after entering it. From that, Drumont inferred that he had been pressured by Loew into bearing false witness and subsequently felt remorseful. But by February 7 Lejeune would have been satisfied that justice was being served and that the courts would eventually extract some compensation from the authors of his misfortune. In any event, the warrant to arrest Bontoux and the declaration of bankruptcy were based mainly on a preliminary audit of the Union Générale's books rather than on Lejeune's allegation. Most economic historians agree that nothing could have been done at a meeting on February 3 to save the bank, but for Drumont and Bontoux its thwarted salvation was an indispensable fantasy.

Not every victim danced to his tune. Drumont fulminated against cosmopolitan aristocrats who befriended the enemy. When titled residents of the Faubourg Saint-Germain should have been wearing black, they dressed as animals for the Princesse de Sagan's costume ball and cavorted with rich Jews. When Alphonse de Rothschild should have been ostracized, the Duc de La Rochefoucauld-Bisaccia accepted an invitation to his salon. It astonished Drumont that some otherwise enthusiastic readers of *La France juive* could reproach him for criticizing the duke. He had not called into question La Rochefoucauld-Bisaccia's "private virtues," he protested, only his public deportment. An aristocrat of ancient lineage should have recognized that his elementary duty was to spurn those whose greed had ruined so many lives. "If, instead of worshipping at the humble parish of Saint-Pierre-du-Gros-Caillou, I had met La Rochefoucauld-Bisaccia at Saint-Clotilde," wrote Drumont,

> I would have candidly said to him while offering him the holy water: "My brother, it will not do for a leader of the Catholic party to go dancing at the home of Jews when so many miserable victims of Israel are in tears over the loss of their savings or killing themselves out of despair. Your place is not at those balls where violins can't quite muffle the distant rattle of the dying. Before entertaining yourself among the Rothschilds, wait until those of your brothers in Jesus Christ whom the Rothschilds condemned to death have stopped swaying at the end of their ropes."

Among Christians, such language was entirely permissible, he insisted. "The Gospel says: *Unicuique mandavit Deus de proximo suo.*"*

Drumont considered the Crash one more baleful event in a cultural and racial war undermining France's soul. Ironically, his screed comports with a myth, embraced by the Jacobins during the French Revolution, according to which noblemen and commoners sprang from different stock, commoners being Gauls and aristocrats descendants of the Germanic Franks.† In Drumont's transposition, a Germanic tribe had again conquered France, but as "Jewish bankers from Frankfurt."

According to *La France juive devant l'opinion,* the Crash had set in bolder relief than any previous catastrophe the opposition between the barbaric energy of Semites and the moral lassitude of civilized Frenchmen. Hun-like was the invader's ruthlessness. If he worshipped

---

*From the apocryphal book *Ecclesiasticus:* "And [God] taught each his duty towards his neighbor." This cosmopolitan aristocracy, which enters Marcel Proust's *À la recherche du temps perdu* in the persons of Robert de Saint-Loup and the Prince and Princess de Guermantes, would enrage Drumont again in the 1890s, when members of it dared to side with Dreyfus.

†A line in the "Marseillaise" refers to this: "*Qu'un sang impur abreuve nos sillons*" (May impure blood slake the furrows of our fields).

a god other than the Golden Calf, it was not one who tempered the wind to the shorn lamb. "Nothing softens his heart, nothing humanizes him. He may mingle with gentlemen at the Jockey Club, but inside him is a savage Shylock." Bred in the bone, like original sin, Jewish avidity was understandable only as a feral instinct exceeding material needs. Predators in the wild cease to hunt when their hunger is sated. Jews, on the other hand, are insatiable.

> Of what use to the Rothschilds was booty from the Union Générale? They didn't need more silver for their table, another painting for their gallery, one more horse for their stables. The men whom they set upon were the most distinguished representatives of a social world that had welcomed these Germans, had opened wide the doors to its salons, had initiated them into its life. . . . Many had bought stock with only one goal in mind: making more money to give away as charity.

So, Drumont concluded, a prouder nobleman than La Rochefoucauld-Bisaccia would tell the "German" bankers who had wrecked Catholic France that "we are the sons of a different civilization and your ways are not ours"; that the anguish of destitute old priests, minor functionaries, and domestics was never to be forgotten; that Jews might have ministers, magistrates, and the press in their pay, but that his people had a homeland they would defend.

EUGÈNE BONTOUX RETURNED from exile in 1888, bringing with him the manuscript of *L'Union Générale: Sa Vie, Sa Mort, Son Programme.* No one welcomed him as warmly as Édouard Drumont, who may have met the fugitive during his clandestine sojourns in Paris. Drumont had already proven himself Bontoux's loyal advocate, and loyal he remained in *La Libre parole,* the daily newspaper he founded in 1892 to expose the machinations of Jews and Freemasons. As we shall see, the Dreyfus affair would be heaven-sent for the journalist standing on an anti-Semitic platform.

In 1902, two decades after "le Krach," when the rage it fueled had been spent on Dreyfus, and when memories had begun to fade, a scandal gave Bontoux the perfect pretext to rehearse his story in *La Libre parole.* Brought to book that year was a swindler named Thérèse Humbert. Passing herself off as the illegitimate child of a great American tycoon and heiress to his fortune, she had defrauded people of millions. It so happened that Madame Humbert was the daughter-in-law of Gustave Humbert, who in 1882, as France's minister of justice, had sponsored Bontoux's indictment. Thérèse had apparently deceived him as well. But without the bona fides his name conferred upon her, her criminal career might not have been possible, and *La Libre parole* made much of this. "Amidst the enormous brouhaha over 'the biggest fraud of the century,' one suddenly hears voices evoking the juridical assassination of the Union Générale," wrote Bontoux. Time had turned the accusations hurled at him twenty years earlier against the accusers. It had given truth the upper hand and shown a minister and a prosecutor for what they were: Humbert a fraud, Loew something even worse. Hadn't Loew, after his appointment to a judgeship on the High Court, voted to grant Captain Dreyfus a new trial, "wrapping the traitor protectively in the folds of his red robe"?

Bontoux's *La Libre* article (published as a pamphlet by Drumont) stops just short of explicitly declaring that Jews committed treason in 1882, when "the Sanhedrin" destroyed a bank whose success would have enlarged the power, prestige, and well-being of France. "We had laid the foundation for substantial enterprises, in which France, her men and industry, would have played an important role." Napoléon never advanced beyond Moscow, but Bontoux, at the behest of General Annenkov, would have crossed Siberia. His would have been the hand controlling rail transportation between Europe and Asia, along three thousand kilometers of track in the Balkan peninsula. Through one of its companies, French Electric Power, the Union Générale would have illuminated France and strung telephone lines across the country. Defeated in war, France would have made good all its losses, and more, in economic conquest.

It did not suit Jews and Germans that France should prosper, in Bontoux's view. Their conspiracy explained what may have seemed fortuitous. It was a key for understanding the apparent randomness of blows to national pride and financial well-being. On the one hand Rothschild wanted no competition from the Union Générale, on the other Bismarck regarded with dismay the prospect of a French company blocking his access to the Orient. "Because it had emerged as a powerful instrument of French expansion, because it served France everywhere and passionately, it was condemned by M. de Bismarck for Germany's sake and by Jewish finance for Israel's. Messieurs Humbert and Loew are secondary figures in a larger drama, that of 'the Jewish jackal clearing a path for the German lion.' "* The "Krach," which Jews and Germans orchestrated, Bontoux concluded, set the country back fifty years.

*As probative evidence of Bismarck's involvement in the bank failure, Bontoux presents the following anecdote: "In October 1881, a great French lady who mixed in German court circles told one of my colleagues after returning from Berlin: 'Beware! The Union Générale is doomed: M. de Bismarck has passed sentence on it.' The remark seemed excessive to us at the time; it proved to be all too exact."

CHAPTER IV

France on Horse

B ontoux's dream of encompassing the globe in a great French web of railroads spoke to his ideological brethren, but not as powerfully as images of France Militant riding horseback. After the Franco-Prussian War, when stone and bronze equestrians sprang up all around Paris, the one that became a rallying point for Catholic royalists was Emmanuel Frémiet's statue of Joan of Arc on the place des Pyramides.

Although she held high the battle flag of French kings, this Joan was not born of deeply sectarian feeling. Jules Simon, the liberal minister responsible for commissioning it six months after "bloody week," had had in mind a monument to national consensus. The statue would stand where it could best express France's valor and resilience, looking south beyond the rubble of a royal palace burned by Communards. At that point, Joan sent mixed messages. Voltaire had derided her "voices" in *La Pucelle* but Friedrich Schiller, among other libertarians, had come to her defense and Jules Michelet, no friend of the Church, portrayed her in his *Jeanne d'Arc* as a freedom fighter from France's peasant heartland.

Joan's confiscation by the Right coincided with the establishment of republican government during the 1870s. Long before the Vatican supported her beatification, one hundred fifty Parisians gathered at the unveiling of Frémiet's statue in 1874. With or without votive tributes, every political creed was represented. "Everyone had something to say about [the recent war]," a police observer reported. "One individual shouted that Garibaldi was nothing but a brigand, whereupon others made him retreat." Republicans confronted monarchists, tempers flared, and a ceremony on which officialdom kept close watch lest it turn too vociferously anti-Prussian ended with gendarmes dispersing the crowd.

Four years later, the threat of a pro-monarchist rally staged under Joan's aegis caused the government even greater concern. By 1878, republicans who had emerged victorious after President MacMahon's high-handed dissolution of the Assembly were beginning in earnest to set their mark on public life. As already noted, the Assembly would move to Paris from Versailles. The "Marseillaise" would become the national anthem and July 14 national independence day. Sainte-Geneviève would become a Panthéon dedicated to "great men of the fatherland" and a government program facetiously referred to as "statuemania" would populate the capital with republican paragons. Streets would be named or renamed. Education would soon be made "free, compulsory, and secular," but a secular bias already imbued new schoolbooks, particularly the one most widely assigned to children learning French history and geography, *Le Tour de la France par deux enfants: Devoir et patrie.*" In it Joan is portrayed as a sublime innocent who "thought" she heard voices commanding her, not as a supernaturally guided instrument of salvation.*

Beaten back by a force that took proprietary liberties with time and

---

*This is the text referred to earlier in the memoir of a schoolmaster at war with the village priest. It first appeared in 1877. Three million copies of it were sold within the first ten years of publication and six million by the end of the century. There were many more readers than that, as children often used copies purchased by their school.

The *Catholic Encyclopedia* states this: "It was at the age of thirteen-and-a-half, in the summer of 1425, that Joan first became conscious of that manifestation, whose supernatural character it would now be rash to question, which she afterwards came to call her 'voices' or her 'counsel.' "

space, Catholic royalists made their stand at Frémiet's statue, treating the square over which Joan cast a shadow as consecrated ground. Rituals of the Left demanded counterrituals, and in 1878 the Right laid plans to remember Joan's martyrdom on May 30. A more symbolically eloquent month than May 1878 can hardly be imagined, for it also marked the centenary of Voltaire's death. Rumor had it that Voltairians, after a commemorative ceremony at his statue on place Monge, planned to march across town and taunt devotees on the place des Pyramides. With such lively prospects of an ideological clash marring the World's Fair, which had just opened, the police intervened. There would be no mourners for Joan, not even wreaths. The entire ceremony was forbidden, and gendarmes took turns guarding against clandestine tributes. "This prohibition will enter the annals of French history," *L'Univers* exclaimed. "Let it be noted that in May 1878, paying homage to the heroine who saved the country and died a martyr was deemed a public danger by the government. Let it also be noted that what provoked the measure was fear of Voltaire's faithless disciples, who, on that day, honored him, much to the delight of the Prussians who had just crushed us!" Several days earlier, *La Lanterne,* a staunchly anticlerical paper, had also, for its own reasons, supported a commemoration. It was high time, its writer noted, that the Church doused with tears of penitence the fire it had lit under Joan's feet after her inquisition.

> Better late than never, and today's clericals are well advised to make due apology at the feet of that glorious girl whom clericals of yesteryear so piously burned. As for us, we can only applaud this demonstration, and we urge all republicans to lay wreaths bearing the following inscription: "To Joan of Lorraine, To the French heroine, To the victim of clericalism."

Sarcasm was lost on the titled ladies who formed a Jeanne d'Arc Committee. Cheated of the ceremony that their president, the Duchesse de Chevreuse, had organized in Paris, they betook themselves to Domrémy, Joan's native village in Lorraine, with fifty crates of wreaths originally meant for the place des Pyramides. All to no avail. The republican subprefect vetoed a procession through the village.

Not until May 1898, four months after Émile Zola exposed the military conspiracy against Captain Dreyfus in *J'accuse,* would there be an annual commemoration of Joan that threatened to end violently. During that interval, the dream of national salvation arriving on horseback attached itself to a cavalier with ambiguous credentials and the least aristocratic of names, Georges Boulanger.

BOULANGER'S COMMON PATRONYMIC* was deceptive. Hailing from Brittany, where his father, Ernest, practiced law, he had connections to the Anglo-Welsh aristocracy through his mother, Mary Ann Webb Griffith, daughter of Sir Edmund Griffith of Llaneravon, who had met her husband during a summer holiday outside Rennes. Born in 1837, Georges grew up in the Breton port of Nantes and attended lycée there at the same time as another famous Georges: Clemenceau.† When debts forced Boulanger senior to auction his practice, the lawyer accepted employment as an insurance inspector. The social consequences of his family's improvidence undoubtedly affected Georges, but in fact one can only surmise how, for little is known about his early life. There was a long sojourn in England organized around the Crystal Palace Exhibition of 1851, during which he became a fluent English speaker. There was also much romping on horseback, with encouragement from Ernest, who had maintained a stable in palmier days. Young Georges demonstrated superior horsemanship at an early age. Dreaming dreams of military adventure, he was said to have learned all he could about Napoléon's campaigns before ever reading Perrault's fairy tales. "Georges has always been a soldier," said his mother. At seventeen he set his course for the Saint-Cyr military academy, took competitive examinations, passed them, and entered in 1854, shortly after the outbreak of war in the Crimea.

Acquaintances observed of Boulanger, then and later, that traits not

---

*Boulanger being French for "baker."

†A previous alumnus was Jules Verne.

often found in combination created an illusion of depth. Vain yet self-denying, he loved the ordeals of officer school as much as its fancy trappings. One would not have thought that his mother's blue-eyed boy could become an immensely popular comrade in arms. Popular he became, however. Making himself conspicuous with his courage in the face of the enemy, he repeatedly risked his life for others, but never lost sight of the main chance. Some were struck by his single-mindedness, others by his labile relationship to principle. What everyone noted was that Boulanger could be tenacious when the goal seemed important enough, and his tenacity carried him through Saint-Cyr closer to the top of his class than to the bottom. He graduated in 1856.

For the Saint-Cyrian with dreams of glory, 1856 was a good year to be earning one's commission. History would offer up several wars during the next few decades, and although a large proportion of Saint-Cyrians died on battlefields in Europe and the colonies before reaching middle age, those who survived often advanced quickly through the ranks. The roster of Boulanger's fellow cadets eventually came to include half a dozen generals.

Boulanger's initiation took place in Algeria. After thirty-six years of intermittent warfare—first with the Turks who ruled it, then with native tribes led by Abdelkader—France occupied most of the "Tell," the fertile region stretching along the coast from Morocco eastward past Algiers, where Louis-Philippe had settled a hundred thousand colonists. The one expanse of seabord yet to be subdued was a mountainous enclave called Kabylia, whose Berber inhabitants held the French at bay from villages perched high above the Bejaïa plain. In 1856, when most Algerian regiments were absent in the Crimea, Muslim holy men or marabouts exhorted their fellow Kabyles to rise against the occupier. It was under these circumstances that Georges Boulanger found himself posted to Blida, in the north, in January 1857. Before long the junior lieutenant was leading a regiment of Algerian riflemen—"Turcos"—up a mountain defended by Aït Iraten tribesmen and capturing a redoubt, Soug-el-Arbâa, thought to be impregnable. Soug-el-Arbâa became Fort Napoléon. Other skirmishes followed, but Boulanger's most spectacular exploit brought the Kabylian campaign to a successful conclusion in July 1857. It involved crossing a narrow pass high in the Djurdjura range at night, through mist, and capturing entrenchments guarded only by day. This feat later inspired comparisons with Corneille's Don Rodrigue—"Le Cid."

Peacetime service did not suit Boulanger. Napoléon III's invasion of Austrian-ruled Lombardy therefore came as welcome news, and in April 1859, after almost two years of garrison life, the lieutenant gladly shipped out for Genoa with his Turcos. At Robecchetto, some miles west of Milan, where the French army, fighting under General MacMahon's command in the Italian War of Independence, routed the Austrians in a bloody prelude to its victories at Magenta and Solferino, Boulanger was seriously wounded. The bullet earned him a promotion, a knighthood in the Legion of Honor, and a scar, to which he called attention as best he could by wearing his uniform laced up over his wound long after it had healed.[*]

The Boulanger saga resumed two years later on the other side of the earth, in Southeast Asia. Jesuits had been evangelizing Indochina since Louis XIV's day. The French traders who followed had established outposts on the peninsula. Their sphere of influence was fortified when Gia Long, the founder of the Nguyen dynasty, welded the three provinces that correspond to modern-day Vietnam into an Annamite empire. Having gained power with weapons and ships supplied by Louis XVI, he rewarded Frenchmen with high office and throughout most of his reign favored a French presence. But Gia Long's hospitality did not outlive him. Foreigners were anathema to his successors, who blamed them for every instance of social unrest. As believers in a strict Confucian order, they set their faces against missionaries in their midst, slaughtering dozens of them. With Catholics at home outraged and French commercial interests imperiled, Napoléon III could not stand idly by. On February 18, 1859, an expeditionary force bent on annexing the Mekong River delta con-

---

[*]His wounds healed, but pain would be his constant companion until Marguerite de Bonnemains, the woman with whom he fell in love, introduced him to morphine. He became addicted.

quered Saigon. The campaign was well under way when Boulanger disembarked in January 1862.

An opportunity to show his mettle presented itself almost as soon as he arrived. Sent upriver to disarm pirates harassing the French, he surprised them with much the same cunning and élan that had succeeded so well in Kabylia. His men then joined in the siege of a citadel on the Mekong. Monsoon rains gave him time to convalesce from a thigh wound, but ultimately nature proved more daunting than enemy lances. When the push toward Cambodia resumed across fetid marshland, Captain Boulanger, like half the army, fell victim to a tropical fever, temporarily going blind; he received in the hospital at Go Cong the good news that his comrades had prevailed. Not until January 1864 did he return to Saigon. It was midyear before he took up quarters again at his home base in Algeria. Of the three hundred members of his regiment who had left Blida on September 16, 1861, only seventy came back.

One might not have been surprised to find the omnipresent Boulanger in Mexico during the mid-1860s, among French troops defending Emperor Maximilian against Benito Juarez's republicans. But the last years of the Second Empire were years of domesticity for Boulanger. He married Lucie Renouard, the daughter of a career diplomat, and fathered two children. In 1867, he joined the staff of the military college. The Boulangers moved to Saint-Cyr, where Georges became a much-admired instructor.

Then, in July 1870, the Franco-Prussian War erupted. While many of Boulanger's cadets saw action at the Front soon after graduation, Boulanger himself didn't face the Germans until late November. Paris was under siege and all attempts to reprovision the capital had failed. One of the bloodiest had occurred at Champigny-sur-Marne, where, after five days and nights of close combat, several thousand corpses lay strewn over a snowy hillside. Boulanger had dumb luck to thank for not lying among them. He survived the charges he had led at Champigny with nothing more than a shoulder wound. And his luck held in another fierce battle at another suburb, Le Bourget, against German troops twenty times more numerous than his regiment. Attentive to the men under his command, he cut a figure of gallantry and bravura, ostentatiously exposing himself to sniper fire on the earthworks while rallying Turcos at the forward posts.

His bravura was much in evidence the following May. By then, an armistice had been negotiated, an election had been held, the government that dared not yet call itself a republic had been established at Versailles, Paris had been taken over by Communards who seceded from the nation, and Germans besieging Paris had been replaced by a French siege force loyal to the elected government. On May 21, 1871—the first day of "bloody week"—government brigades entered the city through lightly defended gates. Mounted on a chestnut horse, Lieutenant Colonel Boulanger rode at the head of a column that fought its way east across the Left Bank as far as a warren of little streets behind the Panthéon. There he suffered yet another wound. He also received another promotion. That he did his bit to suppress the Commune might have dampened the enthusiasm of Paris's working class for "Boulangism" several years later, when that term came to define a rabidly nationalist movement in French political life. But it didn't.

Most alive on the battlefield and in the public eye, displaying his prowess as a warrior and a womanizer, Boulanger felt emasculated by his country's defeat. Provinces had been lopped off, and Germany would not completely evacuate what remained of France until the French government paid the last installment of a huge indemnity in September 1873. These humbling circumstances gave rise in Boulanger to convulsions of vanity. Garrisoned at Belley, midway between Lyon and Geneva, he spent his time (when not wooing the wives of the local gentry or obsessively training his horse in equestrian maneuvers) lobbying for yet another promotion. The colonel wanted a generalship, and to obtain higher rank every hypocrisy was authorized. Knowing that Louis-Philippe's son the Duc d'Aumale, who served as inspector general of the army, had strong ties to the Church, Boulanger made a great show of religiosity. Monarchist deputies must have noticed him sitting in the Church of the Sacred Heart at Paray-le-Monial during the postwar pilgrimage. He regularly visited the bishop of Belley. He insisted that his staff attend mass every Sunday, and, Tartuffe-like, walked to church with a deluxe, gilt-edged prayer book tucked under his arm. "His reputation in the garrison was that of an ardent clerical," according to a secret report received by the ministry of the interior. But the putative clerical, who exercised his horse in a gutted chapel, readily assumed an entirely different guise to court anticlerical republicans when the latter gained power in 1879. He ingratiated himself with Léon Gambetta, president of the Chamber of Deputies, who subsequently championed his promotion. Colonel Boulanger became General Boulanger in April 1880, at age forty-three, two months before the government amnestied fugitive Communards and expelled the Jesuits.

Boulanger's elevation gave him not only a generalship but a mount. Having won his spurs many times over in the infantry, he was rewarded with a cavalry brigade at Valence on the Rhône, near Avignon. Here he demonstrated his allegiance to Gambetta's party by keeping company with an old republican warhorse named Madier de Montjau (who liked to boast that his father had voted for Louis XVI's execution during the Terror). Boulanger not only called upon him regularly but escorted him on his political rounds. This friendship excited great interest beyond the confines of Valence, as the French cavalry, with its aristocratic tradition, boasted few general officers well disposed to the Republic. The brigadier was a rare bird, and republicans in Paris reacted to news of his sighting like grackles suddenly befriended by a raptor. It followed that when a French delegation was appointed in 1881 to visit Yorktown in Virginia for the centennial celebration of the final battle of America's Revolutionary War, it included Georges Boulanger. Among his fellow delegates was a descendant of the Rochambeau whose troops had helped Washington's Continental Army defeat Cornwallis on October 19, 1781.

The handsome, bemedalled general had no sooner set foot on American soil than he became Rochambeau incarnate, a conquering hero, a popular idol. Tricolor flags draped buildings; handkerchiefs fluttered; hats waved to the Frenchman wonderfully fluent in English. How could fantasies of demagogic power not bloom in the praise showered on him for no other reason than that he looked the part of savior? "It was beautiful, it was grandiose, it was gripping," he wrote after one pageant. Bands blaring the "Marseillaise" greeted him at every stop. And the delegation traveled extensively. Fifty years after a young lawyer named Alexis de Tocqueville visited Niagara Falls, Boulanger arrived in a train fitted with two parlors, a dining room, and a kitchen run by Delmonico's restaurant. From there, he criss-crossed the continent, inspecting army garrisons as far west as Cheyenne, in Wyoming Territory. Gala events allowed little time for reflection, but when left alone to think about the American political system, he concluded that Jacksonian democracy worked better than French republicanism. The National Assembly, which had toppled one prime minister after another, wielded disproportionate power. What France needed, if it were ever to regain its greatness, was an American-style president, and a method of voting that encouraged unmediated relations between the strong executive and the populace.

Popularity abroad boosted him at home. On April 16, 1882, soon after succeeding Gambetta as prime minister, Charles Louis de Freycinet appointed Gambetta's protégé inspector of infantry. Boulanger proved to be an aggressive reformer, much loved by younger officers, and, when invited to lecture, a full-throated chau-vinist rousing audiences with talk of blood and sacrifice. But army headquarters on the rue Saint-Dominique were also an excellent post from which to observe parliamentary proceedings at the Palais Bour-bon. The brigadier never took his eyes off them. Had he done so, or blinked, he might have missed the fall of a government. Administra-tions revolved like horses on a carousel. During his two-year inspec-torship, Boulanger counted four prime ministers and sixty-five ministers, leading him to wonder, as ambitious generals often have, whether mayhem in parliament, like confusion on a battlefield, might not favor the bold. What we know beyond all doubt is that political advantage dictated an alliance with his fellow Breton, Georges Clemenceau, and the radical leftist opposition.

Their alliance would have had no immediate consequences, for in February 1884 Boulanger was made commander of the army of occu-pation in Tunisia. The war ministry wanted him there to pacify a restive population, which included not only Arabs who found them-selves treated by rapacious colonial powers as a bone of contention but well-established Italian merchants resentful of France having wrested Tunisia from Italy. Back in North Africa after twenty-eight years, Boulanger—now Lieutenant General Boulanger—quickly made his presence felt everywhere, riding with his armed escort from one Saharan village to another, greeting sheiks, camping in oases, touring Roman ruins. The protectorate required a show of Gallic virility, and for showmanship he had no peer. His public appearances, especially the cavalcade staged on Bastille Day, were great entertainment. To the resident minister, Paul Cambon, we owe a candid portrait of him. "[Boulanger's] chief attribute is his savoir-faire," he wrote.

> He needed it to reach the position he holds at his age, but he lacks a cultivated mind. He has no conversation, either. You feel that here is a man who has read little, thought little about higher things and who has no wide-ranging ideas. His whole mind is bent towards advancement and personal politics. Never under any circumstances have I heard him express an idea or an opinion about what should be done out here. He is quite indifferent to it all.

Cambon knew whereof he spoke. Disdainful of shared authority, Boulanger saw in the minister an obstacle to his advancement and challenged him. After much sparring, word came from Paris that Cambon was to be regarded as minister plenipotentiary in the fullest sense. The order infuriated Boulanger. Like a slighted proconsul with designs upon Rome, he abandoned his command and made for the capital, intending to save face by every means.

Bluster may have been a more effective weapon than diplomacy. As soon as he reached Paris, in April 1885, journalists flocked to his apartment at the Hôtel du Louvre and came away with defamatory tales about his rival. The press, especially Clemenceau's *La Justice,* accepted on faith his assertion that Cambon had not upheld France's honor, that he had on the contrary brought shame upon the country he represented by appeasing truculent Italians, that he was neither a republican nor a patriot.* What to do? As the government had weight-

---

*A fatuous incident provided the basis for his accusations. After her performance at a theater in Tunis, an Italian singer rejected the bouquet thrown onstage by a French

ier matters on its mind than this feud—above all, the Treaty of Tientsin with China, which ended a long struggle for control of Annam, now part of Vietnam—it appointed a commission of enquiry. The latter found Cambon blameless, and amends were made by conferring upon the slandered minister a higher rank in the Legion of Honor. But Boulanger's petulance brought more substantial rewards. In December 1885 the government fell. Charles de Freycinet, who had twice served as prime minister, agreed to serve a third time, on condition that republicans both moderate and radical agreed to sit together in his cabinet. "One of my choices would receive inordinate attention, that of [General Boulanger] as minister of war," he later noted.

> His turbulent history in Tunisia piqued my curiosity. I summoned him to the quai d'Orsay and began our interview with a harsh question: "You've given us much grief, general. For what reason?" He excused himself amiably, granting that his temper had run high. "It was necessary," he declared, "to maintain troop morale." He promised that in some other circumstance he would ask for instructions from the minister. I then questioned him about various reforms on my agenda. . . . His answers were those of a man who had observed and reflected.

Freycinet, intending to curry favor with the hundred or more radical deputies aligned with Clemenceau and to tie down a loose cannon, offered him the ministry. Deeper-dyed republicans wanted a minister of war eager to enforce universal military service and create a democratized army. Clemenceau's one proviso was that Boulanger should consult him before doing or saying anything of an overtly political nature. Boulanger agreed. He had moved onto the great stage.

The new minister could not keep his promise to Freycinet, except within the narrowest definition of "politics." Reforms would adver-

---

officer and pinned to her corsage the tribute of an Italian admirer. In the mêlée that followed, another French officer was mugged. Boulanger issued an order authorizing his men to draw their swords when attacked or insulted. Cambon feared that the order would result in more violence between Italians and French, and revoked it.

tise an ideological bias, universal military service most of all. Before the late 1880s, service was compulsory in name only, the grounds for exemption being so numerous as to make a mockery of the term. Exempted were family breadwinners, the elder sons of widows, the brothers of serving soldiers, educational administrators, and priests, among others. Men who didn't qualify could, for fifteen hundred francs (a sum beyond the means of most working-class families), have their obligation reduced from five years to one. Boulanger's draconian proposal was that recruits serve only three years but that every male citizen serve, without exception. The rich were to camp with the poor and the representatives of God to train with the sons of Mammon. Appalled by the prospect of losing potential recruits for its own army, the Church preached against the measure. Republicans fought back and in due course won the day.*

Officers who had served at Belley during the 1870s still remembered their commander insisting that they attend military mass. The colonel with a prayer book at the ready was now the war minister insisting that priests, of whom there were some fifty-five thousand, bear arms. It was not the first ironic turnabout in Boulanger's career, nor the last. Another one involved the Duc d'Aumale, under whose wing he had sought to place himself fifteen years earlier. In 1886, when rumors spread of a royalist plot against the Republic, Louis-Philippe's grandson and heir to the throne, the Comte de Paris, was expelled from France. Boulanger decided, on his own, to strip d'Aumale, the count's uncle, of military rank. Was this overzealous gesture a pitch for applause from the galleries, as Freycinet believed? Or had he hoped, by demoting the Duc d'Aumale, to absolve himself of his fawning correspondence with a man once powerful enough to recommend his promotion? "We questioned him," wrote Freycinet. "He excused himself, saying that . . . he had applied the law in good faith;

---

*"Universal" was soon qualified to allow for the exemption each year of five hundred students of law, medicine, and several other liberal professions.

The democratization of the army was one priority of "radical" republicans. Another was the complete and immediate separation of Church and State. Unlike the moderates, who preferred a gradualist approach, the radicals sought to have public funding of all religious groups subtracted from the budget.

that his decrees having been published and made known to the men concerned, he could not very well withdraw them; that in any event if the law had been violated, . . . the injured parties could always ask the Council of State for redress." Boulanger's erstwhile benefactor did lodge an appeal, but in vain, and wrote a letter to the president of the Republic haughtily refusing to acknowledge the divestiture ("Military ranks are above your reach, and I remain General Henri d'Orléans"). He followed his nephew into exile.*

Boulanger's military reforms exacted one or three years from the lives of men who might previously have received exemptions. In return he made army life less squalid, continuing what he had begun as inspector of infantry. The common soldier, who was now compelled to grow a beard, could thank Boulanger for the mattress he slept on rather than a straw pallet, for better food, for a more comfortable uniform. And any officer who had personal business at the ministry was liable to be received by the minister himself, chainsmoking cigars. "He seemed scarcely forty," wrote one astonished captain. "No superfluous fat, thickset, his complexion burned by wind and sun. His hair was abundant, fair, and greased so as to keep the parting on the right side perfectly straight. The reddish beard made such a splash of color that I couldn't stop looking at it. The light blue eyes were a bit restless, it seemed to me. . . . He had a benevolent expression on his face and swung back and forth a big pair of eyeglasses on the end of a gold chain. When he replied, his voice, with its low and very masculine sound, had a soft inflection." To be sure, members of the general staff punished for speaking out against the Republic could not stomach Boulanger, but rankers loved a minister whose concern for their welfare was unlike anything in their experience. "He came here to the barracks once," an old veteran remem-

---

*In Belgium, d'Aumale claimed the moral high ground with an announcement that he was bequeathing his entire estate, including his château at Chantilly and the artistic treasures contained therein, to the French nation. Royalist newspapers published three of the letters Boulanger wrote to the Duc d'Aumale in 1880 soliciting his recommendation. The Comte de Paris had served as a captain in the Army of the Potomac, under McClellan, during the American Civil War and fought in the Peninsular Campaign. Afterward he wrote a history of the war.

bered. "He told us something or other about France in his speech. All that I remember is that I wept. If he'd told me: 'Throw yourself onto your bayonet,' I'd have done as he commanded." Boulanger did much visiting of barracks during his administration. The veteran's sentiments would have been echoed by sergeants everywhere and, before long, by the nation at large.

If Boulanger came to embody an image of *la furia francese*—of France bold and triumphant—the occasion that engraved his popular image was the military review at Longchamp on Bastille Day 1886. He prepared for it by acquiring, at great expense, a magnificent black horse that showed his person and his horsemanship to great advantage. He prepared well. So did the horse, named Tunis. Frock-coated, top-hatted government leaders were lost in a sea of more than a hundred thousand spectators, and shouts of *"Vive Boulanger! Vive l'armée!"* drowned out *"Vive la République,"* as the general, white plumes fluttering, cantered around the racetrack. When, at his command, twenty brass bands struck up the "Marche Indienne," troops paraded past the official grandstand, saluting Jules Grévy, president of the Republic, with drawn swords. But when the aged Grévy left Longchamp, his departure passed almost unnoticed. Boulanger was the cynosure of all eyes. And in the end, far more people than a police cordon could restrain mobbed their idol. Men shouted, women wept. The jubilation continued all evening on city streets and in music halls such as the Alcazar d'Été, where the popular chanteur Paulus regaled his audience with the jaunty lyrics of what became Boulanger's theme song: "En Revenant de la Revue" ("On Returning from the Review").* It was a spectacle that Jules Lemaître—a famous literary

---

*The second of many verses, with many dropped syllables, reads as follows: *"Ma soeur qu'aim' les pompiers/Acclam' ces fiers troupiers;/Ma tendre épouse bat des mains/ Quand défilent les Saint-Cyriens;/ Ma bell' mèr' pouss' des cris/ En reluquant les spahis;/ Moi, j'faisais qu'admirer/ Not' brav' général Boulanger."* A literal translation would be: "My sister who loves the fire brigade acclaims its stalwart ranks. My dear wife claps her hands when the cadets march past. My shrieking mother-in-law can't take her eyes off the spahis [irregular Turkish cavalry]. Myself, all I could do was admire our brave General Boulanger." The military review calls to mind Émile Zola's brilliant description in *Nana* (written six years earlier) of an ecstatic crowd at the races at Longchamp, cheering both Nana, the winning mare, and Nana, Paris's reigning courtesan.

journalist, staunch nationalist, and founding member of the Ligue de la Patrie Française—would remember twelve years later, during the Dreyfus Affair, when he wrote, "The crowd feels instinctually . . . that, despite all the sophisms [of Dreyfus's intellectual champions], France's army, today as in the past, is France herself."

Long before this apotheosis, Clemenceau began to question the wisdom of having nurtured Boulanger's career. "There's something about you that appeals to the crowd," he warned. "That's the temptation. That's the danger I want you to guard against." He might as well have asked Zephyr to guard against blowing. The born actor in a star role on France's most prominent stage could not resist playing it for all it was worth. Every morning a coach hitched to a handsome team of horses, with a footman in turtle-colored livery and tricolor rosettes, fetched him at his apartment in the Hôtel du Louvre and drove him to the ministry. There, on the rue Saint-Dominique, clerks chronicled all the events of his professional life. Not a movement, not a decision wasn't instantly reported. The press received from the ministry thrice-daily bulletins announcing banquets to be chaired, meetings to be addressed, troops to be inspected, army orphanages to be visited, foundation stones to be laid. Word of mouth carried through the hinterland, and literate peasants whose reading was restricted to farm almanacs learned the name of at least one minister. Boulanger himself traveled ceaselessly, carrying his baggage of patriotic hyperbole everywhere. "General Boulanger . . . has become so popular in the army and among his people," a visiting Russian colonel observed, "because he works with both intelligence and self-denial to exalt the national spirit and inspire in all men confidence in themselves and in the future of the nation." Being "offensive-minded" was his passionate rule, his *Carthago delenda est.* While it thrilled the masses, it unnerved his political confrères, and unnerved them all the more when monarchist papers seized upon one of Boulanger's more provocative speeches to argue that under a Republic, France was riding for another fall. In Berlin, Otto von Bismarck argued the same. "We have to fear an attack by France, though whether it will come in ten days or ten years is a question I cannot answer," he told the Reichstag. "If Napoléon III went to war with us in 1870 chiefly because he

General Boulanger, minister of war, on his black horse Tunis, at the military review of July 14, 1886.

believed that this would strengthen his power within his country, why should not such a man as General Boulanger, if he came to power, do the same?"

On April 20, 1887, a dispute at France's border with the partially ceded province of Lorraine (now called Lothringen again) ignited the tinder of jingoistic sentiment stored up in France. German police seized a French border official named Schnaebelé at the line of demarcation, accused him of espionage, roughly interrogated him, and threatened a court-martial. It seems certain that he had indeed engaged in espionage, but since, on that particular occasion, he was entering Lorraine officially, and at the behest of his German counterpart, the police breached international law in seizing him. A trap had been set, and as a result, tempers flared even among normally unvindictive French. The situation might have deteriorated further if the new prime minister, René Goblet, had not insisted upon diplomatic pourparlers—unlike Boulanger, who proposed to mobilize troops on the Eastern Front without delay. Aware that Germany's provincial police had blundered, though in a just cause, Bismarck grudgingly freed Schnaebelé ten days after his arrest.

Public opinion credited Boulanger with the surrender, and newspapers sang his praises. One can hardly imagine to what extremes of adulation the crowd would have gone in 1887 had he again pranced at Longchamp, judging by patriotic verse of the day:

> *Tu seras plus qu'un roi, tu seras plus qu'un Dieu*
> *Car tu seras la France, O Général Revanche!*[*]

His new cognomen, General Revenge, voiced the dream of a nationalist Second Coming.[†] However tall Boulanger had stood before 1887, he stood taller after the Schnaebelé affair, when La Ligue des Patriotes, an organization whose membership dwelled fanatically on the deliverance of Alsace and Lorraine, formed up behind him. The league's founder, Paul Déroulède, became Boulanger's knight-errant. Known for his patriotic poems (*Chants du soldat*), his duels, and his monomaniacal oratory, Déroulède traveled the length and breadth of

---

[*] "You will be more than a king, you will be more than a God/For you will be France, O General Revenge!"

[†]*L'Instruction primaire*, a professional journal for primary school teachers, would regularly suggest composition topics, one of which was: "*The Fatherland*. To serve one's country is a *duty* and an *honor*. The *fatherland*, our great family, deserves our entire affection, our entire devotion. We should sacrifice ourselves for it; we were not born for ourselves but for it. The flag is the symbol of the fatherland. To surrender it to the enemy is an act of enormous cowardice. . . ." Another read: "In the Toulon hospital, a young sergeant wounded at Tonkin has a limb amputated. Upon awakening, he regards the amputation and says: 'Better this than being Prussian.' The sergeant came from Metz"—in Lorraine.

France beating a drumroll of revanchism. "Throughout the whole of my journey," he told a large crowd that gathered at the Gare du Nord to welcome him home after one tour, "the name of a single man, the name of a brave soldier, has been my touchstone. It is the name of the supreme head of our army, the name of General Boulanger!" What he had to say reached an even larger audience through the league newspaper, *Le Drapeau*, edited by Maurice Barrès. Its circulation might not have numbered three hundred thousand, as he claimed, but it exceeded most others. And Déroulède could rally leaguers at a moment's notice.

Courted by people high and low, Boulanger attracted a heterogeneous crowd whose individual members had little in common but contempt for parliamentary moderation. From beyond the fringe came the Marquis de Rochefort-Lucay, known only as Henri Rochefort, a journalist of anarchical and contrarian humor, who had spent time in prison, fought duels, joined French exiles in Belgium, served up diatribes in the Chamber of Deputies under Napoléon III, served up more in the National Assembly under Thiers, defended the Commune against Versailles, and, during two decades of vituperation, founded two newspapers: first *La Lanterne*, then *L'Intransigeant*. Rochefort escaped from the French penal colony in New Caledonia, to which he had been shipped after "bloody week," and returned to France in 1880, when ex-Communards were granted a general amnesty. Born to hate men in power, he hectored them impartially. And Boulanger served his malice. The general was a splash of red in France's dun-colored politics, a petard hoisted against the bourgeois Republic, a sword for smiting the Establishment.

Another paradoxical courtier, Arthur Meyer, saw only white, the color of French royalty. His paper, *Le Gaulois*, which circulated like a house organ among Paris's upper crust, offered sufficient proof of his anti-Semitism to earn him forgiveness for having been born Jewish. Infatuated with all things aristocratic, he had married a descendant of the great Marshal Turenne. Conversion came naturally to him. The Jew converted to Catholicism. The Bonapartist converted to royalism. And the royalist embraced Boulanger as a manifestation of Providence. "Boulangism," Meyer wrote years later, shortly before World

War I, "was the collective yearning of a people wounded in its national pride . . . for the man providentially chosen to liberate [Alsace and Lorraine]. France is essentially messianic; it combats the true God and at the same time deifies a false idol." Not that Boulanger replaced the exiled Pretender, the Comte de Paris, in his affections. With Meyer, idolatry and opportunism cleaved together. If events unfolded as he wished, the general would play Joan of Arc to the Comte de Paris's Charles VII or Georges Monk to his Charles II. In an ideal political sequence, Boulanger would wage war, gain power, recover the lost provinces, save the throne, and efface himself before a Christian king.

Thanks to the photoglyptic process, photographs could now be turned out en masse, and photographs of Boulanger inundated France. The newspaper *L'Estafette* alone printed eight hundred thousand copies of a full-length portrait. In bistros and cottages he was prominently displayed, as the *pater patriae*. Framed chromolithographs hung in town houses and mayor's offices. The general was everywhere. A memento industry reproduced his image on dinner plates, in pottery, as sculpted pipe bowls, in soap, on shoehorns, silk handkerchiefs, the handles of shaving brushes, quill pens. A hagiographical biography sold a hundred thousand copies within days of publication. Pamphlets, songs, and odes extolling Boulanger abounded. One poetaster wrote forty-seven rhapsodic stanzas, all variations of:

> *Boulanger! La France répète*
> *Ce nom-là, comme un saint espoir*
> *De revanche, après la défaite,*
> *De victoire, au jour du devoir!*
> *Boulanger! C'est le synonyme*
> *De France, de Gloire, d'Honneur.**

---

*"Boulanger! All of France repeats that name, like the sacred hope of revenge after the defeat, of victory on the day men answer a call to arms. Boulanger! It is the synonym of France, of Glory, of Honor."

Itinerant peddlers hawked the verses in towns and villages on market day.

Enthusiasm was by no means universal, least of all among moderates (who still outnumbered radicals) such as Jules Ferry and Freycinet. Jealousy played a part, no doubt. But they had better grounds than jealousy for their wariness. It alarmed them that Boulanger, far from being the passive object of hero worship, played to the passions he roused, and that his rich friends swayed opinion-makers with well-placed largesse. They saw Boulanger's immense popularity as a dark shadow cast upon the Republic itself. Well before the Schnaebelé affair, during the summer of 1886, Jules Ferry wrote to a colleague that France's neighbors, even the most benevolent, would never trust a government inclined to look away when its chief of staff publicly flirted with civil and military demagogy. "The renown he craves, his verbal imprudences, the fantasies aired around him . . . have unleashed in the German press and public a bellicosity of which we should take careful note." Boulanger was, he concluded, a danger to the cabinet, to the army, and to national security. "I will not dwell on his shameless, intolerable associations with all that is worst on the extreme left, his absolute subordination to M. Clemenceau, his debasing intimacy with the men of *La Lanterne.*"

Since mayhem might have resulted if Boulanger were dismissed outright, moderates devised a Machiavellian strategy. They would bring down the otherwise acceptable prime minister, Goblet, on some extraneous issue and thus make way for a new cabinet from which Boulanger could be excluded with relative impunity. It meant sacrificing the bathwater to get rid of an unwanted baby, but circumstances demanded it. And so it came to pass that Goblet fell in May 1887, when the Chamber of Deputies rejected a budgetary proposal. His successor did as bidden. Dropped from the new cabinet, Boulanger was, instead, made commander of the 13th Army Corps at Clermont-Ferrand, in south-central France: an assignment tantamount to exile. Should he opt for civilian life after thirty-three years, he wondered? Freycinet, in whom he confided, urged him not to resign his commission, to accept the obscure posting, to leave Paris quietly, and to make the best of a bad bargain. "May it be said of you that you have the smartest army corps in France. Therein lies your future and not in the political games of chance to which people lure you with glittering prospects."

His departure was the opposite of quiet. It proved to be an occasion for mob protest as hysterical as the jubilation on Bastille Day one year earlier. Paris had no sooner learned that he would leave from the Gare de Lyon shortly after 8 p.m. on July 6, 1887, than thousands gathered outside the station, some to bid him farewell, others to intercept him. The latter nearly unhorsed his carriage and gave the police all they could handle until reinforcements arrived. Gendarmes cleared a path through the crowd as Boulanger, in civilian dress, held his top hat high for everyone to see. Inside, the police encountered thousands more, thronging the great hall, barricading platforms, standing four deep on coaches, on girders, on canopies. Scrawled across a locomotive was the newly coined slogan *"Il reviendra!"*—"He will return." But it seemed he would never leave. The roar died down only briefly when Déroulède pleaded for decorum: "Citizens! Your presence here says all that need be said. You will be understood. Make way! *Vive Boulanger! Vive la France!*" At length, Boulanger, besieged in a train compartment, was hustled over to his private coach. Maniacs lying on the railroad track like prostrate dervishes waiting to be trodden underfoot by the Holy Litter had been removed, and the train began its run south. "I absolutely blame the demonstrations that took place," Georges Clemenceau asserted in the Chamber of Deputies several days later, distancing himself from a phenomenon that he, too, now perceived as subversive of the Republic. "General Boulanger's popularity came too early to a man too enamored of ballyhoo."

Singing "En Revenant de la Revue," the crowd that greeted Boulanger at Clermont-Ferrand rivalled in lung power the one that had seen him off at the Gare de Lyon. What then was its disappointment, a week later, when Boulanger did not lead the July 14 military review. Is it that he found the stage too small for his star turn? Or that he tried to heed Freycinet's sage advice? Either way, the general, once settled at Clermont-Ferrand, made common cause with the actor he couldn't subordinate, dutifully touring his military district but not before assuring himself that villagers notified of his itinerary in advance would line the road to watch him ride past. One thing changed, however. Somewhat less time was spent on exertions of self-display, and more on a private life that no longer included his wife. Lucie had left him when he began to consort with a much younger woman named Marguerite Brouzet, the Vicomtesse de Bonnemains. Separated from her own unfaithful spouse, Marguerite lived on the fashionable rue de Berri, near no. 20, where Napoléon Bonaparte's niece, Princesse Mathilde, held court. During his provincial banishment, Boulanger arranged clandestine meetings with Marguerite outside Clermont-Ferrand, in a hotel frequented by clients of the local spa. The proprietress chronicled their trysts.

While Boulanger marked time, Boulangism marched forward and continued to raise alarms. Jules Ferry, who understood the revolutionary impetus of revanchism in what was fast becoming a widespread movement, deplored its brutish character. "For some time we have been witnessing the development of a species of patriotism hitherto unknown in France," Ferry declared. "It is a noisy, despicable creed that seeks not to unify and appease but to set citizens against one another. . . . If one believes its spokesmen, love of country belongs to one party alone or to only one sect within that party, and all who do not think as they do, who would not wish to substitute . . . the impulse of irresponsible crowds for the free and reflective action of the public powers, all who do not worship their idols and trot alongside them behind the chariot of a sham Saint-Arnaud, all are held indiscriminately to be partisans of the foreigner!"* During troubled times, the "popular imagination," as Ferry put it, wanted its passions and fantasies embodied in one man. "That is how messiahs and mahdis suddenly loom up in the Muslim world." Ferry might have found analogies closer to home. What distressed him was not nationalist sentiment per se but the tribal character of Boulangist national-

---

*Marshal Jacques Leroy de Saint-Arnaud superintended the military operations of Louis-Napoléon's coup d'état in December 1851. Louis-Napoléon had recalled him for this purpose from North Africa where, like Boulanger, he had led expeditions into Kabylia. He later commanded at the victory of Alma in the Crimean War. Everyone knew that *"un Saint-Arnaud de café-concert,"* in Ferry's words, was a reference to Boulanger.

ism, its Robespierrian exploitation of patriotic virtue, its intense xenophobia, its spurning of individual judgment and its quasi-religious allegiance to a leader, its clamorous irrationalism. Where this new ethos prevailed, Montesquieu's humanist oath—"If I knew something useful to my family but not to my country, I would endeavor to forget it; if I knew something useful to my country but harmful to Europe, or useful to Europe but harmful to the human race, I would reject it as a crime"—spelled treason. Indeed, Ferry the consummate liberal was, by Boulangist lights, more "foreign" than the Austrian demagogue Georg von Schönerer, whose nationalist association, the Verein der deutschen Volkspartei, founded in 1881, had much in common with French populism. Warmongering hung a light veil over hatred of one's bourgeois compatriots.

The conviction upon which Boulangism thrived, that France needed a hero to clean house, was greatly strengthened in September 1887 by a scandal. It began, like the play illustrating Eugène Scribe's dictum "Great effects from small causes," with two courtisans quarreling over a dress, and it ended three months later with Jules Grévy, president of the Republic, resigning from office. What came to light that autumn was the existence of an influential ring trafficking in decorations awarded by the state. Implicated were three generals, one of whom had been financially ruined six years earlier in the Union Générale fiasco. Their confessions led investigators to Daniel Wilson, a prominent deputy who resided at the Élysée Palace with his wife, President Grévy's daughter. Simply put, Wilson used his strategic position to raise revenue for his newspapers, selling membership in the Legion of Honor to well-connected nouveaux riches who wanted their mercantile success consecrated with a ribbon or rosette. Wilson conducted his operation from the Élysée, on presidential stationery.

Confusion, which had assisted Boulanger more than once, would favor him again during the parliamentary embroilment surrounding Grévy's resignation. Among presidential candidates Jules Ferry enjoyed an advantage in intellect and character, but Ferry was anathema to almost every party except his own—to the Right Wing for having secularized institutional life, to the Left Wing radicals for having expanded a colonial empire that benefited financial and industrial interests, to Boulangists for having disparaged Boulanger, to nationalists all together for having had excessively cordial relations with Bismarck.* Moreover, intellect and character were not prerequisites for the presidency. Neither parliamentarians who wanted a figurehead nor antiparliamentarians who wanted a savior insisted upon real greatness. Inoffensiveness was bound to emerge the victor from this scrum, and so it did in the person of Sadi Carnot, whose chief claim to fame was his family name.† Elected president by the National Assembly on December 3, 1887, Carnot invited another reputable moderate, Pierre Tirard, to serve as prime minister. With the political landscape thus cleared of tall trees, a Parisian horizon opened for Boulanger in Clermont-Ferrand.

December 1887 and January 1888 played out like the fantasmagoria of Saint Anthony's temptations. Malcontents right and left viewed Boulanger as the charismatic partner who would dance them into power. He was a soldier, pure and simple, he declared. But the soldier, being all things to all men, welcomed all comers. Radical Republicans proposed to make him minister of war in a future cabinet. At the same time, Arthur Meyer, the editor of *Le Gaulois,* learned from Boulanger's confidant Arthur Dillon that the general would not turn a deaf ear to plans for a restoration. "[Dillon] told me frankly that Boulanger was being solicited by many factions to enter political life," Meyer wrote in his memoirs.

People were imploring him to assemble men of good will, to create a national party, to become leader of the malcontents. He added that everybody was already betting on his popularity. I

---

*Ferry was responsible for other secularizing laws besides the one that made public school education "free, lay, and compulsory." During his first stint as prime minister it became legal to work on Sundays and Catholic holidays. During his second, divorce was legalized, recitation of prayer at the opening of parliamentary sessions was abolished, and magistrates who had protested the expulsion of Jesuits were removed from the bench.

†Sadi was the grandson of Lazare Carnot, who had demonstrated military genius in organizing the defense of French territory against invading armies during the French Revolution. He came to be known as "l'Organisateur de la Victoire."

believed I understood that Count Dillon had royalist sympathies. I think in any event that we had to do whatever we could
to prevent the Bonapartists or the plebiscitarians from confis-
cating this great popular force and I immediately contacted
the Marquis de Beauvoir [the Comte de Paris' principal private
secretary].

In making the ex-minister of war a pawn, his royalist cohorts ran the
risk of fashioning a Bonaparte instead, but Meyer argued that the risk
had to be run, as it could not gain power otherwise. Boulanger, who
had stripped Louis-Philippe's son of military rank eighteen months
earlier, was forgiven his transgressions (Meyer called upon royalists to
wield the sword without examining its hilt). In due course, an
immensely rich noblewoman, the Duchesse d'Uzès, would subsidize
his political campaigns. Other titled ladies opened their salons to him
and, rumor had it, their boudoirs as well. Aristocratic Paris wore his
emblem, the carnation, at parties in the Faubourg Saint-Germain.
Equally forgiving of his radical past was the Church. If Boulanger
could arrange to restore a king, would he not abolish anticlerical laws
passed since 1880? Behind him, side by side, marched the militant
Catholic Eugène Veuillot of *L'Univers* and the priest-eating Rochefort
of *L'Intransigeant.*

   Two monarchist suitors, Baron de Mackau (descended from an old
Irish family that emigrated after James II's dethronement) and the
Comte de Martimprey, conferred with Boulanger at a midnight meeting in December 1887 and received assurances of his devotion to the
Comte de Paris. Five days later, the general, like an eligible bachelor
playing the field, slipped across the Swiss border for talks with
Napoléon Bonaparte's nephew Jérôme, known as Prince Napoléon.
When Franco-German relations came under discussion, the prince,
who possessed famous memorabilia, told Boulanger that Napoléon's
sword would be his to keep if he recovered Alsace and Lorraine. It
was a safe offer, Jérôme later confided to his secretary. "He has all
that is needed to succeed, but nothing of what he needs to stay the
course. He will soon be our man."

   Like disparate elements of an army advancing in the dark, Bonapartists, royalists, and radical republicans pretended not to notice who their allies were, or to forget and forgive until the regime they despised had been routed by the hero they embraced.

A pivotal event in the hero's career lay at hand. Boulanger had two self-styled impresarios, one being the aforementioned Count Arthur Dillon, a financier of low repute who sported a title of dubious authenticity; the other a journalist, Georges Thiébaud, who had arranged the meeting with Jérôme Bonaparte. In February 1888, on the eve of seven by-elections, Thiébaud launched a publicity campaign urging people to make Boulanger their write-in candidate. Fifty-five thousand voters heeded him. The repercussions in Paris were immediate. Asked to explain himself, Boulanger assured General Logerot, minister of war: "I had and still have no knowledge of anything connected with the legislative elections of February 26." On March 3, he assured the minister less succinctly that his military duties occupied him to the exclusion of everything else. Logerot might have clucked or gasped, for the secret service had meanwhile intercepted letters that proved Boulanger's political involvement. This correspondence, having been unlawfully gathered, could not be used against him, but another, admissible infraction supplied Logerot with all the evidence he needed: Boulanger had made three unauthorized trips to Paris, in disguise. Logerot suspended him from active service. Left-wing radicals took up arms on his behalf, sponsoring him for inclusion in two by-elections to be held that March, as a protest against a government not sufficiently imbued with patriotic feeling. In one of them he would garner more votes than both official candidates combined. The next day, March 26, a council of enquiry saw fit to discharge him. Boulanger, who must on some level have regarded his electoral victories as a celebrity poll, was flabbergasted. No less important to him than proof of the public's adulation were the security and prestige of high rank. When he lost them, the ground in which he had always found purchase fell from under him.

Boulangists—the young Maurice Barrès among them—stood ready with a platform. In mid-March the first issue of a daily called *La Cocarde: Organe Boulangiste* appeared at kiosks. It featured the three words that ultimately became Boulanger's mantra: *"Dissolution,*

An electoral poster with a Boulanger slogan: "Révision, Constituante, Référendum" (calling for the election of a Constituent Assembly to revise the constitution, then a national referendum).

Révision, Constituante." Parliament should be dissolved, a new assembly elected, the constitution revised.

News that Daniel Wilson had been acquitted made Boulanger the more appealing to all who shared the belief that corrupt oligarchs controlled their destiny. The first issue of *La Cocarde* sold four hundred thousand copies. Papers vied for interviews with the martyred general. A letter from him on page one was sure to double circulation. Songs and images proliferated. In April 1888, when still reeling from the shock of his discharge, he found himself elected to parliament in the Dordogne, without having campaigned. Had it been possible at that point to discharge him from civilian life, wrote Henri Rochefort, the government would have convened another council of inquiry.

Passionate audiences were the ex-general's elixir. Scarcely a week after his victory in a region he had never visited, Boulanger set out to campaign in the industrial northeast, where, three years earlier, Zola had taken notes for his great saga of proletarian hell, *Germinal*.* The flag was waved and parliament thrashed. "You are called upon to decide whether or not a great nation such as ours can place its confidence in callow men who imagine that suppressing defense will eliminate war," he declared. And again: "Even Parliament is frightened by the results of its inaction. It pretends to be rousing itself but doesn't

*The electoral system allowed candidates to run from multiple districts. If elected by more than one, they sat for the district of their choice.

fool anyone, since every progressive bill approved by the Chamber inevitably comes to grief in the Senate. . . . For the impotence with which the legislative assembly is afflicted, there is only one solution: dissolution of the Chamber, revision of the Constitution." Sympathetic newspapers—*La Lanterne, L'Intransigeant, La France, La Cocarde*—were hawked wherever Boulanger spoke, some with a free portrait and a musical score included. The refrain of one new song had crowds singing, *"Le peuple entier,/Dont il s'est fait aimer,/ réclame Boulanger./ Faut qu'il revienne . . ."** And *"le peuple entier"* did indeed appear in their thousands: half-starved miners from the Anzin coalfields and peasants barely subsisting on the fruit of their labors. They heard Boulanger denounce the "five hundred slackers" in parliament more concerned with their own perquisites than with the country at large.

Although Boulanger's rhetoric was plebiscitary rather than evangelical, it made any rally a revival meeting. He addressed the abject misery of his audience but also spoke to a yearning that transcended material interests. For many people, he embodied "the Way." Ferry had noted as much in 1887. Eight years later the social psychologist Gustave Le Bon used Boulangism to exemplify what he called "the religious instinct" of crowds. "Today, most great soul-conquerors no longer have altars, but they still have statues or images, and the cult surrounding them is not notably different from that accorded their predecessors," Le Bon wrote in *La Psychologie des foules*. "Any study of the philosophy of history should begin with this fundamental point, that for crowds one is either a god or one is nothing." Could anyone still believe that reason had firmly gained the upper hand of superstition? He continued:

In its endless struggle with reason, emotion has never been vanquished. To be sure, crowds will no longer put up with talk about divinity and religion, in the name of which they were held in bondage; but they have never possessed so many fetiches, and the old divinities have never had so many statues and altars

---

*"All the people, whose love he has won, demand Boulanger. He must return . . ."

raised in their honor. Those who in recent years have studied the popular movement known as Boulangism have seen with what ease the religious instinct of crowds can spring to life again. There wasn't a country inn that didn't possess the hero's portrait. He was credited with the power of remedying all injustices and all evils, and thousands of men would have immolated themselves for him.

As with all popular creeds, Le Bon observed, Boulangism was shielded against contradiction by religious sentiment.

Boulanger won the North handily, in what Freycinet later called an "inexplicable vertigo that gripped the masses and left no room for rational thought." Now representing a populous region, he planned to take his new seat four days later, on April 19. A landau (resembling "a harlot's carriage," wrote the Russian ambassador) fetched him at the Hôtel du Louvre. Drawn by two magnificent bays with green-and-red cockades pinned behind their ears, it circled the obelisk on the place de la Concorde to the acclaim of ten thousand Parisians and continued past mounted soldiers guarding the bridge. Déroulède accompanied Boulanger as far as the Palais Bourbon, where ladies had packed the gallery. At that inaugural session, Boulanger said nothing. When Charles Floquet, a radical who had recently become prime minister, declared that parliament should postpone debate on constitutional change until time had allayed suspicions that the issue might be a monarchist snare or "a cloak for dictatorship," Boulanger held fire. On April 27, three hundred acolytes, all prinked with carnations, met to celebrate their new party, the Comité Républicain de Protestation Nationale—Comité National for short—at one of Paris's most fashionable restaurants. Presiding over them was their Leader, who exhorted Frenchmen to join him in creating an "open, liberal Republic." Opponents on the Left might have responded with a version of Voltaire's famous quip about the Holy Roman Empire, that it was neither holy, nor Roman, nor an empire.

At Boulanger headquarters near the Arc de Triomphe, a portrait of the general astride Tunis hung behind his desk. Other walls displayed his collection of trophy arms. The atmosphere exuded Bonapartism, but Boulanger the deputy, like Boulanger the minister, welcomed all and all alike. Members of his party wore the carpet thin.

Well-wishers were sparser in parliament. Fellow deputies outraged by his characterization of the Chamber as a gang of slackers seized the opportunity to avenge themselves on June 4 when Boulanger presented his brief for constitutional revision. What they heard was not so much a carefully reasoned argument as a catalogue of ambiguous measures. He denounced the regime in the strongest possible terms ("sound and fury, disorder, corruption, sterility, and lies") but otherwise spoke by rote, like a man going through the motions of parliamentary discourse.* Georges Clemenceau, Boulanger's erstwhile sponsor, rose to the occasion. "These discussions for which we are castigated only prove our desire to deal more knowledgeably with matters of great political and social import," he asserted.

Yes, glory be to countries in which discussion takes place, and shame on those in which it doesn't. You raise your hand against parliamentarianism, but parliamentarianism is representative government. It is the Republic itself against which you raise your hand.

Openly contemptuous was prime minister Charles Floquet, who declared that young Napoléon returning from a victorious campaign did not address the Council of Five Hundred as haughtily as Boulanger did the Chamber of Deputies. By what right did he talk down to it? he asked. What deeds authorized his impudence? "At your age, Monsieur le Général Boulanger, Napoléon was dead. And you, sir, you will be nothing more than the Sieyès of a stillborn institution."†

---

*The French diplomat and writer Eugène Melchior de Vogüé remarked upon Boulanger's conversation: "All visitors, after meeting him, were stunned by the hollow sound the idol made when they tapped him."

†Emmanuel Joseph Sieyès, the eighteenth-century statesman, is especially remembered as the author of a pamphlet titled *What Is the Third Estate*, which became a manifesto of the French Revolution. After Napoléon's coup d'état on 18 Brumaire, he drafted a constitution for the Consulate. Napoléon reshaped it to his liking.

Nothing daunted, Boulanger mounted the tribune again five weeks later to demand that a stale, impotent, unrepresentative legislature be dissolved and new elections held before the World's Fair of 1889. Once again, Floquet refuted him, mocking the pretensions to open, liberal government of a man who had spent more time in "sacristies" and "princes's antichambers" than in republican forums.

Boulanger's secret pact with the monarchist party, which underwrote his campaigns, did not embarrass him. He resigned his seat in high dudgeon and, declaring that his honor had been impugned, challenged the prime minister to a duel.

Floquet accepted his challenge. The combatants met on July 13 in the garden of Arthur Dillon's town house at Neuilly. No friend of Floquet imagined that the prime minister, whose witness was Clemenceau, would gain the upper hand, but he did, and buried the point of his foil in Boulanger's neck. The general reportedly lay near death for two days. Boulangists rushing to the nether side of the Arc de Triomphe gathered outside Dillon's gate, where medical bulletins were posted every six hours.

Instead of puncturing his balloon, the wound inflicted by a feisty, potbellied, bowlegged, sixty-year-old lawyer earned Boulanger political kudos. Humiliated at the hands of the bourgeois establishment as France had been humiliated at the hands of Germany, Boulanger could still do no wrong. He was a martyr. On July 28, the man recently said to have lain near death rose from the grave for a spin in the Bois de Boulogne. His landau, followed by sixteen carriages and several hundred people, circled the lake and proceeded at a solemn pace down the Champs-Élysées. This public resuscitation made front-page news.

Soon afterward, when Floquet scheduled elections to fill three vacant seats, including the one vacated by his antagonist, Arthur Dillon insisted that Boulanger run for all three and launched France's first true publicity blitz. Inspired by the American practice of "selling" political candidates, he arranged to have more songs composed, pamphlets written, posters drawn, flyers circulated. He papered the countryside. Lithochromatics showing Boulanger on horseback were bundled off trains and carted to rural inns and cafés. An industry in

Boulangeriana sprang up, with merchants peddling souvenirs all over the departments of the Somme, the Charente-Inférieure, the Nord. Boulanger's dynamic impresarios, Dillon and Baron de Mackau, never doubted the truth of Maurice Barrès's political dictum: "The important thing about popular heroes is not so much their own intentions but the picture of them that people create in their own minds."

For funds, Dillon could thank the Duchesse d'Uzès, who pledged a huge fortune to the Comte de Paris on the condition that he, in turn, give his blessings to her protégé.* The duchess had satisfied herself, at a rendezvous with Boulanger, that the restoration of the monarchy was his ultimate goal.

And the Church had satisfied itself that he stood squarely against anticlerical legislation. Despite the inconvenient memory of his edicts at the War Ministry and the shrill support he received from France's preeminent blasphemer, Henri Rochefort, clergy joined his camp, or camped within hailing distance. "I shall never, whatever the circumstances, countenance religious persecution, for if I did, I would be acting against my conscience and interests," Boulanger told *La Croix,* the Assumptionist newspaper read in every French presbytery. Police agents reported from provincial outposts that priests had been touting Boulanger as "God's emissary." An article in the quasi-official *Moniteur de Rome* declared that the Church "might have much to gain" if Boulanger became head of state.

Boulanger in the Élysée Palace seemed a much realer prospect after the three by-elections of August 1888. He won all three by substantial margins, leading Jules Ferry, among others, to anticipate that another Napoléon III might institute another plebiscitary dictatorship. "The arithmetic of our defeat is appalling and it can't be denied that the Republic has been wounded grievously," Ferry said. Common sense dictated that leftist parties locked in combat over constitutional revision should suspend their differences before Boulanger's populist movement swept them over the edge. An effort at communality had indeed been made the previous May. On the twenty-third of that

---

*They conferred in the symbolically apt setting of Coblenz, in Germany, where, during the Revolution, many French émigré nobles had taken refuge.

month, four hundred anti-Boulangists convened at Masonic head-quarters, with its symbolic aptness in mind, to found the Société des Droits de l'Homme et du Citoyen. Its manifesto read in part:

> We are devoted to the policy of revision, but we want the sincere application of this policy and not its exploitation by a general who poses as a pretender and who recruits his followers from all parties. . . . It is understood, moreover, that revision alone cannot suffice. We must take up the national movement of the French Revolution from where it has been halted and become its perpetuators. We must protect individual and public liberties, freedom of the press, of reunion, and of association, guaranteed by Republican institutions. We must continue the integral development of the Republic—that is, the progressive realization of all constitutional, political, and social reforms contained therein. Such is our goal.

The group drafted reforms aimed at improving the condition of the industrial masses and diverting their support from Boulanger. It demanded the repeal of a law that banned the International Working-men's Association. It called for the establishment of union-controlled labor exchanges. But, rife with internal dissension, its membership didn't grow. Snubbed alike by moderate republicans and by extremists content to sit above the fray, like a marble effigy of Patience, the Société des Droits de l'Homme had little effect.

How ineffectual it was became quite clear in January 1889, when France slipped farther down the slope of antiparliamentarianism. During the previous months, rumors of the imminent collapse of the Panama Canal Company, whose bonds had once been considered a golden investment, stoked widespread discontent. And discontent inevitably benefited Boulanger. His victories in three provinces where opposition had been divided or weak were the springboard for a leap into the heartland of republican strength—Paris.

A by-election to fill a Paris seat provided the occasion. Electioneering began in mid-January and was in full swing by the twenty-first, six days before the event. Republicans had chosen a candidate, Édouard

Jacques, whose joviality made him acceptable to most factions. The poster campaign that had littered three provinces now disfigured the capital. To approach the Orangerie was to encounter Boulanger's face on the flanks of lions overlooking the place de la Concorde. To enter the Opéra was to see his name stencilled on the steps. Boulanger stumped neighborhoods rich and poor, running with the hares and hunting with the hounds. Often accompanied by Paul Déroulède, he had the full support of the militaristic Ligue des Patriotes. To radical republicans he spoke as a radical, with revisionist committees in every ward. Catholic clergy embraced him despite the misgivings of their prelates (who nicknamed him General Géraudel, after a ubiquitously advertised cure-all of the period). The Comte de Paris waffled, but royalist papers uniformly endorsed him. And indispensable to the movement was a large population of the generally disaffected. "If I had voted," wrote Edmond de Goncourt, "I would have voted for Boulanger, even though it's the unknown. But if it's the unknown, it's deliverance from what is, and I don't like what is."

On the twenty-seventh, Boulanger garnered far more votes than Jacques. Parisians in the dead of winter looked as if they were celebrating springtime. Crowds chanting *"Vive Boulanger!"* filled the boulevard des Italiens, the place de la Concorde, the boulevard Saint-Michel. Workers who had streamed down from Montmartre joined well-groomed gentlemen from the *beaux quartiers*. Trumpets blared the "Marseillaise" outside the offices of *L'Intransigeant* while Arthur Meyer at *Le Gaulois* prepared to toast the future restoration. Recognizable anti-Boulangists risked being set upon, or worse, if they ventured outside. Everyone remembered that in December 1887 a patriotic zealot had shot Jules Ferry twice as he entered the rotunda of the Palais Bourbon.*

Election results reached Boulanger at Durand's restaurant on the place de la Madeleine, where his patroness, the Duchesse d'Uzès, presided over one banquet table and his herald, Paul Déroulède, over

---

*Léon Blum, eighteen at the time, would have remembered this incident forty-eight years later, in February 1936, when, as prime minister of the Front Populaire government, he was dragged from his car by right-wing demonstrators and badly beaten.

another. News of a landslide, the prodigal flow of champagne, thousands outside shouting *"À l'Élysée! À l'Élysée!"* made thoughts of a coup d'état suddenly thinkable. Boulanger's entourage believed that a march on the presidential palace could be accomplished without serious opposition from gendarmes, Republican Guards, or regiments garrisoned in Paris. Déroulède urged Boulanger to wait until the morning, when his Ligue des Patriotes would have assembled twenty thousand strong at the Palais Bourbon. Boulanger himself fought shy of danger, arguing that regimes born of coups d'état died of original sin, and that in any event he stood to gain power legally six months later, at the general election. Militants felt that something or other had sicklied over the native hue of resolution. "January 27, 1889, is a date worth noting," wrote Charles de Freycinet, "for it marks the highest point of Boulangism's ascending curve. Thenceforth it descended with surprising rapidity."

Five months earlier, in August 1888, after his electoral sweep, Boulanger and Marguerite de Bonnemains had spent six weeks in Spain and Morocco, traveling incognito. No one knew his whereabouts. Now, after a more portentous victory, he disappeared once again into Marguerite's bosom. The new deputy from Paris didn't take his seat in the Assembly on February 1 but instead boarded a train for Clermont-Ferrand with his mistress. He would not reemerge until the fifth and even then eschewed the Palais Bourbon, preferring to make his views known in salons or over meals, as at a banquet on March 17 in the city of Tours.

This banquet would be remembered as Boulanger's last performance on French soil. So many thousands greeted him that seven police brigades were needed to maintain order. Tours itself was Boulanger's audience, and Tourangeaux not lining his route sat at a table one hundred yards long in an industrial hangar that served as a banquet hall. The Georges Boulanger who spoke that day wore his customary headgear of two caps, with the right one tipped farther forward in deference to the Catholic deputy who had invited him. Did his conservative followers, he asked rhetorically, suppose that he affirmed the Republic in order to betray it? "They clearly understand that a royal or imperial restoration, if such a thing were possible, would leave the nation as divided, more so perhaps, than it is at the present time." But the Republic he professed to love was not the Republic whose politics had been aggressively anticlerical for a decade. A "liberal, tolerant" regime was what he envisioned. It behooved France to

> break with the system of oppression that lacks even the grandeur of our forefathers' warfare. . . . The Republic must repudiate the Jacobin inheritance of our Republicans in power.

Journalists lost no time dubbing him "the Boulanger of curates" and "the Jesuits' revenge." His protestations of loyalty rang false to them. Who was Boulanger after all? Was he the former minister of war who insisted that priests do military service? Or was he this pro-clerical impersonator? Did he himself know? Royalists still riding his coattails were troubled. "There were two successive political agendas," he later explained. "One was mine; it chimed with my feelings and opinions, which were republican, democratic, reformist. . . . The other was equivocal. It had been devised with electoral considerations in mind and inspired the speech I gave at Tours."

As his electoral strength had always drawn upon anger or illiberalism, the speech at Tours would probably have produced more defections than endorsements in the general election, all else being equal. But the government resolved that all else should not remain equal, and most resolute of all was a minister of the interior named Ernest Constans. Well acquainted with the lawyerish adages that recommended obliquity over direct confrontation, the minister, a seasoned veteran of political infighting, attacked Boulanger's flank with a legal maneuver that justified the dissolution of the Ligue des Patriotes. Then, through agents planted in the Boulangist Comité National, Constans spread rumors that the general himself would soon be indicted on charges of plotting to subvert the legally constituted government, hoping to scare him out of France before holding a trial whose outcome he could not predict. Constans knew his man. After a brief interval, during which Boulanger's dual privy councils—royalist here, republican there—asked themselves in feverish debate whether he would lead more effectively from exile or from prison, he arranged to flee with Marguerite de Bonnemains. On April 1, the two, trailed by police, boarded a train at the Gare du Nord, and two hours later they crossed into Belgium, where Boulanger's henchman, Arthur Dillon, awaited them.

His flight, which stunned the nation, bolstered Constans's case. Baron de Mackau urged Boulanger to stand trial. The dock, he argued, was a stage from which every word spoken against parliamentary ineptitude would resound through France. But Boulanger was content to issue written manifestos. He would doubtless have continued to do so from Brussels if the Belgian government, fearing political embroilments, had not insisted that he leave. On April 24, 1889, he and Marguerite sailed for England and settled in London with secretaries, cooks, and chambermaids, all at the expense of Marie-Clémentine d'Uzès and contributors to the royalist war chest.* A loyal equerry named Giraud managed his stable. Riding Tunis in the park every morning, dictating letters, and conferring with Dillon or another member of the Comité National on strategy for the fall elections, he conducted himself to all appearances like an exiled head of state, and English society helped maintain the fiction. Summer arrived. There were garden parties, including one given by Queen Victoria's rakish son, the future Edward VII, who had once rubbed elbows with Boulanger in an ill-lit Montmartre cabaret.

Summer also brought the long-awaited trial. The government accused him of conspiracy, but also prosecuted his character, claiming that he had financed a reprehensible private life with money diverted from the war ministry. He was found guilty by the High Court. It handed down its verdict in August, when Parisians who had cheered Boulanger on the place de la Madeleine in January would be least likely to react, and, indeed, with multitudes visiting a universal exposition much grander than that of 1878, his trial took place in the

---

*An especially generous contributor was the financier and railroad builder Maurice de Hirsch, whose widow, as we shall see, would keep faith with the aristocracy in her own way.

wings. Onstage were the Eiffel Tower, a grand Palace of the Arts, banquet tables at which the Republic assembled 11,250 mayors. Had Boulanger returned, he would have been apprehended at the border. But Constans need not have put border guards on high alert. Despite his party's complete disarray and an electoral reform calculated to work against him, Boulanger saw himself returning after the September 22 elections in triumph. Several confidants tried to convince him that the role of victor would be his only if he played the shackled martyr first, challenging his judges not from a Georgian town house on Portland Place but from within a French prison. The Comité National needed him *sur place*. He didn't listen.

Although Boulanger was again elected to the Chamber of Deputies from Paris on September 22, his party was crushed everywhere except in major cities, and he, having proved useless as a stalking horse for his royalist allies, found himself disavowed by them. "General Boulanger didn't deceive us," wrote Meyer. "It was we who deceived ourselves. Boulangism is failed Bonapartism. To succeed it needs a Bonaparte, and Boulanger as Bonaparte was a figment of the popular imagination." When Meyer gave him the back of his hand in *Le Gaulois*, Boulanger fired off an irate telegram: "I always thought your defining characteristic was stupidity; now I see that it's betrayal."

The unhappy sequel to this fiasco leaves little doubt that in the realm of self-deception, Boulanger enjoyed pride of place. About finances he could not deceive himself. The duchess's fund had been exhausted, and royalist money was no longer his for the asking. Unable now to afford a retinue of servants, a stable of horses, and a patrician residence in London, he and Marguerite de Bonnemains moved to Saint-Hélier on the island of Jersey. It was October. From his new residence, the Hôtel de la Pomme d'Or, he sent a public letter to his Paris constituents, in the working-class district of Clignancourt, thanking them for their vote. All was not lost, he assured them. "We must reconstitute our movement. This is a momentary setback, trust me. Henceforth we move further Left." (Bereft of Boulangism, many Boulangists would in fact find a new home in the Socialist Party.) On November 8, twenty-five loyal deputies landed at Saint-Hélier and

gathered in a dining hall decked with tricolor flags. They meant to for-
mulate a parliamentary program, but toasting Boulanger was their
first and last collective act. After hours of disputation, they agreed on
nothing. Three days later Boulanger issued a "Manifesto to the
French Nation." To anyone listening, it must have sounded like a
voice from beyond the grave.

The wraith of his party struggled on for another season, until April
1890, and breathed its last in Paris's municipal elections. Boulanger
despaired when his lieutenants, most of whom had pleaded with him
to repatriate himself, resigned from the Central Committee. "I didn't
believe that I would ever in my life witness such a shameful flight,"
the fugitive declared. Matters would have been worse if Marguerite
had not unexpectedly inherited enough money to cushion their fall.
They moved to a seaside villa.

Tunis remained from his glory days. Boulanger rode his black horse
every morning and at the Mont Orgueil cliffs, on a clear day, scanned
the French coast thirteen miles away. There was little else to distract
him. His mother, a widow in her dotage, had joined him. Visitors were
few. At the theater in Saint-Hélier, his presence ceased to cause a stir.

While Boulanger began to look the paunchy squire, Marguerite's
health was failing. Afflicted with tuberculosis or stomach cancer or
both, she fell desperately ill in January 1891, during a sojourn in
Paris. As soon as word of her condition reached him, Boulanger
arranged a rendezvous in Brussels. There they remained, transferring
their chattels from Jersey to a rented flat. Marguerite was beyond
help. She wasted away and died on July 16.

Arthur Meyer's epitaph for Boulanger—"The horseman fell from
his mount because love was riding pillion with him"—was widely
quoted by believers disposed to blame his collapse on a femme fatale.
The day after Marguerite's death, Boulanger confided to a friend that
if he thought he had the right to kill himself, he would already have
done so. "It would be a cowardly act to shirk what I consider my duty
and to bankrupt the hopes of so many good people." But when
Déroulède urged him once again to confront his foes, he refused, saying, "My obligation is to this tomb." One week later, he wrote, "I'm

weeping like a child. I can't do anything, I can't work, I can't think. I would never have believed that one could live this way, with one's heart torn apart. Ah! If only there were a battle to be fought somewhere, a war, how willingly I would volunteer! What frightens and terrifies me is that my pain grows worse, more bitter, more difficult to overcome, with each passing day. Can I bear this grief? I begin to doubt it." The woman whose companionship had been his refuge from the dangers and impostures of public life was now the absence that left him homeless. Sitting beside the bed in which Marguerite died and placing flowers at her tomb were the chief rituals of his day. He no longer rode Tunis. A saga whose early chapters had promised the coronation of a latter-day Bonaparte was ending with the sorrows of a fin-de-siècle Werther.

Boulanger's spirits lifted when news arrived from Paris of loyalists invoking his name in anti-German riots after a performance of Wagner's *Lohengrin*.* But only briefly. During the last days of September 1891 he put his affairs in order. On the thirtieth he took a coach to the Ixelles Cemetery in Brussels, sat with his back against Marguerite's tombstone, and blew his brains out.

Had Boulanger died in Paris two years earlier, the constabulary would have been overwhelmed. Even in Brussels, where he was buried next to Marguerite, police had difficulty controlling the crowd of 120,000 who witnessed the funeral procession. People climbed over the cemetery walls and broke past gendarmes at the gates. The Church refused Boulanger holy rites. Déroulède sprinkled a handful of French soil over the coffin. Another mourner added red carnations. There were no eulogies.

In life, Boulanger hardly acknowledged the existence of a wife and daughters. Neither did he do so in his will. To the French nation he offered this posthumous apologia:

---

*Other loyalists saw Boulanger as an avatar of the Swan Knight. Wagnerian opera, which had passionate enthusiasts in France and acquired more with a performance of the *Die Walküre* in 1893, was hospitable to the fantasies of glory and salvation that invented a Boulanger.

I am convinced that my many, devoted partisans will forgive me for not being able to bear a burden of grief so heavy that all work had become impossible. In any event, *uno avulso, non deficit alter.**

So, may they continue the struggle against those who, flouting legality, make me die far from my country. I shall be gone tomorrow. Today I loudly declare that I have nothing to reproach myself for. I have always done my duty, nothing but my duty.

History will treat me leniently. It will not spare those who banished me, who tried to besmirch a loyal soldier with a political judgment. . . . In departing life, I have only one regret, and that is not to be dying on the field of battle, as a soldier, for my country.

THOSE WHO READ the political testament as a last, cracked blast of his trumpet, believing that Boulangism had been buried once for all, would learn otherwise. Boulanger was right. The illusionist in whom so many had vested so much became the martyred hero of a generation whose watchword was "renewal" and whose populist creed, as we shall see, was a glorification of the instinctual, the affective, the inborn, the racial. "Intelligence, what a very small thing on the surface of ourselves!" wrote the fervent Boulangist Maurice Barrès, founder of *La Cocarde*. Rationalism and individualism were seen as the baggage of an alien culture to which the bourgeois—above all, the bourgeois timeservers responsible for banishing General Boulanger— held France hostage. Intelligence undermined an organic, historical community the paramount virtue of whose institutions was their age. It set the French against "la France profonde." It hollowed them out. It exorcized their collective soul. It was, as the xenophobic Barrès put it, a "surface," and, by metaphorical association, a foreigner. Its concomitants were betrayal and disgrace.

Léon Blum, a three-time prime minister of France, believed that Boulanger's mercurial career gave rise to the civil war that tore France

---

*From Virgil: "When one is torn away another succeeds."

apart in the 1890s and colored opinion throughout the Western world. "One cannot understand the Dreyfus Affair unless one remembers that it broke out less than eight years after a failed revolution. The Boulangists sought revenge . . . and the discrediting of institutions and parties."

CHAPTER V

THE OGRE OF MODERNITY: EIFFEL'S TOWER

A MONUMENTAL POLITICAL argument" is what one contemporary called the Eiffel Tower, which bestrode the Universal Exposition staged in 1889 to celebrate the centenary of the French Revolution. His point was driven home by an accident of history: only hours after the tower's inauguration, on March 31, General Boulanger slipped out of the country.

The Revolution, which laid the groundwork for a community that transcended national boundaries, had marked the beginning of a new era, according to Édouard Lockroy, minister of commerce and industry. Releasing creative energy into an untrammeled world, it had fostered the progress of mankind as a whole. The fair, he declared in his preface to an official report, glorified revolutionary ideals and displayed their fruitfulness.

Lockroy had statistics at hand to demonstrate the fraternal reach of France's birthday party. Crammed onto the fairground were far more products than in 1878, bigger machines, more ornate pavilions, more *pompier* art, a "Retrospective of the History of Work and the Anthropological Sciences, including military arts," a "History of the

Human Habitat in 44 separate displays," a replica of the Bastille, and 55,486 exhibits altogether.*

As for the Exposition tower, with its immense steeple poking into the clouds, it was, he wrote, "the image of progress such as we conceive of it today: a pole around which humanity spirals eternally upward." But where Lockroy saw a steeple, others—and not only aggrieved Boulangists—saw an insult. What enraptured the republican minister dismayed compatriots who associated republicanism with impotence, "progress" with movement away from the true center, universality with alienation, and the tower itself with Babel.

LIKE THE New York World's Fair of 1939, the Paris Exposition of 1889 gave a proud face to a harrowed nation. On November 8, 1884, when the government decreed that an exposition should open in five years' time, distress was widespread and vocal. Strikes at the coalfields of Anzin, Decazeville, and Vierzon lasted for weeks or months. The metallurgical industry and building trades languished. Two hundred thousand Parisians, many of whom demonstrated on the place des Invalides in March 1883, were said to be unemployed. Many others, calling themselves les Affamés ("the Famished"), assembled in April 1885 on the place de l'Opéra, where the bourgeoisie, less familiar with the sight and smell of misery since Baron Haussmann's earthmovers had driven the urban poor from Paris's center to its outlying *banlieue,* could not easily ignore them.

The discontented spoke loudest in the general elections of October 1885. Voter sentiment gravitated to extremes. While Clemenceau's party gained on the Left, Bonapartists and monarchists made even

---

*No one knew better than the minister, however, how many exhibits represented foreign interests authorized to join the fair by governments that would not do so in their own name. Monarchies, especially moribund ones, could not openly participate in the celebration of a historical event invoked by subjects plotting their demise at home. Officially absent, then, were Austria-Hungary, Belgium, Brazil, China, Spain, Great Britain, Italy, the Low Countries, Portugal, Romania, Russia, Denmark, Sweden, and Norway.

more significant gains on the Right. Republicans still held sway, but only when radicals and moderates, each other's bane, agreed to cooperate. More often than not, they presented a cracked façade, which boded well or ill for all who read the crack as a sign of the Republic's fragility. The diplomat Paul Cambon, who had recently called Boulanger's bluff in Tunisia, thought that circumstances favored the restoration of a king or the rise of a demagogue. "The general impression is that the Republic is at its wits' end. Next year we shall see revolutionary excesses, then a violent reaction. What will come of it? Some kind of dictatorship, no doubt." His friend Jules Ferry wrote ruefully that monarchism was once again a force to be reckoned with, only four months after half of Paris had thronged the boulevards between the Arc de Triomphe and the Panthéon for the funeral procession of the Republic's poet laureate, Victor Hugo— "one of the greatest pageants ever seen in France," according to *The New York Times*. Given a state of affairs that revived hope in lost causes, the symbolic role of the Exposition acquired peculiar importance, and historical symbolism imbued everything associated with it, not least of all the stage chosen for its mise-en-scène: the Champ de Mars. During the 1880s, this enormous sandlot at Paris's western edge was a military drill ground. Older Parisians would have remembered it from 1867 as the site of the Palace of Industry in Napoléon III's prewar Exposition. But cultural memory reached back much further, to an event some of whose rubble might still have lain underneath that vacant expanse. On May 7, 1794, at Robespierre's behest, the Revolutionary Convention, which had outlawed Catholicism five months earlier, proclaimed the sanctity of a deistic substitute for the Christian God and decreed that a festival be held every June. The first—and only—Fête de l'Être Suprême (Festival of the Supreme Being) took place on June 8. It began in an amphitheater improvised outside the Tuileries Palace, where Robespierre, standing on an upper tier, spoke of the need to root out vices leagued against the Republic and exhorted the assembled thousands to honor the "Author of Nature." It continued across the river at the Champ de Mars, with deputies, citizens, foot soldiers, cavalry, floats, bands, and drum corps moving from one site to the other in a long procession elaborately choreographed by the painter Jacques-Louis David. What awaited everyone on the Left Bank was, remarkably, an artificial mountain.* Broad enough to accommodate the entire Convention, whose several hundred members, led by Robespierre, climbed a steep path to its summit and disposed themselves there under a real tree, this impressive facsimile beetled over the choruses singing accompaniment to patriotic rituals that evoked ancient Sparta. With swords drawn, adolescents swore to defend the fatherland, as young mothers held their infants above their heads in pledges of sacrifice.

Four generations after David designed his altar to the Supreme Being, an engineer of genius wrought a monument to the god of scientific progress. Where the mountain had stood, a tower rose. The structure that Gustave Eiffel envisioned in the 1880s was to serve as the centenary's portal and its beacon. It would introduce visitors to the fairground and lift them high above the city. It would be an arch evoking the Arc de Triomphe and a spire contesting the Sacré-Coeur's command of the sky over Paris.

GUSTAVE EIFFEL, who would have ranked high among candidates for the mandarinate ruling France if the social theorist Henri de Saint-Simon's ideal of a scientific oligarchy had ever been realized, was bred to the roles of engineer and entrepreneur by an ambitious family. His father, Alexandre, had joined the Grande Armée in 1811 at age sixteen and fought against the Austrians in Northern Italy. Wounded twice, he returned to field duty in 1815 and rose to the rank of sergeant-major during the so-called Hundred Days of Napoléon's second reign. Marooned after Waterloo in a civilian world he knew almost nothing about, Alexandre enlisted in the royal army as a private. (Wanting his combat experience under Napoléon recognized, he would vainly petition every successive regime for membership in the Legion of Honor and concede defeat only when Louis-Napoléon informed him in 1852

---

*The mountain alluded to the political party known as la Montagne, which had acquired its sobriquet by occupying the uppermost rows of the tiered legislature. It became virtually synonymous with "Jacobin."

that his exploits at Mincio and Borghetto had been insufficiently heroic to warrant commemoration.) Under Louis XVIII, the private rose in the ranks once again, concealing his Bonapartist sympathies. Army service under the Bourbons was an anticlimactic affair, but for Eiffel it became something else during a stint at the garrison in Dijon. There he met and married the daughter of a lumber merchant, Mélanie Moneuse, an indomitable Burgundian whose conjugal plans did not square with the peripatetic life of a noncommissioned officer.

Gustave's entrepreneurial spirit came from his mother. Bent on staying in Dijon, where she would in due course set up shop, Mélanie insisted that her husband resign and accept civilian employment. Her business was the storage of coal shipped to Dijon on the Canal de Bourgogne from fields southwest of the city. With the industrial development of the Ouche valley, furnaces at Le Creusot smelted around the clock, and the mines that fed them reached deeper below the countryside. For Mélanie, industrialization spelled prosperity. From modest beginnings her operation became a network of wagons, barges, and warehouses. By the early 1830s, Alexandre had quit his job—a clerkship at the prefecture—and joined her in business. The couple lived only yards away from the company's wharf. Their first child, Gustave, was born in 1832, eight years after their wedding. "[My parents] worked relentlessly," he remembered. "From dawn to dusk they supervised the unloading of boats and the loading of wagons, in every kind of weather. This struck my imagination. They had had a series of boats built, the first of which was named *Le Beau Gustave* and the second *La Petite Marie,* for my sister."

When Gustave witnessed his parents at work on the quai Nicolas Rolin, it was as a sojourner. Lacking the time to raise her son, Mélanie boarded him with her widowed mother, in whose household the boy breathed the incense of Catholic France. A half-blind, pious old lady, Mme Moneuse had priests for company, and Gustave's main chore after school was to read her the daily office under pain of having his knuckles rapped. This closed world would have been unrelievedly dismal if not for the presence of a high-spirited uncle (by marriage) whose oaths of allegiance to the secular Republic rang loud and true. "I particularly remember," wrote Eiffel, "how [his uncle, Mollerat] looked at me fixedly from behind his large spectacles and bushy eyebrows and said, 'Remember, my nephew, that all kings are scoundrels,' emphasizing the point with his index finger." What lent authority to this admonition, besides Mollerat's physical stature and a tale about Robespierre's having befriended him during the Revolution, were his scientific credentials. As a successful chemist who manufactured products that carried his name, Mollerat spoke from a bully pulpit. Gustave listened, perforce, and at an early age adjusted to the family supposition that chemistry was his calling.

When, in 1841, the newly affluent Eiffels retired to a country villa, they delivered their nine-year-old son from Mme Moneuse. Reading the daily office was a ritual soon forgotten, and in adolescence Gustave took full advantage of parents who may have wished to atone for their neglect by cosseting him. Not until the last year or two of high school did his intellect awaken. He took first prize in Greek translation (French to Greek), and his honorable mentions in physics and chemistry banished any misgivings the family might have had about the path laid out for him. He would study at the Collège Sainte-Barbe, a school in Paris that prepared candidates for the École Polytechnique. He would become a chemist. He would return to Dijon, or Pouilly-sur-Saône, and take over Uncle Mollerat's plant.

In fact, the path he followed was far more aleatory. His parents' fears that once in Paris he might, like Balzac's provincials, succumb to the lure of Babylon were not groundless. Preoccupied with clothes and theater, Gustave courted failure at Sainte-Barbe, relying upon his natural facility to muddle through. It served him most of the way, but on the entrance examination for the Polytechnique he came up short, and enrolled instead at a marginally less prestigious institution—the École Centrale des Arts et Manufactures.

Uncle Mollerat's heir apparent entered Centrale with the knowledge that its founders included a world-famous chemist, Jean-Baptiste Dumas. This endorsement might have been more consoling if he had shown greater aptitude for the science to which his family had assigned him. Chemistry was not his first, or second, love. Low marks tell the story. He nonetheless bent himself to expectations and graduated in 1855 (during the first Paris Exposition, which enthralled him).

Life then took a fateful turn. His father and his uncle quarreled bitterly. While political differences may not have caused bad blood to flow, they justified the feud. Mollerat inveighed against Louis-Napoléon's coup d'état; Alexandre Eiffel applauded it. Close relatives of the two could not occupy neutral ground, least of all Gustave. With the family split, all communication with his uncle ended. Mollerat died soon afterward, and his business failed as a consequence. Eiffel the reluctant heir found himself mercifully disinherited.

Disinherited but unemployed. Seeing in the person of her son an inert object that wouldn't move unless pushed, Mélanie appealed to her former clients for help. One of them introduced Gustave to Charles Nepveu, a brilliant alumnus of Centrale and the founder of a company that manufactured tools, forges, steam engines, boilers, sheet iron, and rolling stock. Separated in age by only six years, the two men clicked.

Their brief collaboration was intense, and Gustave, whose strong suits had never been single-mindedness or ambition, now worked as if a bottled-up genie had suddenly leaped free. Nepveu accumulated projects and Gustave organized them. "I'm at the office by 8:15 every morning," he wrote to his mother, whose approval (not easily gained) he would always seek. "At a quarter to eleven I take off for lunch and must be back at noon to confer with M. Nepveu. . . . Dinner is at a quarter to six. But don't imagine that my day is over. Not at all. Except on Mondays, when M. Nepveu receives friends, he has me work with him until 11 or midnight. . . . If I stay here, my future is assured. Whatever happens, I will learn a great deal, for M. Nepveu puts a lot on my plate." He was soon to learn something as well about the darker side of his mentor's exuberance. Having undertaken more than he could afford, Nepveu, faced with mounting debt, vanished one day and reappeared a week later, unable to explain his absence or to remember that during it he had written a suicide note. By then, the company had run aground, stranding Gustave's dreams of an assured future on an unmapped shore. Equally unforeseen were the events that floated those dreams again several months later. Early in 1857, a Belgian manufacturer of railroad materiel, François Pauwels, bought the insolvent firm, with an eye to Nepveu's contracts. Of particular interest was an iron bridge over the Garonne River at Bordeaux, to be built for a railroad network owned by the immensely powerful financiers Isaac and Émile Pereire.* Requiring three thousand tons of girders, it would yield handsome profits, and Nepveu, however unreliable in other respects, was an engineer qualified to solve the technical problems involved. Furthermore, Gustave Eiffel's remarkable talent for organization had not gone unnoticed. At age twenty-five he was made project manager, equal in rank and authority to Nepveu.

Managers far more experienced than he might have begged off. The task was formidable. Iron caissons in beveled concrete mantles would be sunk eighty-two feet under the riverbed to provide a base for iron cylinders stacked like segments of a classical column. These would make six piers supporting a span five hundred sixty yards long—the longest in Europe at the time—with thick girders reinforced by iron latticework and massive abutments at either end. The new technology of air compression would enable workers to operate below water level. But first a wooden service bridge would be needed upriver from the construction site. Problems abounded, and the Garonne at Bordeaux, where swift currents flowing down from the Pyrenees met high tides rolling in from the Atlantic, was dangerously turbulent.

In less than two years, Eiffel accomplished a feat of major proportions. "The general aspect of the bridge, whose design varies infinitely according to one's vantage point, is at once elegant and majestic," *Le Monde illustré* reported on August 25, 1860. "So simple, so untrammeled, the roadway barely flush with pillars that support it, it compels one's admiration! . . . The interior offers truly remarkable effects of perspective. It is an immense gallery stretching beyond eye's reach, in which light flooding it from all sides sharply outlines every structural feature and rivet." The young man was rewarded with the title of engineer, a substantial salary, and a commission on projects secured for Pauwels in the future. Projects there would be, in abundance. Having greatly impressed colleagues at the Pereires' Compagnie du

---

*In the same year, 1857, young Eugène Bontoux was hired by the Pereires at the Staatsbahn in Austria.

Midi, he was set to play his part in the conquest of space by rail before tilting his vision upward. This project launched him. Nepveu, to whom he owed so much, became irrelevant.

The bridge had not yet been completed when Eiffel was asked to build a small viaduct over the Garonne, also at Bordeaux. During the next year his work took him farther afield in southwestern France, with plans for bridges over the Lot and Dordogne rivers. *Le Moniteur,* the official government newspaper, ran a long article about the new technology implemented by Eiffel in a lattice bridge over the Nive at Bayonne. His reputation therefore preceded him when he bade farewell to Aquitaine and came north in 1862, newly wed, to manage Pauwels's Paris operation. He lived near the factory in Clichy before moving to an apartment on the rue de Saint-Pétersbourg (almost next door to Édouard Manet).

The Pereires' empire began crumbling in the early 1860s, and industrialists heavily dependent on it found themselves mired in financial difficulties. Pauwels and Company, which supplied the Compagnie du Midi with locomotives as well as bridges, was starved for business, and Eiffel, networking feverishly, scratched together only enough to maintain a faint professional pulse. It turned out once again, however, that an employer's reverses ultimately advanced his career. Driven as never before, and bolstered by admirers well placed in the engineering community, he struck out on his own. The year was 1864. He had a delicate, acquiescent wife, three babies, no capital, and a contract to organize the production of thirty-three small steam locomotives (called "locomobiles") for the Egyptian government.

Egypt, where he spent almost four months arranging delivery, exposed him to spectacles of grandeur and backwardness that stretched his mind in opposite directions. Dilatory government officials, for whom terms of a contract were as elastic as the quoted price of articles at the souk, exasperated him. "You can't imagine the time wasted here in paltering and the kind of distracted people with whom one must deal," he wrote to his father. "One never knows on what ground one stands. I've been here for twelve days and am frightfully bored." So obtuse were Alexandrians that news of Abraham Lincoln's assassination, when it arrived in early May, perturbed them "only to the extent that it might affect the market price of cotton." But there were also the pyramids to take in, and the Suez Canal, which had been under construction since 1859. He toured the area at the Canal Company's invitation, and marveled at it all—the stupendous trench, the blooming green markets at a city built by Ferdinand de Lesseps on the shore of Lake Timsah, the railroad and freshwater canal running from Ismailia west to Zagazig. "After having seen the desert, the immense, desolate expanses deprived of water and vegetation, one understands first of all what boldness was required to place thousands of workers on such soil, then to sustain them beneath the torrid sun," he noted. "The impression one gets of man as supreme conqueror of the desert is all the more striking because its conquest took so little time and cost so few victims." Not that he was as blind to natural beauty as his imperial language suggests. He was enraptured by the sight of islands seemingly afloat in the vapor rising from Lake Menzaleh and of flamingos trolling its shallow waters. But where literary pilgrims such as Gustave Flaubert sought refuge in the "Orient" from bourgeois France, Gustave Eiffel thrilled to evidence of mankind's mastery of nature.

It followed nicely, then, that after his return, several of the men planning an event designed to celebrate France's modernity, prestige, and global reach should solicit his collaboration. By designing the armature of buildings that would stand no longer than needed for a six-month fair, Eiffel planted himself on the Champ de Mars for the first time.

In April 1867, Louis-Napoléon, who had been at work reinventing Paris ever since he had proclaimed himself Napoléon III fifteen years earlier, inaugurated his second Universal Exposition. Among the six million people who eventually attended, those who came by special invitation included the czar and the czarina, the king of Prussia, the khedive of Egypt, the Japanese mikado's brother, the sultan of Turkey, the Hapsburg emperor, and the Prince of Wales. During several months, hardly a week passed that Louis did not have occasion to greet some panjandrum alighting at a railroad depot and lead him in military pomp to the Tuileries Palace, where gala after gala preempted other, more banal affairs of state. Economic misery was rampant, but

A photograph of the Palace of Industry, which covered much of the Champ de Mars at the Exposition Universelle of 1867.

few looked backstage. All along the boulevards, theaters, restaurants, and boutiques drove a thriving trade as Paris mobilized its vast pleasure industry for visitors who arrived by the trainload or boatload.

"French is the language least heard on Paris streets," declared one chronicler, and this polyglot horde was indeed ubiquitous. It filled the Théâtre des Variétés when Offenbach's *La Grande-Duchesse de Gérolstein* opened there on April 12. It fed its eyes on women high-kicking at dance halls (to which it found its way by following a guide titled *Parisian Cytheras*). It oohed at fireworks in the Tuileries Gardens and aahed at gorgeous carriages in the Bois de Boulogne, where Society paraded its wealth every afternoon. Gravitating to light, to movement, to fanfare, to novelty, it did not neglect Paris's venerable monuments but often glimpsed them en passant, as did Mark Twain, who wrote in *The Innocents Abroad*: "We visited the Louvre, at a time when we had no silk purchases in view, and looked at its miles of paintings by the old masters." Old masters couldn't quite compete against Charles Blondin waltzing on a tightrope with blazing Catherine wheels fastened to his body. When the aerialist performed in a suburban pleasure garden, the horde of visitors flowed away from Paris like the sea at ebb tide. And when in October they left Paris for good, laden with silk from the great textile mills at Lyon, the image graven on their minds was more likely to be of machines in the Palace of Industry than of *Le Déjeuner sur l'herbe* in Manet's little pavilion.

The Palace of Industry occupied the Champ de Mars. Looming above gardens and grottoes laid out by Adolphe Alphand, architect of the Bois de Boulogne, this industrial-age Colosseum was an immense iron-and-glass oval whose bulk dwarfed the minarets, the pagodas, the domes, the cottages, the kiosks built to represent various nation-states. Unlike the Eiffel Tower, the Palace of Industry did not outlive the abuse heaped on it by those who lamented France's "Americanization"; but while it stood, it advertised more comprehensively than any American structure the materialist worldview against which Pope Pius IX had inveighed in *The Syllabus of Errors*.

Had Pius ever seen the Palace, its six concentric galleries might have put him in mind of Dante's Hell, especially by day, when a roar of machinery drowned the hubbub of the crowd and vapor from steam engines billowed toward the glass roof. To tour these mile-long galleries was, if one believed in progress, to rejoice in man's victory over nature or, if one did not, to witness the spectacle of pride running before a fall. Here industrial Europe displayed itself at its most vainglorious. There were machines of every order and dimension: textile machines, compressed-air machines, coal-extracting machines, railway equipment, electric dynamos, hydraulic lifts. There were locomotives and large-scale models of those railroad stations that enshrined the nineteenth century's architectural historicism. There was a show on the history of labor, where working-class visitors (those who could afford the price of admission) were given to understand that they did not lack basic necessities but, quite the reverse, had earned enough since 1848 to afford the clothes, utensils, and gadgets laid before them in grotesque profusion. Beneath this glass roof nothing gainsaid Louis-Napoléon's optimism, not even a fifty-eight-ton steel cannon made by Krupp of Essen for Wilhelm of Prussia. With political reality suspended for the moment, inklings of doom were as unwelcome as early Impressionist paintings. Tourists pressed on heedlessly, orbiting through Wonderland until their journey led them to the outermost ring, where they restored themselves in cafés and restaurants. To Epicurus Rotundus, a pseudonymous Englishman reporting for *Punch,* nothing about the Palace of Industry was so clearly reflective of its nature and purpose as the garden around which it had been built. "My dear Sir, the heart of this garden, the center of all these monster rings, which made you feel as if you had got into Saturn, was a little money-changing office. I like this cynicism."

Eiffel's advocates had given him the task of conducting experiments to test the elasticity of structural iron pillars. By the time the Exposition opened, he had also accomplished the design of a large aquarium (called Neptune's Realm) and engineered the skeleton of a gallery five hundred meters long reserved for art and archaeology. His work earned him an invitation to the ball held for eight thousand notables at the Hôtel de Ville on June 8. "The two emperors, the king of Prussia, and every imaginable highness will be there and I've ordered for the occasion an outfit befitting a courtier—tight-fitting trousers with silk stockings and pumps," he wrote to his parents. "Marie [his wife] is also quite excited; she will certainly never have seen nor will ever see again anything so splendid."

Intoxicated by this grand festival and buoyed by the memory of Suez, Eiffel was not to be deterred by sober counsels from taking a longer leap into the entrepreneurial void. With borrowed money, he rented hangars just outside Paris, built a house on an adjacent parcel, bought the equipment of Pauwels's bankrupt plant at knock-down prices, and opened shop as "G. Eiffel, Ateliers at 48 Rue Fouquet in Levallois-Perret near Paris: Metallic Doors and Pneumatic Foundations, Iron Frameworks, Gazometers, Boilers and Generally All Metallic Constructions."

Barely enough business dribbled in to keep him afloat until the chief engineer of the Orléans Railroad Company, Wilhelm Nordling, whom Eiffel knew from Bordeaux, recruited him to build two viaducts. One of them, at Rouzat, presented formidable challenges. Though much shorter than the Bordeaux bridge, it spanned a deep valley in the Auvergne. Here, Eiffel, no longer relying upon another engineer's technical ingenuity, proved his mettle, in every sense. Max de Nansouty, a devoted confrère, would applaud him for having shown how different kinds of iron can be combined in large structures to achieve both resistance and lightness; how straight-beam bridges can be wheeled out into space at dizzying heights with great precision by means of levers and the tipping slide Eiffel invented; and, finally, how, when mountainous terrain doesn't allow scaffolding, one builds piers up from the chasm floor by winching parts down from the beam they will eventually support. Eiffel's innovations were many. There would be more. But like the elegance of his own person, the looks of what he engineered also mattered to him. The viaduct across the Sioule River was "certainly one of the most beautiful works I've made until now and also one of the boldest," he wrote to his mother, sending her photographs of his high-slung creation.

Eiffel commanded respect. He was on terms with men of influence. He could deal directly with France's most important iron and steel manufacturers. He acquired capital in the person of a wealthy young engineer, Théophile Seyrig, his collaborator at Rouzat, who became his business partner. And, thanks in considerable part to Wilhelm Nordling, he had as much as he could handle of building more bridges for the Orléans line. "This gives us a security we haven't enjoyed hitherto, not to mention the fact that Gustave now stands in the ranks of Paris's premier builders," Marie wrote to her mother-in-law in 1868.

After the Franco-Prussian War and the two sieges that destroyed large areas of Paris, Eiffel, with his equipment intact, took up where he had left off, but reaching far beyond France. During the 1870s, Eiffel & Co. built railroad bridges in Peru, Spain, Portugal, Romania, Indochina. It built gasworks high up in the Andes at La Paz and a breakwater in the then-Peruvian port city of Arica. Churches on either side of the Pacific originated in Eiffel's workshop, along with railroad stations at Santander and Budapest, the Lycée Carnot, the casino of Sables-d'Olonne, and Paris's first department store, Le Bon Marché, whose soaring central atrium is the stage set for Zola's *Au bonheur des dames*. It patented a portable bridge used throughout the colonies, and in 1881, it produced the framework of Bartholdi's Statue of Liberty. There were several lost causes, a notable one being Eiffel's design for the new observatory in Paris. But lost causes were the exception. By 1884, when his company drafted early plans for a thousand-foot tower, his name, stamped in structures all over the world, was synonymous with iron.

Among great Eiffelian structures eclipsed by his tower, the one that most clearly prefigures it is the Garabit Viaduct in the Massif Central, a wrought-iron railroad bridge half a kilometer long whose central piers, reinforced by a sweeping, crescent-shaped truss, support a girder four hundred feet above the Truyère River.* Where river valleys could suddenly become wind tunnels, the vagaries of weather dictated design, and for help in this domain Eiffel relied heavily upon the calculations of a brilliant young assistant named Maurice Koechlin. Koechlin would play an important part as well in designing the Exposition tower—so important, indeed, that the tower might just as rightly have borne his name.

Broadly speaking, the Exposition tower was not one man's creation but the child of an era obsessed by the idea of a one-thousand-foot tower. The nineteenth century had already begotten at least three unrealized projects with which Koechlin must have been familiar. In 1832, when the Reform Bill became law in England, a Cornish mining engineer named Richard Trevithick proposed commemorating the event "by the erection of a stupendous column, exceeding in dimensions Cleopatra's Needle, or Pompey's Pillar and symbolic of the beauty, strength and unaffected grandeur of the British Constitution." When, in 1852, the House of Commons voted not to save Joseph Paxton's Crystal Palace, an architect named C. Burton suggested that iron and glass salvaged from the demolition be used in a cluster of telescoped towers rising one thousand feet. Two decades later, the Philadelphia Centennial celebrating American independence inspired the design for a tapered one-thousand-foot tower replete with viewing galleries and four elevators running up a central shaft thirty feet in

---

*One admirer of the Garabit Viaduct was Le Corbusier. As a young architect, he wrote to Eiffel with questions about it.

diameter. "Whenever men have become skilful architects," John Ruskin said in *Lectures on Architecture and Painting*, "there has been a tendency in them to build high; not in any religious feeling, but in mere exuberance of spirit and power—as they dance or sing—with a certain mingling of vanity—like the feeling in which a child builds a tower of cards." A "certain mingling of vanity" understates the preening of *Scientific American* in an article about the Philadelphia project: "As did the descendents of Noah, so propose we to do. . . . And to its prototype, Babel, a pile of sun-dried clay which the authorities assert, at the hour of the confusion of tongues, had not attained an altitude of over 156 feet, the graceful shaft of metal, rearing its summit 1,000 feet above the ground, forms a fitting contrast, typical of the knowledge and skill which intervening ages have taught mankind."

The millennial demon visited Koechlin on June 6, 1884, when he crudely sketched a tower and, next to it in vertical sequence, seven famous monuments—Notre-Dame cathedral, Saint Peter's, the Statue of Liberty, the Vendôme and Bastille columns, the Arc de Triomphe, and the Luxor obelisk in the place de la Concorde. Piling Pelion on Ossa was no mere fantasy. His mathematical calculations as to weight and wind resistance convinced him that the fabled height could be reached. Another Eiffel engineer agreed, but Eiffel himself demurred. Wary of a dangerous enterprise, he had serious misgivings about throwing pride and money into a short-lived structure. Even if the tower stood, it would last only as long as the exposition itself, and ephemerality didn't sit well with him. But three months later, he and Koechlin obtained a patent for "a new scheme rendering it possible to construct metallic piers and pylons more than 300 meters in height." What explains this about-face? It is thought that with the refinement of Koechlin's design, Eiffel's imagination caught fire; that the adventurer in him, overruling the prudent bourgeois, decided to risk it, and to win a contract on his own terms. There would be competition, but he could marshal behind him a group of influential men. As early as October 22, 1884, *Le Figaro* was touting Eiffel's custom. "Among the most extraordinary projects born of the announcement that another Universal Exposition will be held in 1889 is that of an iron tower 300 meters tall. It is on the drawing-board of M. Eiffel, the builder well-known for his bold modern constructions and notably the Garabit Viaduct. This tower on the fairgrounds would stand twice as tall as the highest monuments in the world." Three months later, *Le Temps* followed suit with a front-page article contending that an industrial fair needed new, extraordinary proportions. "The grandiose is called for. Everything that has been done hitherto seems small. Industry must push the ultimate limits of the materials it uses. Among the new projects to which this presumption has given rise, we call attention to the one that bears the name of M. Eiffel, whose artistry in iron is the object of universal admiration."

Certainly, political sentiment helped Eiffel warm to the prospect of having his creation arch over the Centennial fairgrounds. Although Uncle Mollerat would not have found his nephew's republicanism robust enough, it was unambivalent. He had provided his bona fides on the municipal council of Levallois-Perret during the 1870s, when members repeatedly demanded the separation of Church and State. In 1884, a colleague through whom he ventriloquized, Max de Nansouty, dressed his skeletal tower in the rhetoric of republican triumphalism. Echoing Condorcet's *Esquisse d'un tableau historique des progrès de l'esprit humain* ("Outline of a Historical Tableau of the Progress of the Human Mind") in which the eighteenth-century philosopher foresaw a universal language emerging from the Revolution, Nansouty declared that the confusion of tongues that doomed its biblical ancestor would not affect "this Babel of modern industry," for its language would be "the universal language of humanity making a common effort to achieve boundless progress and measured freedom."

But ideals aside, professional pride is what ultimately motivated Eiffel. No one explained with greater relish the anatomy of his virtual behemoth. Its piers, he wrote, introduced a method of construction all his own, using curved edges to blunt the wind's cutting power. "Before coming together at the high pinnacle, the uprights appear to burst out of the ground, and in a way to be shaped by the action of the wind." Knowing that judges disposed to admire his engineering against wind resistance might still be reluctant to commission a display of technology for its own sake and to let it stand longer than necessary, he equipped it with practical purposes. It would serve as a sentinel in time of war and a scientific workshop in time of peace, giving meteorologists and astronomers an incomparable observatory. And as we have seen, Eiffel also vested pride in the looks of his work. Technology for him was inextricably bound up with an aesthetic creed amalgamating form, material, and function. "The fact is that this tower resembles nothing known, which is why certain architects reject it," he wrote in 1886 to Adrien Hébrard, director of *Le Temps*. "Being made of iron, it exemplifies no architectural style—neither Greek, nor Gothic, nor Renaissance; its form rationally comports with the nature of its materials." At the École des Beaux-Arts, where, in his words, one "learned very little about iron," the material was a pariah. "It eludes [architects trained there]. But they will eventually accept it, just as engineers have done."

Competition came from Jules Bourdais, the architect of the Trocadéro Palace and darling of the Academy, who had his own three-hundred-meter tower to propose: the Sun-Column, as he called it. A granite shaft eighteen meters in diameter, sheathed in spun copper, surmounted by a beacon powerful enough to light all of Paris, and built on a foundation large enough to house a museum of electricity, it would rise above the esplanade des Invalides. Each of five levels would have sixteen rooms, in which penurious invalids likely to benefit from diminished atmospheric pressure could undergo "aerotherapy." The architect dismissed the engineer as a philistine unworthy of consideration. He claimed, on dubious grounds, that Eiffel's metal tower would weigh almost eight times more than his stone column. It would make Paris a prime target for lightning bolts. And officialdom couldn't grant it longevity since iron was inherently corruptible. If Greek and Roman monument-builders had worked with iron rather than with stone, would anything remain of classical antiquity? As for Eiffel's contention that the tower would "personify the modern engineer's art and a century of industry and science for which the groundwork was laid by the Revolution of 1789," the centennial deserved better. It deserved art, real art, an architect's art.

These contestants jousted furiously. While Eiffel refuted Bourdais's argument point by point before the Society of Civil Engineers, citing the troubled history of the Washington Monument, architects heaped scorn on Eiffel in their trade journal, *La Construction moderne.*[*] Dogged efforts were made to influence the administration. Eiffel put his case to Alphonse Alphand, the director of public works for the city of Paris, whom he had known since 1867; Bourdais, in turn, lobbied Édouard Lockroy, the minister of commerce and industry, whom he mistakenly believed favored his design. Lockroy played a Machiavellian role in the politics that ultimately rewarded Eiffel. Well acquainted with technical reports describing the Sun-Column as no match for the forces of wind and gravity, but careful not to offend academic pooh-bahs by rejecting it outright, he invited wider participation, set a draconian deadline, received 107 proposals all told, and quickly herded them through a gauntlet of committees. On June 12, 1886, Eiffel's, the preordained winner, won.

Already rich, Eiffel stood to become much richer after negotiating a brilliant contract. Unless neighborhood residents who had initiated a lawsuit succeeded in blocking construction and, for that or any other reason, the tower was not completed by April 1, 1889, he would pocket all income from its business operations for twenty years. Moreover, the government provided an "indemnity" of 1.5 million francs.

It all began with concrete foundations, gravel laid in clay soil, and beds of masonry reinforced by bars of puddled iron to cramp the stone together. Hydraulic derricks and winches positioned parts on the lower level. Once the tower's first platform had been hoisted and bolted to its pillars, heavy lifting was accomplished by a steam crane sitting on the platform's girders. This spectacle enthralled Paris for twenty-six months. Eighteen thousand numbered pieces traveled from Levallois-Perret to the Champ de Mars with military precision. As time wore on, the workforce employed at ground level dwindled to a

---

[*]Political as well as structural problems plagued the Washington Monument. The cornerstone was laid in 1848 but construction halted ten years later, for lack of funds, and resumed twenty-one years after that, in 1879. Stone from different quarries mark the hiatus. The foundation had to be redesigned, and the monument was moved at one point, to firmer ground.

Gustave Eiffel, photographed by the Nadar studio.

much smaller crew high above Paris—so high that their welding was almost inaudible, and so often obscured by low-lying clouds or autumn fog that the tower seemed to be rising of its own, like a gigantic stalk. Except for forges glowing in the sky at dusk, wrote the Vicomte de Vogüé, one would not have guessed a human presence. Reporters brave enough to ascend the unfinished tower described another scene. "A thick cloud of tar and coal smoke seized the throat, and we were deafened by the din of metal screaming beneath the hammer," wrote Émile Goudeau. "Over there they were still working on the bolts: workmen with their iron bludgeons, perched on a ledge just a few centimetres wide, took turns at striking the bolts"—these in fact were the rivets. "One could have taken them for blacksmiths contentedly beating out a rhythm on an anvil in some village forge, except that these smiths were not striking up and down vertically, but horizontally, and as with each blow came a shower of sparks, these dark figures, appearing larger than life against the background of the open sky, looked as if they were reaping lightning bolts in the clouds."

On Sunday, March 31, 1889, four hundred dignitaries, including Prime Minister Pierre Tirard (who had earlier disparaged the tower as "American" in spirit), gathered for inaugural ceremonies under the tower arch. Framed by an iron semicircle were the Exposition's central dome, its esplanade, and a statuary fountain featuring a winged *Progress* with enraptured acolytes at her feet. Under the tower itself stood another statuary group, *La Nuit essayant d'arrêter le génie de la Lumière qui s'efforce d'éclairer la Vérité* ("Night trying to prevent the genius of Light from illuminating the Truth"). Allegorical figures representing five continents as five stages in humanity's quest for enlightenment surrounded the antagonists, Night and Light.*

The tower was complete except for elevators, which would not be installed until the exposition opened to the public in May. On inaugural day, Eiffel, followed by a delegation, began to climb the 2,731 steps to the summit. Delegates who had attended too many banquets in political life fell by the wayside at each successive platform, pant-

*Asia, for example, was a languid odalisque and Europe, a scholar pictured with a book and a printing press.

Engraving of the Eiffel Tower, by Fraipont, as it appeared on
Bastille Day, 1888, eight months before completion.

ing from their exertions, but Eiffel persevered, along with Édouard
Lockroy. After more than an hour, the survivors, journalists and
politicians alike, crowded onto a small round platform in the campanile. There, at Lockroy's behest, Eiffel unfurled a large flag, and
with the tricolor flapping in the wind and cannons below firing a
twenty-one-gun salute, everyone sang the "Marseillaise." Afterward,
on a lower platform, Tirard promoted Eiffel to the rank of officer in
the Legion of Honor. The ironworkers then offered him a bouquet of
white lilacs.

History offered him its own bouquet of sorts one day later, when a threat to the Republic was averted. On April 1, General Georges Boulanger sought asylum in Belgium, and the Eiffel Tower seemed to plant a gigantic exclamation mark after the announcement of his flight.

PUBLIC COMMENT ON the tower did not argue a neat correlation between taste and politics. Some political conservatives liked it, some republicans found it abhorrent. Among the latter, for example, was Guy de Maupassant, one of whose characters (in the short story "La Vie errante") claims that he fled Paris because of the Eiffel Tower.

> Not only is it visible from every point in the city, but it is to be seen in every shop window, made of every known material—an unavoidable and tormenting nightmare. . . . I wonder what will be thought of our generation if, in some future riot, we do not dismantle this tall, skinny pyramid of iron ladders, this disgraceful giant skeleton with a base that seems made to support a formidable monument of Cyclops and which aborts into the thin, ridiculous profile of a factory smokestack.

On February 14, 1887, when it stood no higher than its cyclopean feet, Maupassant joined forty-six artists and writers in an open letter of protest to Alphonse Alphand, minister of public works. "Writers, painters, sculptors, architects, passionate lovers of the heretofore intact beauty of Paris, French taste has been flouted, French art and history are threatened by the erection in our midst of the useless, monstrous Eiffel Tower, and we protest against it with all our strength and indignation," they declared, presenting themselves as devout partisans of stone.

> We are not being fanatical chauvinists when we proclaim publicly that Paris is unrivalled in the world. Along its streets and wide boulevards, beside its admirable riverbanks, amid the magnificent promenades, stand the most noble monuments to which

Engraving of the Eiffel Tower in La Revue illustrée, *1889. "The Eiffel Tower and the highest monuments on Earth."*

human genius has ever given birth. The soul of France, the creator of masterpieces, shines from this august proliferation of stone. Italy, Germany, Flanders, so rightly proud of their artistic heritage, possess nothing comparable to ours, and Paris attracts curiosity and admiration from every corner of the universe.

The sacred city was being profaned by Mammon. The "mercantile fantasies" of an engineer were fouling Paris's noble mind. France was becoming more American than America.

Inauguration of the Eiffel Tower, 1889.
"M. Eiffel unfurling the tricolor flag at its summit."

Do not for a moment doubt that the Eiffel Tower, which even commercial America would not want on its soil, disgraces Paris. Everyone feels it, everyone says it, everyone is profoundly saddened by it, and we are only a faint echo of public opinion. When foreigners visit our Exposition they will cry out in astonishment, "Is this horror what the French have created to display their vaunted taste?" They will be justified in mocking us, for the Paris of sublime gothic, the Paris of Jean Goujon, of Germain Pilon, of Puget, of Rude, of Barye, etc., will have become the Paris of Monsieur Eiffel. To understand our case, one need only imagine a . . . gigantic, black smokestack beetling over Notre Dame, the Sainte Chapelle, the Tour Saint Jacques, the Louvre, the dome of the Invalides, the Arc de Triomphe, humiliating our monuments with its barbarous mass, dwarfing our architecture. . . . And for the next twenty years we will see this city, still vibrant with the genius of so many centuries, overshadowed by an odious column of bolted metal.

Published in *Le Temps,* the "Protestation des Artistes" was signed by such guardians of artistic propriety as Ernest Meissonier, Charles Garnier (architect of the Paris Opéra), William Bouguereau, Alexandre Dumas fils, Sully Prudhomme, Leconte de Lisle, Charles Gounod, and Victorien Sardou.

But like Joan of Arc, the Eiffel Tower came to reflect even more

The 1889 Exposition Universelle, photographed from the Trocadéro.

sharply the ideological rift in fin-de-siècle Paris. While republican newspapers published panegyrics, *L'Univers,* the Catholic daily now managed by Louis Veuillot's brother Eugène, inveighed against it. Its only point being to reach three hundred meters, the ill-proportioned tower would, like an arriviste forever climbing, always find true height beyond its reach. Naked and pointless, it was dwarfed in every way by the Gothic church. Medieval architects, *L'Univers* declared, accomplished marvels of construction that far surpassed Eiffel's by "raising edifices 150 meters long, covered with stone vaults 25 to 30 meters wide, as high as 50 meters, with flying buttresses, with clerestories, with glass all around." And unlike republican engineers, medieval architects eschewed the work site on Sundays. Was it not on a Sunday that Sadi Carnot, president of the Republic, paid an official visit, and on another Sunday, three months later, with construction still in progress, that Prime Minister Pierre Tirard inaugurated the tower? Until the very end, the Lord's Day was profaned to meet a

*The central dome of the Palace of Diverse Industries at the 1889
Exposition Universelle, engraved by F. Méaulle.*

deadline. "The point had to be made that this was a completely secular enterprise and that the tower showed no sign of clericalism. The
ceremony was entirely civil: no benediction, not the least little prayer,
not the least homage to the God of heaven and earth. The Republic
does not recognize the Creator, and the engineer believes himself to be
perhaps the equal of He who made mountains." Hubris would not go
unpunished, the paper prophesied. Dominating all of Paris's crosses,
the vainglorious tower erected as a symbol of the Revolution would
eventually fall or be eclipsed by a taller structure crowned with the

sign of Redemption. "Official France" was "prey to the enemies of God," but "God's hour" would sound, the true French reduced to private devotions would emerge, and *Te Deums* of victory would be sung in "the national sanctuary"—the Sacré-Coeur.

In *Remarques sur l'exposition du centenaire,* Melchior de Vogüé imagined a dispute between Notre-Dame and the Eiffel Tower, with an ethereal moderator trying to reconcile the adversaries.* "Things down below, heavy things," his moderator says to the cathedral towers, "your words are unjust and your view shortsighted. You, pious Gothic towers, why do you forbid your young sister to be beautiful? If an Athenian Greek had been present when master masons were sculpting you, he would have said of you what you say of her today. He would have treated you as barbaric monsters, as an insult to the sacred lines of the Parthenon." Then, addressing the Eiffel Tower: "And you, daughter of knowledge, curb your pride. Your science is beautiful, and necessary, and invincible; but you accomplish little by enlightening the mind if you do not cure the eternal wound of the heart. Your elder has been giving mankind what it needs: charity and hope. If you aspire to succeed her, arrange to found the temple of the new alliance, the accord of science and faith."

But the argument for rational cohabitation could hardly make itself heard. Scorn spoke too loudly, in too many voices. For aesthetes, Eiffel's tower was the grotesque child of the industrial age, desecrating a museological city. For Catholics, it was the sport of revolutionary Nimrods expounding their secularism in Notre-Dame's parish with phallic arrogance. And for nationalist zealots, who joined the chorus, the wrought-iron tower incommensurate with everything else in Paris was a tyrannical mutant, a foreigner lording it over the French past and future, a cosmopolite aspiring to universality, a potential instrument of treason. As such, it could only be the invention of "Israel." One Jacques de Biez enlarged upon this idea in *La Question juive: La France ne peut pas être leur terre promise* ("The Jewish Question:

*De Vogüé is best known for having introduced France to the Russian novel—the works of Dostoyevsky in particular—which he discovered for himself during a stint at the French embassy in Saint Petersburg.

France Cannot Be Their Promised Land"). Published soon after *La France juive,* it continued Drumont's work of showing Jews to be ubiquitous saboteurs of the French soul. Eiffel was identified as Jewish. Worse yet, the tower destined to bear his name embodied a Jewish conspiracy. "I am dismayed, but hardly surprised," wrote de Biez. "There are ideas that spring only from Jewish brains. Only a Jew could have submitted such a project. Only a Jew like the engineer Alphand could have recommended its construction. Only a Jewish ministry like the Lockroy-Ollendorff ministry could have imposed the project." True France was France of the soil. Imposters were rootless. Touted as a sentinel guarding the homeland, Eiffel's tower would, on the contrary, operate as a spy betraying Paris to "hordes from the East." The Jew who "brought it with him from Germany" entered France in the bowels of a Trojan horse.*

Master and disciple, cofounders of the National Anti-Semitic League of France, took turns decrying the tower. It had just been completed when Drumont, in his book *La Fin d'un monde,* drew a parallel between its erection and the trappings of victory worn by Byzantine emperors marching back to Constantinople after disastrous defeats at the hands of Bulgars or Goths. With France's economy in shambles, the three-hundred-meter tower was a comparable deception. And whose interests did it serve? Those of the cosmopolite. "We sons of

*Gustave Eiffel's great-grandfather, Wilhelm Bonickhausen, had indeed emigrated from Westphalia in the late seventeenth century, settled in Paris, and changed his name to that of a Westphalian mountain range, the Eifel, adding a second "f." There was nothing remotely Jewish in Gustave's family background, however. Nor were the others in this indictment Jewish. It will be recalled that Loew, the Alsatian Protestant prosecutor of Eugène Bontoux, had likewise been Judaized. Biez quotes here from a magazine interview in which Eiffel explains that the tower would be visible, by optical telegraphy, from as far away as hilltops in the Côte d'Or, and goes on to explain how useful this will be for national defense. "That station would be linked by optical telegraphy to the one on Mont Afrique, which communicates in turn with the Eastern Front. . . . Should there be another siege of the capital, one would be able to follow all of the enemy's movements from the tower's cupola." Biez comments as follows: "Thus, everything has been plotted in advance by the German Jew Eiffel, even, and above all, a new siege of Paris by the Germans . . . Babel! This monument to the Jew's inexorable internationalism."

France would like our mother to face our trials with dignity," wrote Drumont, whose nostalgia for the "organic" city—the higgledy-piggledy of preindustrial centuries sacrificed to Napoléon III's abstractly conceived capital—inspired his first book, *Mon vieux Paris*.

> The Cosmopolites, who have substituted themselves for us, don't see things the same way. They absolutely insist that France appear before the universe covered in ridicule. Having been cruelly humiliated isn't enough; it must make itself a laughing-stock by declaring that it has never been so great, so powerful, so daunting, and rich. In all its imbecility, bad taste and foolish arrogance, the Eiffel Tower has risen for the express purpose of braying this message to heaven. It is the symbol of industrialized France. Its mission is to be insolent and stupid, like modern life, and to crush under its mindless height the Paris of our fathers, the Paris of memories, old houses and churches, Notre-Dame and the Arc de Triomphe, prayer and glory. This delirium of vanity signals the death throes of a society.

"Cosmopolite" being a familiar code word for Jew, Drumont agreed with de Biez that the misbegotten tower sprang from the mind of a Semitic race that did not hesitate to sully Mother France. And the incongruous growth reflected that mind not only in its lust for money and power, but in its natural penchant for deformity. "With its instinctual hatred of all that has inspired our respect and enthusiasm, with its need to blaspheme, this race is incontestably gifted with eyes for perceiving the grotesque side of everything moving and beautiful," he asserted. "Jewish artists and writers show us the world through lenses that are dirty or askew, lenses that conform to their astigmatic brains and make everything on earth seem deformed, ill-fitted, incoherent, extravagant, and baroque."

Several years later, Drumont presented much the same argument, applying "modern" to Jews as a term of abuse. "In reality, Jews—these Moderns, these ultra-civilized people with their excesses, their fevers, their constant hungering—wreak more havoc wherever they go than Goths and Vandals."* Powerful beyond his numbers, the Jew, like Faust, rode on the devil.

The journalist who had predicted that hubris would not go unpunished was to credit himself with having been half right. He would see punishment inflicted only four years after Eiffel unfurled a flag over the tower. The tower didn't fall, but its creator did, in a scandal that tainted not only him but the visionary whose accomplishment at Suez had inspired him to undertake epic tasks of his own—Ferdinand de Lesseps.

---

*Drumont, who wrote the article from Sainte-Pélagie Prison, where he was serving a brief sentence for libel, signed it with the nom de plume Sylvio Pellico. The original Pellico, an early-nineteenth-century Italian patriot imprisoned by the Austrians, is known for his own prison memoir.

It is ironic that the allegedly "Jewish" features of modernism in Drumont's portrait reappear four years later as symptoms of degeneracy in Max Nordau's famous disquisition on modernism in art, literature, and mores, *Degeneration*. Nordau was a founder of the Zionist movement.

CHAPTER VI

THE PANAMA SCANDAL

In May 1879, long before Gustave Eiffel and Ferdinand de Lesseps had ever sat down together, their names became linked in a clash of ideas from which de Lesseps emerged the blind victor. It took place at an international congress convened in Paris under de Lesseps's auspices to study the digging of a canal across the Central American isthmus. Plans for one had been laid as early as 1876, with the establishment of the Société Civile Internationale du Canal Inter-océanique, which had obtained a concession from Colombia, but which, with nothing to show for it after two years, had failed.* The congress, half of whose delegates were French, resolved that a canal be built, that it be built in Panama rather than Nicaragua, and that Suez be its model. Upon adjourning, its prime movers organized a company under French law with de Lesseps as president. They acquired the concession for ten million francs—approximately two million dollars—and within a year raised enough money in a stock offering to launch the colossal operation.

De Lesseps, whose dream of completing a water circle around the

*Colombia governed Panama until 1903.

Ferdinand de Lesseps as Sphinx.

The biblical de Lesseps: Samson-like, but also invertedly Mosaic (dividing the rocks to let water pass through). Caricature by Carjat.

earth by means of a sea-level canal between the Atlantic and the Pacific had lured him out of a venerable retirement at age seventy-four, did not welcome dissent. A controversy about how to construct the canal had split the international congress. Panama was not Egypt, prominent engineers asserted; locks would be needed to raise the water level and float ships across the country's hilly backbone. In every imaginable way, a canal *à niveau constant* defied common sense. On the technical committee, Eiffel argued against it, and a mining engineer well acquainted with Panamanian geology declared that its rock, far from being friable, as de Lesseps's partisans maintained, would splinter steel. But de Lesseps was a man disposed to take Ernest Renan at his word when the latter welcomed him into the French Academy by quoting Saint Matthew: "If you have faith as a grain of mustard seed, ye shall say unto this mountain, Remove hence to yonder place; and it shall remove." The man of faith swept aside objections. Had he not already done as he pleased with natural impedimenta? De

Lesseps wanted "a new Bosporus" whatever the cost and brought all his prestige to bear upon delegates, a majority of whom undoubtedly voted against their better judgment in endorsing the project. Many abstained.

De Lesseps's grandiosity, or capacity for self-delusion, made him, like Eugène Bontoux, an exceptionally effective promoter. In a report to the company's general assembly, he reassured shareholders that everything bode well. Panama would be far less inhospitable than Egypt, where he had had to contend with muddy lakes, fractured shelves of earth, and loose sand. The Central American isthmus was comparatively straightforward: a mountain mass sixty-five kilometers wide flanked at either end by deep bays. To be sure, the Rio Chagres, swelling under two hundred inches of rainfall a year, often flooded, but a dam would be built at its headwaters to contain it. As for rock, not even granite could resist the new technology. "The Panama canal may thus be seen as an operation whose precise mathematics are known, and the enormity of the enterprise does not alarm us." Compliant engineers estimated that the canal would open in 1888; de Lesseps advanced the date by a year or two, and, for public consumption, reduced its probable cost commensurately.

De Lesseps visited Panama to preside over a ground-breaking cere-mony on New Year's Day 1880 at the mouth of the Rio Grande. The boat transporting him and other dignitaries arrived behind schedule, and low tide prevented their landing. The ceremony was therefore improvised on deck, with de Lesseps allegedly swinging a pickax into a box of soil while all aboard raised glasses of champagne.

Wise investors would have interpreted this contretemps as an omen. The intransigence of nature and the distance from reality that marked the inaugural rite were to doom the entire enterprise. Excavation at the all-important Culebra Cut—a man-made valley to be bored through the Continental Divide—did not begin until January 1882. Two years had been spent in recruiting a huge workforce of French and West Indi-ans, in assembling machinery (much of it inadequate), in making sur-veys (most of them slipshod), in erecting hospitals (staffed by untrained Sisters of Charity), in building a mansion for the director-general, Jules Dingler, who would never occupy it (it came to be known as Dingler's

Folly). When excavation began, it proceeded furiously, but after removing almost 30 million cubic meters of earth the French had shaved only twenty feet off a ridge over two hundred feet high. Mishaps were of every kind. With deforestation came landslides; landslides led to more futile excavation; men were buried; tracks for the trains that removed excavated earth repeatedly slid into the trench. By December 1882, the general contractors, Couvreux et Hersent, concluded that the project would bankrupt them, and withdrew. De Lesseps made a virtue of their departure, as he did of every setback. Now that subcontractors were no longer answerable to a director-general, he declared, work would proceed apace. "During his recent voyage to the isthmus, the vice-president of our Society, M. Charles-Aimé de Lesseps [Ferdinand's son, who had originally tried to dissuade him from undertaking the project], noted the felicitous results of this modification."

Official reports also papered over the disastrous toll taken by tropical diseases. Sooner than pay the fee for a hospital bed, contractors often allowed infected workers to die on the job. But just as many succumbed under medical care as not. (In the early 1900s, Colonel William Gorgas, who directed sanitary services during American construction of the Panama Canal, estimated that something over twenty-seven thousand employees, laborers, and engineers alike, had died between 1881 and 1889. Included among them was Dingler's entire family—wife, daughter, son.) Since doctors misunderstood the pathogenesis of yellow fever and malaria, they couldn't know that hospitals at Ancon and Colón served as ideal nurseries for mosquitoes. *Aedes aegypti* and *Anopheles* bred prolifically in ornamental basins and in tins of water placed under the legs of beds to prevent insects from crawling up. Windows, which the nuns left open by day and shut after evening prayer lest poisonous jungle mist enter at night, were unscreened. Everything promoted disease. De Lesseps, meanwhile, strove to assure investors that reports about the deteriorating health of workers were patently absurd. "Fevers prevalent in that region, while they weaken, rarely kill," he declared in June 1882. "They are our only adversary; we have undertaken to conquer them by a series of preventive measures, and success is at hand. The latest report of our chief physician, dated May, ends as follows: 'Despite the anxiety that April may have caused, the health of our personnel is satisfactory. . . . Our hospitals are emptying.' "

Obfuscation dictated financial reports as well. What passed for accounting concealed the true state of affairs, which was that nothing flowed between the Atlantic and Pacific but mud and money. The trench, never deep enough for water, proved to be bottomless for francs. Between 1882 and 1888 there were six bond issues, totaling 781 million francs.* Banks that underwrote them knew that the company was riding for a fall, but commissions spoke louder than scruples. Indeed, nowhere up and down the line did scruples speak as loudly as the temptation to milk Panama for all it was worth. Enormous salaries were paid to directors, engineers, and other officers on the isthmus. Clerical workers traded in company furniture. French manufacturers eager to jettison outdated or defective materiel shipped it abroad. Unsupervised contractors excavating earth charged whatever they pleased and avoided the harder spots. Graft, extravagance, and waste were rampant. In May 1885, with funds depleted, de Lesseps applied to the French government for legal permission to issue forty million francs' worth of lottery bonds (that is, reimbursable for lucky subscribers). An inspector advised that the canal could not be finished within the announced time frame and on budget unless a system of locks was adopted. Two American engineers informed the Navy Department that at its present rate of progress the company would be digging for another twenty-six years.

When de Lesseps yielded two years later, he met reality only halfway. Locks were forced upon him; but the lock canal he envisioned was nothing more than a temporary arrangement that would buy him time to continue work on the canal of his dreams.† In Octo-

---

*One hundred fifty-six million dollars, or at least twenty times that much in today's currency.

†The president didn't willingly give up on anything. One is put in mind of Joseph Conrad's novella *Youth,* where the narrator recalls his young days: "I remember . . . the feeling that will never come back any more—the feeling that I could last forever, outlast the sea, the earth, and all men; the deceitful feeling that lures us on to joys, to perils, to love, to vain effort—to death; the triumphant conviction of strength, the heat of life in the handful of dust." After the inauguration of the Suez Canal, in 1869, de Lesseps, a sixty-four-year-old widower with five sons, married an eighteen-year-old and fathered twelve more children during the next sixteen years.

ber 1887, negotiations began with Gustave Eiffel, who seized this opportunity to prove himself right (at the expense of the man whom Gambetta styled "le Grand Français") and rescue a project that dwarfed his three-hundred-meter tower. Contractual terms specified that the new waterway should have ten giant locks capable of raising vessels above the flood line of the Rio Chagres. It was to be navigable by June 1890. "The confidence that you show in me by inviting my collaboration is not misplaced," Eiffel wrote to de Lesseps on November 15. "Rest assured that I shall devote myself unstintingly to a work on whose success hinge the honor and material interest of France." What profited France profited Eiffel. His collaboration was dearly bought, but it offered hope, and before long, models of the locks shared space with pieces of the tower in Eiffel's factory at Levallois-Perret.

Eiffel arrived too late. After 1887, attention shifted from the pestilential swamp of Panama to a financial morass in Paris. On March 1, 1888, de Lesseps formally announced that the company would need six hundred million francs to complete the redesigned canal by July 1890. When yet another bond issue—the sixth since 1882—yielded only thirty-five million, authorization from the government to lure investors with lottery bonds was strenuously sought. Thousands signed a petition. Five major newspapers—on the canal company payroll, as the public would soon learn—exuded optimism. Financiers lobbied. De Lesseps gave illustrated lectures on progress at the Culebra Cut to the Topographical Society and the Academy of Sciences. Eiffel displayed his model locks. None of this swayed the prime minister, Pierre Tirard (under whose leadership Boulanger was being run out of France). But in the legislature, where opinion was divided, more and more deputies—also on the company payroll, as it turned out—began to favor a lottery. Some supporters cited the example of the Suez Canal in arguing that a year before that magnificent project reached fruition, "experts" had declared it futile. Others claimed to speak for small investors whose financial well-being was at stake. "You must opt between authorization and a refusal that will have easily foreseeable consequences for four hundred thousand French citizens," warned M. Denormandie, a former governor of the Bank of

France. More prolix was M. Léon Renault: "There is a whole clientele of quite ordinary people grouped around the illustrious founder of the Panama Company. . . . Would you say that they don't deserve the interest of Parliament? . . . Is this not something to stir our patriotic feeling, to inspire not so much solidarity with the enterprise as an expression of sympathetic concern?"

In June 1888 the Chamber of Deputies passed a law authorizing lottery bonds, but the public, who had heard about the company's woes, did not invest. Only a third of the bonds issued were sold, and on June 29, de Lesseps, in language reminiscent of Bontoux's diatribes after the collapse of the Union Générale, attributed this latest, and definitive, fiasco to a conspiracy. "On June 18, conditions for the issuing of lottery bonds had hardly been made public when subscribers flocked to buy them," he wrote in the *Bulletin du canal.* "The well-informed press predicted with good reason that there would be more applicants than bonds for sale. On June 22, four days before the subscription closed, at the Paris Bourse, the usual speculators opposed to our enterprise launched a scandalous campaign of shortselling and violently pulled down the price of shares in our company. . . . Coincidentally, fraudulent telegraphic dispatches spread the news that I had died." With the whole edifice of Panama collapsing around him, de Lesseps continued to put a Micawberish gloss on things. The canal would open in July 1890, he assured shareholders at a general meeting in August 1889.

Six months later, the Panama Canal Company was no more. On February 4, 1890, the civil court of the Seine pronounced its dissolution, ordering the company to be liquidated, and appointing as its liquidator a former minister of public instruction, who had its books audited by a chartered accountant named Rossignol.* Rossignol's report, which cast suspicion on individuals and financial practices, paved the way for a more detailed enquiry three years later and a trial that exposed a viper's nest—with some notable political vipers coiled in it—to public view.

---

*His name was professionally inconvenient. A *"rossignol,"* meaning nightingale, is a blackmailer in police slang.

The numbers were damning. An exorbitant proportion of funds raised by the company had been squandered on "publicity" and on commissions to underwriters responsible for placing stocks and bonds. Rossignol noted that the relationship between services rendered and commissions charged became, with each successive issue, progressively tenuous. "I must conclude, until I am presented with more abundant information, that the sums assigned to underwriters in the last four issues were not recompense for services rendered, but outright gifts made to agents who could have harmed the enterprise by exerting their influence negatively but who really did nothing to facilitate the issues." Availing himself of more complete records, Rossignol's successor concurred that the Panama Canal Company had been whale blubber for every shark in the water: banks, newspapers, contractors, administrators, individual financiers. Before each of three bond issues, *Le Petit journal* received more than a hundred thousand francs, *Le Figaro* upward of fifty thousand, and the directors of *Le Gaulois* fifteen or twenty thousand. The Crédit Lyonnais did little to justify its commissions of 3,589,000 francs between 1880 and 1888, and the Société Générale very little more for 4,126,000. De Lesseps was paid 550,000 francs over seven years in addition to a munificent salary. Eiffel, whose locks were of course never completed, came away richer by as much as twenty-one million. All told, after expenses of every other kind, only 559 million francs, or less than 40 percent of its capital, had been invested in actual construction.

Added to these enormities were the sums disbursed to Baron Jacques de Reinach, de Lesseps's personal financial adviser. The son of a German-Jewish financier with European connections, and a Frenchman by choice, Reinach exemplified the internationalist of anti-Semitic lore. Born in Frankfurt, he had made Paris his home after attending the Lycée Condorcet. In 1863, when he was twenty-three, he and a brother-in-law founded the investment bank of Kohn, Reinach & Co. It prospered and Reinach—a figure not unlike Zola's Aristide Saccard (hero of *La Curée* and *L'Argent*) in his shortness, roundness, lavishness, verve, and cupidity—established himself on the social scene. Known far and wide, he entertained an omnium-gatherum of painters and singers, journalists and stockbrokers, academicians and politicians, at his mansion overlooking the Parc Monceau. Through his nephew, Joseph Reinach, who had been Léon Gambetta's protégé and had succeeded him as director of the newspaper *La République française,* Baron Jacques mingled with leaders of the moderate-left republican majority, the so-called opportunists. In Reinach's salon, this appellation, which was intended to describe a party's political pragmatism, came to signify its venality. Many "opportunists" made it known that they had their price, and pledges of support for the Panama bond lottery were secured with a portion of the millions in Reinach's account. (For one bond issue alone, in June 1888, Reinach received 6,190,000 francs.)

Opportunists and radicals might have been on the opposite side of many fences, but lucre established a community of opinion when it came to voting on Panama bond issues, and the associate through whom Reinach swayed Clemenceau's party was a strange figure named Cornelius Herz. Like Reinach, Herz had German-Jewish parents. Born in Besançon, near the Swiss border, he was a young child when, after the Revolution of 1848, his father, a bookbinder, moved the family to America. What little one knows about Cornelius's early years does not suggest that he was obliged to live by his wits, Herz senior having prospered as a manufacturer of packing boxes. He returned to France in his early twenties with a bachelor's degree from the Free Academy (later renamed City College of New York) and seems to have worked in the lowlands of his future profession as a pharmacist's assistant, an orderly at the hospital of Bicêtre, and a nurse in an insane asylum while studying at Paris's École de Médecine. When war broke out, the army, desperate for medical personnel, commissioned him an assistant surgeon major. After 1871 Herz returned to the United States, rich in battlefield experience but lacking academic credentials. That deficiency was soon resolved: he obtained a diploma from the Chicago Medical College in a matter of weeks. He also acquired a wife and headed west, bent upon reinventing himself in California. There the vagabond struck gold. A well-respected physician, who later denounced him as a swindler, took him under his wing. Three years were all Herz needed to mulct the Jewish community of San Francisco, to fleece members of his Masonic lodge, and to separate his patients from their money by propagating the notion that electrodes applied to their temples would cure them of headaches.

Electricity was no panacea, but it became Herz's passport to honor and respectability when he surfaced in Paris in 1877. San Francisco was behind him. Reinventing himself once again, this time as a savant, he founded a journal, *La Lumière électrique,* launched a French syndicate for developing electrical power, and contrived to join two Rothschild barons on the organizing committee of an "electricity fair." With a new telephone system patented as his invention in the United States, he proposed to wire the city of Paris. That project failed, but others succeeded. According to Herz's police file, deals abounded. They begot another fortune, which gave him access to politicians of the Left whose electoral campaigns he financed lavishly. There was Freycinet for one, and Clemenceau for another. James Blaine, President James Garfield's secretary of state, named him an honorary delegate of the United States to the International Congress of Electricians in the summer of 1881. Herz, a foreign member of the Legion of Honor, was promoted to *commandeur* in 1883 at Jules Ferry's recommendation, and *grand officier* three years later.

The "doctor," as he liked to be called, had covered his tracks well. Everyone knew him, but no one knew much about him, making him the paradox of an obscure notability. "I've never witnessed a stranger phenomenon," the columnist Joseph Montet wrote in *Le Gaulois* years after the Panama scandal. "His importance was something specific yet elusive. What were this man's origins? No one could say. A doctor, but of what? No one could question his intelligence, his enterprise, his boldness, his firm handling of men. . . . In the spheres of industry, finance, and politics, everyone reckoned with him. . . . Through a cunningly devised web of associations and friendships, he exercised influence everywhere, from ministerial offices to the inner councils of government. Implementing his wishes were a newspaper, a formidable leader [Clemenceau], very nearly an entire parliamentary faction. . . . Why? How to explain the role he played in the Panama affair?"

Most mystifying was his hold over Reinach, who treated him with such uncharacteristic deference as raised suspicions that Herz had threatened to reveal some dark secret if the baron did not do his bidding. The terms of a contract drawn up between Herz and the Panama Canal Company in 1886 were egregiously generous. Through Reinach, Charles de Lesseps agreed that Herz should receive ten million francs for wielding his influence in parliamentary circles to effect a lottery bond. In the event that parliament rejected the bill (which it did at first), Herz would nonetheless receive six hundred thousand francs, a round sum for which Reinach stood surety. Moreover, Reinach subsidized Herz's own ventures, making large loans on request. In September 1886, for example, Herz wrote to Reinach: "You have lent me today 100,000 francs . . . it being understood that you pledge to lend me an additional 400,000 francs in September or October, if necessary." And in April 1887: "I request that you guarantee payment to M. Schwob of the 150,000 francs that I must pay him as follows: 50,000 on May 31, 50,000 on June 31, 50,000 on July 31. If you should have to make good on your guarantee, I promise to reimburse you as soon as possible and in any event by the end of the current year." Before long, their relationship soured. Each rogue accused the other of bad faith. In 1888, when parliament finally voted the issue of lottery bonds, Reinach declared that Herz would receive the ten million francs stipulated in their original contract, less all of Herz's outstanding debts to Kohn, Reinach & Co. The balance, a mere five million francs (or twenty million dollars in twenty-first-century currency), did not satisfy Herz. "Your friend is trying to trick me," he complained to the administrator of the Panama Canal Company. "Either he pays or I bring him down, and if he goes down, his friends will go down with him. I'll wreck everything sooner than be robbed of one centime. Please advise, it's high time." Within forty-eight hours, men in high places, all of whom had skeletons to hide, were hard at work placating Herz. The minister of war, Freycinet, summoned de Lesseps's son Charles, now president of the Panama Canal Company, and urged him to accept Herz's ultimatum. Clemenceau and Prime Minister Floquet followed suit. Reinach struck martial poses. "Not only do I refuse all further payment to Dr. Herz, but I shall sue to be reimbursed for all he has taken from

Panama if he doesn't keep quiet. Nothing is due him, either legally or in fact. He has done nothing and deserves no remuneration." But in July 1889, the discomfited baron would give Herz a large I.O.U., bringing to twelve million, by one estimate, the sum total of the doctor's booty.

BY 1889, the jungle had begun to reclaim the Culebra Cut and senility to cloud de Lesseps's mind. While a handful of men profited enormously from the fiasco, tens of thousands—more than had been ruined in the crash of the Union Générale—lost their life savings.* Of the Panama Canal Company nothing remained but ashes. Its liquidation did not end the matter, however. Beneath the ashes were live embers, and after three years of smoldering, they burst into flames. In 1892, the Panama affair became the Panama scandal.

During that interval it had been crowded out by social strife, grand entertainments, an epidemic, and one major bank collapse. After 1888 the episodes of Boulanger's rise and fall were, like installments of a feuilleton, inexhaustible grist for the newspaper mill. The Universal Exposition, whose most obvious purpose was to argue France's power and prosperity, gave the government every reason to impose de facto censorship on bad economic news. In the early 1890s, troops confronted striking miners at the huge coalfield of Carmaux, anarchists hurled bombs, influenza claimed hundreds of lives in Paris and cholera hundreds more. Above all, members of the ruling party caught with their paws in the honeypot wished they could consign the whole Panama fiasco to oblivion. Boulanger or no Boulanger, it worried them that disclosure of their misdeeds would unleash enough anger in investors to topple the Republic. Was Boulangism really dead? Might it rise from the grave in general elections scheduled for 1893?

Dilatory tactics didn't work. In June 1891, a minister of justice assigned the Panama affair to a sluggish magistrate, but eight months

---

*The Panama fiasco was called the "*Krach des bas de laine,*" the "woolen-stockings crash"—referring to money saved in a woolen stocking by people of modest means.

later, in February 1892, parliament, having received numerous petitions, instructed the government to act "swiftly and energetically." A new prime minister, Émile Loubet, took office in February, with a minister of justice less solicitous for the well-being of compromised colleagues than his predecessor had been, and in September the attorney general, Jules Quesnay de Beaurepaire, concluded that the State should prosecute Panama Canal Company executives. At that point, Loubet panicked. Three members of his cabinet—the ministers of finance (Maurice Rouvier), commerce and industry (Jules Roche), and the navy (Auguste Burdeau)—would almost certainly not escape unsullied from a trial. The prime minister implored Quesnay de Beaurepaire to nullify his decision, arguing that the Republic itself was in danger. Sadi Carnot, president of the Republic, whom an anarchist would assassinate two years later, repeated the argument. All to no avail.

By October 1892, much of the dirty linen had already been aired. Indeed, "The Dirty Linen of Panama" was the title of a series of articles featured on the front page of *La Libre parole,* the newspaper Édouard Drumont launched in April 1892 with the motto *"La France aux français"*—France for the French. Written pseudonymously by a banker named Félix Martin, who had drummed up business for Panama lottery bonds, "Les dessous du Panama" struck terror into the hearts of all concerned. "Thanks to the hospitality of *La Libre parole,* the only newspaper independent enough to allow an attack against the Golden Calf of yesteryear, I shall state impartially, for the benefit of shareholders, what I saw and noted each day, either at the isthmus of Panama itself or in Paris," he wrote in the September 6 issue. "There will be many gaps in these articles, but the latter will not be without interest even so, I hope. I shall examine the relationship of the Panama Company with entrepreneurs, finance, and finally the parliamentary world. I was well placed to observe the last of these." Seven articles containing a plethora of detail and naming names appeared during the next ten days. Admittedly enraged by a campaign of deception that had led him, a trusted banker, to deceive his modest clients, he spared no one: neither de Lesseps nor his son Charles, nor past prime ministers (Freycinet, Floquet), nor moneychangers in

Panama converting piasters into francs for workers at usurious rates, nor Eiffel, who had negotiated his contract with Jacques de Reinach, nor the venal press. "The Press, liberally compensated, sang the company's praises, more out of duty than conviction; and only the *petit peuple*—the concierge and clerk and pensioner, all of whom had been deliberately gulled—remained confident and credulous." Historical scholarship has validated most of the indictment, but for all his professions of impartiality, Martin had his bugbears, the most conspicuous being Jews and Freemasons. This "occult power," as he called Freemasonry, had served de Lesseps well. All but one member of the first board of inquiry responsible for examining charges of corruption against legislators were, he noted, fellow Masons. When Martin pressed charges in a letter sent to the board shortly before parliamentary debate on a lottery bond, hoping to thwart the machinations of Reinach's agents, the board did not respond until the bond issue was a fait accompli.

Martin's last article appeared on September 16. Weeks passed before *La Libre parole* served up more scandal, and this time the disclosures came from an entirely unexpected source: Baron Jacques de Reinach. Although cited only once by Martin, Reinach lived in fear of an all-out assault. To ward off Drumont's blows, he offered him the names of several deputies whose votes had been bought. (Their prosecutors dubbed them *"chèquards"*: recipients of checks, or "checksters.") Such was the explanation later given by Louis Andrieux, an embittered Boulangist and former prefect of police who had acted as Reinach's go-between with the deputies. "When offered arms against the political party I was fighting, I had no qualms about their origin or the purity of their source," Andrieux testified. "I grabbed them, concerned only that the intelligence be correct. That is the background of the spirited campaign against deputies and senators launched on November 8 in *La Libre parole*." *La Libre parole* honored its agreement, but another journal, *La Cocarde,* was not a party to the conspiracy of silence and aimed its full battery of execration at Reinach. On November 19, 1892, the minister of justice informed parliament that five men faced charges of fraud (Ferdinand de Lesseps, his son

Charles, two more administrators of the canal company, and Gustave Eiffel). Later that day, Reinach, accompanied by Clemenceau and the minister of finance, visited Cornelius Herz, who, for whatever reasons—out of sheer vindictiveness, to purchase favor with the opposition, or to extort more money from Reinach—had been leaking prejudicial information to the right-wing press. They begged him to desist. He refused.

The next morning Reinach was found dead in his mansion. Rumor had it that he had killed himself. Cornelius Herz immediately fled to England, where he sheltered under the cloak of invalidism at a seaside

Cornelius Herz and his wife before the profiteer's flight to England.

resort. "Cornelius Herz received notification of the English mandate issued against him yesterday evening at the Tankerville Hotel in Bournemouth, where he is laid up, suffering, it seems, from complications of diabetes," a skeptical French detective reported to the Sûreté, the criminal investigations branch of the French police. "Our investigations reveal that Mr. Cornelius Herz has acquired one of the most beautiful properties in Bournemouth, which he intends to renovate and occupy, health permitting. . . . I believe he is not as sick as he purports to be." Ultimately an English magistrate deferred to the doctors who had examined him (Jean Charcot delegated from France and Sir Richard Quain, physician extraordinary to Queen Victoria, appointed by the crown). There would be no hearing before a rogatory commission and Herz remained in Bournemouth, taunting French authorities with hints that they might yet convince him to disclose the secrets he harbored. On one occasion he received the chairman of a board of inquiry. But nothing of significance was ever wormed out of him, and all attempts to extradite him failed. He took his intelligence to the grave in 1898, much to the relief of several dignitaries.

In Paris, the drama unfolded simultaneously on many stages: in the Palais Bourbon, where denunciations flew like cawing crows across the Assembly chamber and suspect deputies were stripped of immunity; on a field outside Paris, where Clemenceau, who avoided prosecution but lost his seat in the 1893 elections, dueled the Boulangist standard-bearer, Paul Déroulède, to a harmless draw; before an enlarged board of inquiry appointed by parliament; and in the courts. On January 4, 1893, police arrested a representative of the Crédit Lyonnais on charges of having given the disgraced minister of public works, Baihaut, 375,000 francs to endorse a lottery bond for the Panama Canal Company. Three days later police arrested Baihaut himself. The board of inquiry had meanwhile learned that almost six hundred "publicists" had been on the company payroll. In February 1893, de Lesseps father and son were each sentenced to five years in prison and Gustave Eiffel to two and a half. Freed on appeal in June, Eiffel was compelled, the following year, in a civil suit, to reimburse Panama bondholders ten million francs. Three banks were assessed a like amount. Many of the venal deputies escaped justice, as not all the coded names on a list of *chèquards* confiscated by investigators could be identified.* In due course, Charles de Lesseps's prison term was reduced from five years to two. The High Court of Appeals annulled his father's sentence. Ferdinand was in his dotage by then and died in 1894.

There were enough sinners to keep magistrates well occupied for years. The sordid tale of Panama illustrated, if nothing else, the democracy of greed. But antirepublican papers intent on exploiting public rage wanted a satanic malefactor into whom all sinfulness could be cast, and three men prominently embroiled in the scandal justified their choice of the Jew. *La Libre parole* (along with prominent socialists) declared Panama to have been a "Jewish disaster" in an article with that name. Tribunals and investigative committees would pass judgment on one French culprit or another, declared *La Libre parole*, but no matter: Jews were behind it all. The Jew was the puppet master.

> It seems that all of Jewry, high and low, congregated beneath the udder of this milch cow. In the disaster that cost so many French their savings and so many good deputies their reputations, one encounters Jews wherever one turns. They were the authors of this foul mess. It was they who organized the siege of consciences, who finally strangled the enterprise. And while they divvy up the fruit of their rapine with impunity, the unfortunate administrators of the Society, Lesseps first of all, are being dragged before tribunals. In a few days the thieves in their rich equipages and their expensive fur-lined coats will come to the Court of Appeals and see judgment passed on those whom they callously robbed.

The author challenged any man capable of seeing beyond his political prejudices to deny that the collapse of the venture was "a fla-

---

*The checks had been made out to proxies. The names of the real recipients were recorded in code on the stubs.

grant instance of the Jewish peril to which we have so often drawn attention."*

"The Jewish Disaster" followed on the heels of a more elaborately racist brief against Jews titled "The Jewish Drama." With Jacques de Reinach dead, *La Libre parole,* released from its vow of discretion, avenged itself upon his corpse. According to Drumont, Reinach exemplified a species of characteristically Jewish neurasthenia undermining French society. "Those people [Jews] have differently configured brains; their evolution has not been ours; and everything about them is exceptional and bizarre," he wrote.

> They come from heaven knows where, they live wrapped in mystery, they die in the space of conjecture. . . . They don't strive, they suddenly appear, dazzling European capitals with the millions they have acquired by unknown means. They don't die, they disappear as suddenly as they arrived, in a dramatic flurry. They stir everything up, they bring drama with them into the countries they unsettle and the interiors they invade. The Crash, the sensational event, the financial killing, the unforeseen . . . are their natural element.

Being overcivilized and uncivilized and everything except conscionable, Jews fostered and thrived on unreality. Frenchmen had roots. Jews had a diaspora. Drumont pictured them as merchants of illusion or actors loyal only to their own kind, moving from capital to capital on a revolving stage. The wreckage of Panama was their handiwork.

> What would you have them do, the autochthons [i.e., the French], the natural inhabitants of the country traversed by bands of Bedouins dressed in the latest fashions? Violently torn from their traditions, separated from all the hereditary sentiments that constitute a race, a people, a Fatherland, these poor

---

*The quoted passage was taken by *La Libre parole* from an article by Henri Rochefort in the equally rabid *L'Intransigeant.*

natives are experiencing the bewilderment that characterizes modern times. . . . Indeed, there is nothing left; neither hearth, nor family values, nor social principles, nor religion, nor the fixed constitution of property. Property worth 1,000 francs today won't be worth a sou tomorrow, when the Jew who ascribes a fictitiously inflated value to the deed or certificate will, like Reinach, have swallowed a phial of aconite.

Drumont's harangues were the litany of diocesan newsletters all over France. *La Semaine religieuse de Mende,* for example, informed its readers in the Cévennes region, "We are being pillaged, dishonored, exploited, and emptied by the Jew. . . . Servile, slithering, artful, filthy, and vile when he is the weaker one, he becomes arrogant when he has the upper hand, as he does now. The Jew is our master. . . . When one of these vultures swoops down on the finances of a people, he pilfers, ransoms, tears, flays, strangles." Several months later, in December 1892, the valiant, independent-minded Abbé Frémont noted regretfully in his journal, "Hatred of the Republic and of Jews is today the sustenance of French clergy. Drumont is their preceptor. Above all, don't tear this choice morsel out of their mouths: if you try, you will immediately be smeared with ink and blackened with calumny."

THE THREE MODELS for Drumont's racial portrait were Jacques de Reinach, Cornelius Herz, and Léopold Émile Arton, an Alsatian Jewish bank broker and representative of the dynamite industry, who served as Reinach's surrogate, helping the financier bribe politicians. Arton had already disappeared when Herz fled. It was 1895 before police tracked him down. Extradited from England, he admitted having paid twenty-six legislators 1.1 million francs. A tribunal sentenced him to eight years in prison. Eventually the twenty-six were acquitted in trials that lasted for months. Arton himself was pardoned. This flagrant *blanchissage* would have received more prominent notice if the Dreyfus Affair were not by then monopolizing headlines.

Reinach, Herz, and Arton, who saw almost nothing of the twentieth century, were destined to live on as exemplary agents of the Jewish world conspiracy in *The Protocols of the Elders of Zion.** This fabrication of the Okhrana, the czarist secret police, which began its sinister tour of the West after World War I, was published at Tsarskoe Selo in 1903, two years before Arton committed suicide. But its Russian author only used a full-blown myth, to judge by the reflections of Marcel Proust's friend Daniel Halévy. In January 1898, when *J'accuse* appeared, the young historian noted that the Panama scandal had bred nationwide suspicion, asperity, and unhappiness, sickening France's soul. Blame for it had fallen on Jews, and especially on "that mysterious triad" of Reinach, Herz, and Arton. "The three had gone unpunished and the country, silent but deeply distressed, bided its time, filled with hatred and spoiling for vengeance."

*The portrait of the three as an all-powerful triumvirate was inspired by Drumont, who undoubtedly served as Edmond de Goncourt's informant (the two were friends). "To think—and it's undeniable—that for almost twenty years, the three absolute masters of France were the baron de Reinach, Cornelius Herz, and Arton," Goncourt wrote in February 1893.

CHAPTER VII

THE DREYFUS AFFAIR

O_N N_{OVEMBER} 1, 1894, *La Libre parole* announced in bold headlines that charges of espionage were to be brought against "a Jewish officer" named "A. Dreyfus." Shortly before Christmas, seven military judges deliberating inside the Cherche-Midi Prison found the thirty-five-year-old artillery captain guilty as charged.

The affair began with the discovery of a secret memorandum addressed to Maximilian von Schwartzkoppen, military attaché at the German embassy on the rue de Lille. This so-called bordereau, which reached French spymasters in September 1894 after a charwoman in the employ of the French intelligence service fished it from Schwartzkoppen's wastepaper basket, was written in French and read as follows:

I have received no word as to whether you wish to see me, but I nonetheless send you, Sir, some items of interest, viz:
1. A note about the hydraulic brake of the 120 and the manner in which this part has performed. [The reference was to the hydro-pneumatic brake of the French gun called 120 *court*. It was a heavy fieldpiece, recently brought into use; the

mechanism of the brake which overcame the recoil of the gun was a deep, dark secret.]

2. a note on covering troops (some modifications will be carried out, according to the new plan). [These were troops to be called to the frontier at the beginning of mobilization. They were slated to screen the concentration of the rest of the army.]

3. A note concerning a modification in the formations of artillery.

4. A note about Madagascar. [France's ministry of war was preparing an expedition to conquer that island.]

5. An outline of the proposed firing manual for field artillery (March 14, 1894). This document is exceedingly difficult to obtain, and I can only have it at my disposal for a very few days. The minister of war has distributed a certain number of copies among the troops, and the corps are held responsible for them. Each officer with a copy is required to return it after the maneuvers. So, I shall arrange to lay hold of it and you will return it straightway, after gleaning from it what interests you. Unless you prefer that I have it copied in extenso and send you the copy.

I now go on maneuvers.

Colonel Jean Sandherr, director of intelligence, took it for granted, despite evidence pointing elsewhere, that Schwartzkoppen's informant was a general staff officer trained in artillery. General Mercier, the minister of war, concurred. But among those to whom photographic copies of the bordereau were shown, no one recognized the handwriting—neither the heads of general staff bureaus nor the heads of artillery. Sandherr's investigation might have died there had not a colleague, Lieutenant Colonel d'Abboville, revived it. Only someone acquainted with four different bureaus of the ministry could have secured the intelligence offered to Schwartzkoppen, declared d'Abboville, and such widespread exposure suggested that the culprit might be a *stagiaire,* a newly commissioned staff officer serving probationary internships or *stages* in all four bureaus. This conjecture became certainty when Colonel Pierre Fabre of the fourth bureau alighted on the name of Alfred Dreyfus, who had graduated from the École Polytechnique as a student artillery officer, had won captain's rank, and then had attended the War College. It hardly mattered that interns never went on maneuvers. To Sandherr, Fabre, d'Abboville, et al., everything instantly argued Dreyfus's guilt—above all his "racial" origin—and a handwriting analysis prepared by yet another staff officer, Commandant du Paty de Clam,* who dabbled in graphology, furnished them with what they considered absolute proof that the Jew had written the bordereau.

Like a carefully cultivated epiphyte, the case against Dreyfus did not at first thrive outside the hothouse atmosphere of Mercier's ministry. It left President Jean Casimir-Périer unimpressed. It won no support from General Félix Saussier, the military governor of Paris and de facto commander-in-chief of French armed forces (whose mistress had a Jewish husband). And it led Gabriel Hanotaux, the minister of foreign affairs, to state categorically that an investigation or trial based upon one fragile document defied common sense. Mercier persisted, however. Belabored by the right-wing press, which held him responsible for, among other sins, harboring unpatriotic elements (i.e., Jews) in the officer corps, this taciturn, austere graduate of Polytechnique, who had embraced republicanism rather more vigorously than most generals, was receptive to a cause célèbre that might placate detractors. It was so flagrant a crime, he told Hanotaux, that he could not but prosecute its author. Otherwise, he would inevitably be accused by officers in the know of having compromised with treason.

Instead, Mercier betrayed his honor by fostering the nascent conspiracy. When an expert graphologist from the Bank of France concluded after close examination of the bordereau that "someone other than the suspect" could have written it, Mercier recruited other experts, notably Alphonse Bertillon, who ran the police prefecture's

---

*"Commandant" in the French army corresponds to the rank of major in the English and American military.

service of judiciary identity. Bertillon knew what was wanted of him and, being a vocal anti-Semite, complied. To explain the obvious dissimilarity between Dreyfus's script and that of the bordereau, he showed, in great detail, how the traitor had forged his own handwriting with calculated discrepancies. The proof was irrefutable, he wrote. "From the very first day, you knew my opinion. It is now absolute, complete, and admitting of no reservation." The general staff hailed Bertillon's lunatic argument as a scientific tour de force.

To Alfred Dreyfus, for whom religious feeling mattered less than love of country, no insult could have been more heinous than the charge of treason pressed upon him by du Paty de Clam on October 15 at the war ministry. An Alsatian whose family had chosen French citizenship after 1871, when they left Mulhouse (all except one member, who managed the Dreyfus cotton mill), Alfred vividly remembered that calamitous evacuation. Seeing French infantry trudge westward in "despair and humiliation" determined his future career, he later asserted. But if fervent patriotism made him a soldier, so did his profound need for the clear-cut orthodoxies of army life, and it is supremely ironic that that tidy, disciplined, hierarchical world should all at once have become a Kafkaesque enigma. Torn away from wife, from children, from fatherland, this Jew who gave Judaism short shrift found himself shut up first in the Cherche-Midi military prison then in La Santé Prison, accused of high treason. "They put me in the strictest solitary confinement, and all communication with my kin was forbidden me," he wrote in a memoir some years later.

> I had at my disposal neither paper, pen and ink, nor pencil. . . . In that gloomy cell, still under the appalling influence of the scene I had just endured and of the monstrous accusation brought against me, when I thought of all those whom I had left at home only a few hours before in great happiness, I fell into a state of fearful excitement and raved from grief. I paced back and forth in the narrow space, knocking my head against the walls. Commandant Forzinetti, director of the prison, came to see me, accompanied by the chief guard, and calmed me for a little while.

Two weeks passed before he was shown a photograph of the bordereau. Meanwhile du Paty de Clam had searched his apartment on the avenue du Trocadéro and warned Lucie Dreyfus that any attempt to make the arrest public would spell disaster for everyone. "One word could mean war."

Confidentiality became irrelevant after October 29, when *La Libre parole* asked, in its first article on the case, whether an important arrest had not taken place by military order. "The individual arrested has reportedly been accused of espionage. If this item is true, why have military authorities maintained absolute silence?" Other right-wing papers—*L'Éclair, La Patrie*—thereupon bayed in chorus, and the Catholic press joined them. "Whereas Judas belonged to the people of God, being the apostle chosen by the Master, the Jewish officer did not belong to the French Nation," wrote Father Vincent de Paul Bailly, an Assumptionist representing the bigoted salient of French Catholicism in *La Croix*. "Our society has already been punished, but its suffering is not at an end—our treasures, our banks, our papers, our railroads, and our army are caught in the spiderweb of Judaism." The general staff, which had hoped that Dreyfus would confess his guilt or commit suicide, was obliged to go forward. Needing some motive for treason, Major Bexon d'Ormescheville, judge advocate of what was to be the first court-martial, in whose hands the judicial investigation had been placed, sought evidence with which to portray Dreyfus as a debt-ridden gambler, a whoring libertine, or an inquisitive rogue. Classmates from the War College testified that wherever he passed, documents disappeared, and d'Ormescheville concluded as follows:

Along with his extensive knowledge, Captain Dreyfus possesses a remarkable memory; he speaks several languages, including German, which he knows thoroughly, and Italian, of which he claims to have only a vague notion. He is, moreover, of a rather supple—even obsequious—character, quite suited for relations of espionage with foreign agents. He was thus the perfect choice for the miserable and shameful mission that he either inspired or accepted and to which—quite luckily for France, perhaps—the discovery of his intrigues has put an end.

Of such vaporous stuff was his entire report made. Nothing in it promised to nail the captain, and with newspapers predicting that Mercier would fall if Dreyfus went free, consternation grew at the war ministry. "The Dreyfus affair sticks to General Mercier's back as the centaur's tunic stuck to the shoulders of Hercules" is how one journalist put it. "If Dreyfus is acquitted, the minister departs; that much is certain, since he would be crushed beneath the awful responsibility of having frivolously brought about a very grave predicament. But if Dreyfus is convicted . . . Mercier gains stature and, profiting from the trial, becomes his country's savior."

Exasperated by the lack of hard evidence against a man in whose guilt they fervently believed, Sandherr and his assistant, Commandant Hubert Henry, set out to fabricate some—with Mercier's knowledge, no doubt. Rewriting two memoranda dated March 1894, which contained information furnished by a Spanish military attaché, they inserted several quotes, notably this one: "Someone in the ministry of war, almost certainly an attaché, has tipped off the German military attaché. . . . That is further proof that you have one or several wolves in your sheepfold. . . . Find out, I can't tell you often enough, because I am certain of it." The forged papers joined other dubious material in a file to which du Paty de Clam contributed explanatory notes. Dreyfus's lawyer, Edgar Demange, never saw it. It emerged from the war ministry under the seal of secrecy on December 22, when jury deliberations had already begun. Du Paty de Clam handed it to Colonel Maurel, president of the court-martial, which was being held behind closed doors, and declared on behalf of General Mercier that "the most urgent moral imperative possible" argued for showing the jury its contents.

All seven officer-judges followed orders. Not a single one sought to exclude a communication hidden from the defense for being in violation of the law, the military code, or common equity. Indeed, neither Maurel nor his fellow judges needed surreptitious guidance. Swayed by testimony given by Henry two days earlier, they would have convicted Dreyfus anyway. Henry's had been a bravura performance. After declaring that an "honorable person" had twice advised him to watch out for a traitor in the intelligence service, he pointed at Drey-

"The Traitor." A famous portrayal of Captain Dreyfus being publicly stripped of his rank in the courtyard of the École Militaire. The dome of the Invalides rises behind student barracks.

fus and shouted: "This man is the traitor." Demange inveighed against anonymous denunciations and challenged Henry to reveal the informant's name, whereupon Henry, slapping his kepi, rejoined that "there are some secrets in an officer's head that his cap does well to ignore." Colonel Maurel asked him solemnly whether he would affirm on his honor that the treasonous officer was Captain Dreyfus, and Henry swore to it while lifting his hand toward a painting of Christ.

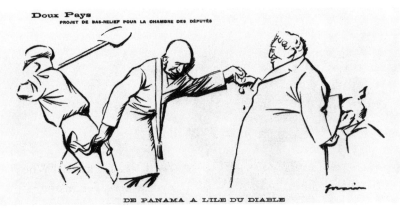

Doux Pays
PROJET DE BAS-RELIEF POUR LA CHAMBRE DES DÉPUTÉS

DE PANAMA A L'ILE DU DIABLE

"A bas-relief for the Chamber of Deputies." Caricature by Forain. It shows a corrupt legislator pickpocketing a canal digger with his right hand and, with his left, pressing coins into the palm of a portly banker (modeled after Baron de Reinach), who holds military secrets behind his back for scrutiny by a helmeted German soldier.

The trial served an exorcistic purpose. Having cast out the alien, France celebrated her salvation. Everyone rejoiced, socialists arm in arm with monarchists, and men of the Left proved, if anything, even more bellicose then men of the Right. "He has no relative, no wife, no child, no love of anything, no human—or even animal—ties, nothing but an obscene soul and an abject heart," railed Clemenceau (who later led the fight for retrial, or *"révision"*). Jean Jaurès, the redoubtable socialist orator, maintained, during a parliamentary debate on the question of restoring capital punishment for high treason, that Dreyfus should have been sentenced to death. "The country sees that simple soldiers are shot without pardon or pity for a momentary lapse or act of violence. . . . We must ask ourselves whether the nation's justice should remain unarmed in the event that abominable acts analogous to that committed by Captain Dreyfus were to recur."[*]

Germany, which looked on nervously, denied that it had ever had any traffic, direct or indirect, with Alfred Dreyfus, but the denial only confirmed his guilt, the French thought. In these circumstances, where

---

[*]Like Clemenceau, Jaurès later became a staunch Dreyfusard. But most socialists were slow to follow him; for them, anti-Semitic and often jingoist, the multiple sin of being a Jew whose family had enriched itself in industry made Dreyfus inherently detestable.

did one seek justice? A petition for appeal fell on deaf ears, and on December 27, Dreyfus, who had hardly eaten or slept since his condemnation, was publicly stripped of his rank in the main courtyard of the École Militaire. Despite frigid weather, thousands had gathered outside on the place de Fontenoy. Pressing against the iron gate, they sent up shouts of *Mort aux juifs! À mort le traître! À mort Judas!* as a burly member of the Republican Guard surrounded by silent troops tore all insignia from Dreyfus's uniform—epaulets, galloons, buttons—and finally broke Dreyfus's sword over his knee. "When he advanced toward us, with his kepi pulled down over his forehead, with his lorgnon perched on his ethnic nose, stone-faced," wrote Maurice Barrès, "he shouted, or I should say ordered, in an insufferable voice: 'You will tell all of France that I am an innocent man.' "

On January 17, 1895, army officials packed Dreyfus off to the Atlantic port of La Rochelle in a convict train. There, too, people gathered, but this mob rained blows upon the "Jew's head" before his escort could intervene. A launch then transported Dreyfus several miles offshore to the Île de Ré, where he spent more than a month under constant surveillance. His wife, Lucie, who visited him twice a week, saw him last on February 21. The following day Dreyfus found himself aboard the ship *La Ville de Saint-Nazaire,* sailing—though he knew nothing yet of his destination—for French Guiana. The transatlantic voyage took more than two weeks; on March 12 *La Ville de Saint-Nazaire* dropped anchor off the Îles du Salut. Devil's Island, a nearly treeless volcanic rock baked by the equatorial sun and plagued with malaria, from which deportees seldom returned alive, was to be his hell for more than four years. The local commandant jailed him in a stone cabin twelve feet square.

Stunned by this arbitrary blow, Dreyfus's family drew close together. The task of rescuing him devolved upon an older brother, Mathieu, who made it his mission. But with nothing to help him argue the case for a judicial error—nothing except the marginalia Dreyfus himself had scrawled on Major d'Ormescheville's indictment—where could he begin? While police agents dogged his steps, he visited politician after politician, all in vain. Only Dreyfus's former wardens showed any real compassion, and one of them

"Story of a Traitor." A cartoon about the Dreyfus Affair.

offered advice from which Mathieu profited greatly. "Your brother's cause must be defended before public opinion," declared Patin of La Santé Prison, suggesting that the collaboration of a militant journalist might prove invaluable. The name Bernard Lazare came to mind.

Lazare must have seemed an improbable ally. Known for his spirited defense of anarchists, he was—although Jewish himself and, like Dreyfus, the son of a textile manufacturer—not disposed to concern himself with the predicaments of well-heeled Jews. In a book titled *L'Antisémitisme, son histoire et ses causes,* Lazare had blamed anti-Semitism on its victims and held the "religious impulse" responsible for impeding revolutionary development. How remarkable, then, that one or two conversations should have converted Lazare to the cause. "Lazare lost no time," recounts one historian. "In the spring of 1895 he was already at work on the first draft of his essay. With very few documents at hand, he made numerous errors. But his intelligence, exactitude and even his prescience were astonishing. A simple and rigorous style shorn of all bombast gave force to the argument."

Lazare would have circulated the essay immediately had not Dreyfus's lawyer, Demange, urged him to wait for a more auspicious occasion. Reluctantly, he heeded this advice and let off steam in bitter exchanges with Édouard Drumont, declaring that the "ancestral tradition of humility" under which his coreligionists labored did not bend every Jewish back. "I know some who . . . have had enough of anti-Semitism," he wrote in *Le Voltaire.* "They are tired of the insults, the slander, the lies, the dissertations on Cornelius Herz and the prosopopoeias on Baron de Reinach. And tomorrow they will be legion, and if they thought as I do they would mobilize openly, courageously, against you, against your doctrines, and no longer be content to defend themselves, they would attack you; and you are not invulnerable, neither you nor your friends." On June 18, 1896, the exchange of invective led to an exchange of bullets, which, however, harmed neither duelist. By then, Lazare had come to view himself as "the spokesman of a Jewish resistance too long deferred."

After eighteen months of largely futile supplication, Mathieu concluded that drastic measures were needed to break the silence enveloping his brother's case. Spurred by terrible news from Devil's

Island (where, according to one published report, Alfred Dreyfus had become "ageless, his body stooped over, his hair white, his face sallow and hollowed, his beard gray, weary and slow of pace"), he hired an English agent to spread the rumor through London newspapers that Captain Dreyfus had disappeared. His strategy worked. The French government set matters straight, but the French press erupted in gossip, second thoughts, and calumny. *La Libre parole* denounced a vastly rich Jewish syndicate for plotting Dreyfus's escape. The conservative newspaper *L'Autorité,* which did not ordinarily sympathize with Jews, dared to wonder whether Dreyfus had perhaps been the victim of a judicial error.

Most important were articles published by the anti-Semitic *Éclair,* whose best-known writer, Ernest Judet, cultivated General Mercier. Eager to banish all doubts about Dreyfus, it naïvely evoked a "secret file" containing, in one decoded letter, irrefutable proof of his guilt.

A song titled "Dreyfus, Reinach & Co.," created at the Paris branch of the organization Anti-Semitic Youth. The Reinach in question is Baron de Reinach's nephew Joseph, a deputy in the legislature and prominent Dreyfusard.

An anti-Semitic flyer, 1897, accusing the "Jewish Syndicate" of framing Commandant Esterhazy. "A Call to All French," "Death to the Traitors!," "The Honor of the Army," "The Indignation of Our Soldiers," "Infamous Machinations," "The Dreyfus Syndicate," "Down with the Jews!" "Where the Money Is Coming From."

"It may be imagined that [the code] was much too useful for public dissemination," *L'Éclair* explained.

> Later on, it will be seen that for this same reason the letter in question was not included in the official dossier and that it was only in secret, in the deliberation room, out of the presence even of the accused, that it was transmitted to the judges of the court-martial. About September 20, Colonel Sandherr, head of the section of statistics,* communicated to General Mercier the letter, which had been deciphered. It concerned the espionage service in Paris and contained the sentence: "Decidedly, that animal Dreyfus has become too demanding."

This disclosure excited Mathieu, and when the government made no effort to refute it, Lucie Dreyfus, armed at last with specific evidence of malfeasance, sent the president of the Chamber of Deputies a petition, which was carried by various newspapers, including *Le Figaro*. "I could not believe [what *L'Éclair* reported] and expected the denial that the semi-official Agence Havas supplies in the case of all erroneous news," she wrote, at the dictation of Edgar Demange. "The denial did not come. It is thus true that after debates shrouded in the deepest mystery, because of a closed session, a French officer has been convicted by a court-martial on the basis of an accusation that the prosecution has produced without his being informed and without his lawyer being able to counsel him. This is a denial of all justice. . . . I have kept silent, despite all the odious and absurd slander propagated amidst the public and in the press. Today it is my duty to break that silence."

Soon afterward, on November 7 and 8, members of parliament and influential journalists received copies of Bernard Lazare's pamphlet *Une Erreur judiciaire: La Vérité sur l'Affaire Dreyfus,* which had been secretly printed abroad. Then, two days later, yet another crucial disclosure strengthened the cause of Dreyfusism. After obtaining a facsimile of the bordereau from one of the graphologists con-

---

* "Section of statistics" was a code name for the intelligence bureau.

LA PLAIDOIRIE DE Mᵉ DEMANGE. (Croquis d'après nature de notre envoyé spécial GEORGES REDON.)

A courtroom sketch by Georges Redon, November 7, 1899, of Alfred Dreyfus seated at his second court-martial, in Rennes, and one of his lawyers, Edgar Demange, pleading from the rostrum. "[Dreyfus] listened to the oration of M. Demange with a mask of impassibility resembling his frozen attitude during the first days of the trial," wrote the New York Times *correspondent.*

sulted three years earlier, *Le Matin* published it on November 10. For Mathieu, no reasonable person could deny any longer that Alfred Dreyfus was innocent, and to drive home this message he had the notorious document, flanked by samples of his brother's handwriting, reproduced as a poster. "Our circle of action was growing, expanding from day to day," he later recalled.

Meanwhile, unbeknownst to Mathieu, a lone truth-seeker had

been at work inside the general staff itself. On July 1, 1895, Lieutenant Colonel Georges Picquart, who had witnessed Dreyfus's court-martial and applauded the verdict, replaced Colonel Sandherr as chief of intelligence. A highly decorated veteran of campaigns in Africa and Tonkin, he did not relish espionage but nonetheless applied himself to it with characteristic thoroughness. Months passed more or less routinely until in March 1896 something deeply disturbing occurred. Schwartzkoppen's fecund wastepaper basket yielded an unsent letter-telegram, or *petit-bleu,* from which French intelligence deduced that the addressee, Commandant Walsin Esterhazy of the French Army's 74th Infantry Regiment, had been passing along military secrets. Was another Dreyfus on the loose? So it seemed to Picquart. Information gathered by the police convinced him that the forty-nine-year-old major, who descended from the powerful Austro-Hungarian Esterhazy clan through a bastard, expatriate line, might well do anything for money. "[He] had serious financial problems. He was keeping a mistress . . . whom he visited every evening before returning to his conjugal home at night. He was renting an apartment for her at 49, rue de Douai, and gave her a monthly allowance. He was saddled with creditors and could not pay his bills on time."

Not every adulterous, debt-ridden officer made a traitor, but Esterhazy had taken unusual measures to familiarize himself with the latest technological developments in artillery. He had, moreover, been spotted on several occasions entering the German embassy. By June, Picquart lacked only some document in the suspect's own hand, and that lacuna was filled during the summer, when Esterhazy persistently requested a desk job at the war ministry. Toward the end of August, two letters of ardent solicitation were forwarded to intelligence (with approval from the minister of war). Picquart was stunned, for what he thought he saw in reading them was the script of the infamous bordereau. A close comparison bore out their identity and left him to draw the painful conclusion that an innocent man had by then served one and a half years on Devil's Island.

After examining the "secret file," which contained no definitive proof against Dreyfus of the kind he had expected to find there, Picquart reported his discovery to General Raoul de Boisdeffre, chief of the general staff. That the file was still intact shocked Boisdeffre, but neither he nor his deputy, General Gonse, expressed chagrin over the apparent miscarriage of justice. On the contrary, they urged him to "keep the two cases separate." How could they be kept separate? Picquart wondered. The obstinate young intelligence officer, whose scruples proved stronger than his own prejudice against Jews, questioned this cynical recommendation, citing the recent disclosure of the secret file in *L'Éclair* as all the more reason to investigate. "In my opinion it is imperative to act without delay," he advised Gonse. "If we wait any longer, we will be overwhelmed, locked into an inextricable position, and we will no longer have the means either of defending ourselves or of ascertaining the truth." His argument went unheeded. Picquart then secured an interview with General Jean-Baptiste Billot, the minister of war, who had not been compromised by the Dreyfus trial, but he, too, wrapped himself in silence. It became quite clear that the general staff had decided to make common cause against any threat of exposure. "What do you care that that Jew is on Devil's Island?" Gonse asked Picquart on September 15, after a heated discussion. "His possible innocence is irrelevant. Such matters ought not enter into consideration." Picquart was appalled. "What you've said is abominable," he replied. "I do not know what I will do. But in any event, I will not take this secret to the grave with me."

Rather than dismiss Picquart outright, the conspirators decided to remove him from Paris on some pretext. He was told that the intelligence service affiliated with military groups stationed along France's eastern border needed reorganization, and on November 14 Billot ordered him there immediately. Six weeks later another order dispatched him to Tunisia, where, though still nominally head of intelligence, he found himself attached to the 4th Regiment of Sharpshooters in the garrison at Sousse. "The minister has just told me that he is expanding the range of your mission and charging you with the organization of the intelligence service in Algeria and in Tunisia," Gonse informed him on December 24. Did his superiors hope that an early grave could more easily be arranged abroad? Apparently so, for in due course Boisdeffre instructed General Leclerc, who commanded the army of occupation, to have Picquart verify at firsthand reports of local tribes gathering beyond Gabès, near Tripoli—a notoriously dangerous region. Picquart had long since taken the trouble to record everything he knew about the Dreyfus case in a codicil to his will.

It was a matter not only of exiling Picquart but of incriminating him, and as early as November the general staff embarked upon a frenzied program of deception that ultimately saw Boisdeffre, Gonse, Henry, du Paty de Clam, and several lesser figures collude with none other than Esterhazy himself. For mischief, Picquart's de facto replacement, Commandant Hubert Henry, had no peer. To bolster the case against Dreyfus, this shrewd, rough-hewn bully decided to prepare yet another bogus document. Borrowing the salutation and signature from a letter written to Schwartzkoppen by his Italian counterpart, Alessandro Panizzardi (and of course retrieved by the charwoman, Mme Bastian), Henry inserted between them the brief message: "I have read that an elected deputy is to pursue questioning about Dreyfus. If Rome is asked for new explanations, I will say that I never had any relations with the Jew. If they ask you, say the same, for no one must ever know what happened with him."

Here indeed was "conclusive proof," and into the Dreyfus file it went as soon as Boisdeffre advised the war minister, Billot, of its existence. Henry then turned his creative pen against Picquart. On November 27, the latter's mail, which had been routinely opened since October, produced a note from a friend alluding to certain mutual acquaintances by their nicknames. This private language inspired Henry, who used it in a letter made up to suggest that Picquart had clandestine relations with a syndicate of powerful Jews who frowned upon his reassignment. Signed "Speranza," the fictional message, which intelligence "intercepted" on December 15, read as follows:

Paris, Midnight 35—I am leaving the house, our friends are in a state of consternation; your unfortunate departure has upset everything. Hasten your return here; come quickly, quickly! The holiday season being quite auspicious for the cause, we count on you for the 20th. She is ready, but cannot and will not act until she has spoken to you. Once the demigod speaks, we will act.

Lest Picquart awaken before the trap had been sprung, rumors of his disgrace or dismissal were floated and categorically denied. At year's end, Henry and Gonse sent the lieutenant colonel expressions of affectionate camaraderie, wishing him "good health" on his "splendid tour of service" in North Africa.

By the middle of 1897 the conspirators felt certain enough of victory to declare war. In May, when Picquart demanded that the general staff clarify his status, Henry sent him a list of charges arising from an investigation of his conduct as intelligence chief. The grotesque truth now dawned on Picquart, who hurriedly arranged to visit a lawyer in Paris, Louis Leblois. Anguished discussions took place during the last week of June. Torn between his military oath and his personal honor, Picquart told Leblois as much about Esterhazy as conscience allowed (conscience forbade mention of the *petit-bleu*). He also gave him power of attorney to inform the government, if need be. Under no circumstances, however, was Leblois to contact Dreyfus's brother or lawyer.

A fortnight after Picquart's departure from Paris, Leblois sought out Auguste Scheurer-Kestner, vice president of the Senate, and unburdened himself. This choice of confidant made perfect sense. Scheurer-Kestner, who had led the protest against Germany's annexation of Alsace-Lorraine in the National Assembly of 1871, where he represented Mulhouse, enjoyed an unparalleled reputation for patriotism and rectitude. As former political editor of Gambetta's paper, *La République française,* he presided over a Gambettist fraternity that included Billot, the minister of war. And finally, he was one of very few politicians known to entertain serious doubts about the Dreyfus verdict. Leblois convinced him that general staff officers had framed Dreyfus. Scheurer-Kestner, in turn, called upon Prime Minister Jules Méline, President Félix Faure, and General Billot, begging the government to initiate a judicial appeal while reluctantly honoring the pledge of discretion exacted by Picquart. Rebuffed at every turn, he suffered abuse from anti-Dreyfusard newspapers, which had been given inside information about his high-level rendezvous. *Le Matin, La Patrie, La Libre parole,* and *L'Intransigeant* vied for honors in defamatory invective. He was called a Kraut of course, but also a lunatic, a "lipomatoid gorilla," and "slime that must be washed into the sewer." To Mathieu Dreyfus, this scurrilous outcry had a reassuring ring, as it meant that his brother's case had been revived.

Fortune then began to smile on Dreyfus's supporters. Early in November 1897, Mathieu received a visit from a stockbroker named de Castro, who, having chanced upon the facsimile of the bordereau distributed a year earlier, recognized his client Walsin Esterhazy's handwriting. De Castro brought along several letters, and Mathieu, after inspecting them closely, made this remarkable development known to Scheurer-Kestner. With Picquart's stipulation thus circumvented, Leblois, Scheurer-Kestner, Mathieu, and Edgar Demange could now work in concert. On November 12 all four held a strategy meeting at which they were joined by Emmanuel Arène, editor of *Le Figaro*. And on November 15, *Le Figaro* published this letter from Mathieu to General Billot:

> The sole basis of the accusation brought in 1894 against my unfortunate brother is an unsigned, undated letter establishing that confidential military documents were delivered to the agent of a foreign military power. I have the honor of informing you that the author of that document is M. le Comte Walsin Esterhazy, an infantry commandant, withdrawn from active duty last spring because of temporary infirmities. Commandant Esterhazy's handwriting is identical to that of the document in question. It will be quite easy for you to procure a specimen of the handwriting of the officer. I am prepared, moreover, to tell you where you may find letters of his, the authenticity of which is incontestable and which date from before my brother's arrest.

He did not doubt, he wrote in conclusion, that the minister of war would act swiftly to see justice done.

A LUNCH ORGANIZED at Scheurer-Kestner's residence on the day after the council marked the beginning of Émile Zola's involvement in the Dreyfus Affair. Recruited for the valuable advice he could give as a famous and forceful writer who knew more than most about influencing mass audiences, he found himself captivated by Leblois's account of events. There was no need to tell those present—Leblois, Scheurer-Kestner, an appeals court judge named Louis Sarrut, the novelist Marcel Prévost—that anti-Semitism disgusted Zola. Eighteen months earlier, *Le Figaro* had published an article titled "For the Jews," in which he declared that for several years he had been following, with surprise and revulsion, the campaign against Jews in France. "I see it as a monstrosity, by which I mean something outside the pale of common sense, of truth and justice, a blind, fatuous thing that would push us back centuries." It stupefied him that such fanaticism should have erupted in an age of universal tolerance "when the movement everywhere is toward equality, fraternity, and justice."

But the Dreyfus drama spoke to Zola in other ways as well. His imagination had always dwelled upon the victim, the alien, the outcast. Characters expunged from a closed, hostile world figure prominently throughout his fiction, shaming bourgeois hypocrisy or political despotism. Two Zolas appeared at Scheurer-Kestner's on that fateful November 13: a man haunted since his own childhood by rigged trials that had robbed him of his inheritance, and a novelist enthralled by persecutional schemes. "Our factual accounts became poetry for Zola," Scheurer-Kestner recalled. " 'It's gripping!' he'd say from time to time. One felt that his little body was clambering up the curtains the better to hear and see. And he exclaimed: 'It's thrilling! It's horrible! It's a frightful drama! But it's also drama on the grand scale!' " The warden of La Santé had once urged Mathieu Dreyfus to defend his brother before France at large, and now, three years later, Zola argued that legal ploys would not suffice. A campaign was necessary, he said, with brief, trenchant articles challenging the enemy and stirring public indignation.

Zola's article on Scheurer-Kestner launched that campaign. Published on November 25 in *Le Figaro*, it celebrates the old man's perseverance and makes an assertion that was to become the *cri de guerre* of Dreyfusards: *"La vérité est en marche, et rien ne l'arrêtera."* ("Truth is on the march, and nothing will stop it.") One week later, on December 1, Zola published another article in *Le Figaro*, this one directed sardonically against the myth of a Jewish "syndicate," the press that propagated it, and the government agencies that fostered it. "Captain Dreyfus was condemned by a court-martial for treason," it begins.

> Since then he has become the traitor—no longer a man but an abstraction embodying the idea of the fatherland bled dry and handed over to the conqueror. He represents not only treason present and future, but also treason past, for people blame our old defeat on him, in the stubborn belief that only treason can explain it. There he is with his black soul and hideous face—the shame of the army, the thug who sold his brethren as Judas sold his God. But since he's Jewish, it's clear what will happen. Rich and powerful as they are—and, moreover, without national allegiances—Jews will work clandestinely, using their millions to bail him out. They will buy consciences, they will envelop France in a damnable plot, they will substitute an innocent man for the evildoer.

Thanks to twenty or so newspapers whose stock-in-trade was xenophobia, Zola noted, the idea of a subversive brotherhood invested with diabolical powers had taken root in the public mind. "How many simple folk have accosted me during the past week, saying: 'What? Isn't M. Scheurer-Kestner a knave? How can you associate with the likes of him? Don't you know that they've sold out France?' Such talk makes my heart tighten, for I know very well that misdeeds will thus be conjured away."

But if newspapers perverted public opinion, behind them lurked the ministry of war. "Who doesn't sense that we stand before the most impervious of ill wills? There are those who won't admit that errors— I was about to say transgressions—have been committed. They persist in shielding the compromised parties. They will stop at nothing to avoid the purge that looms." France, bereft of her reason, Zola declared, had

> turned against a poor wretch who for three years has been expiating in atrocious conditions a crime he didn't commit. Yes,

there exists over there, on a godforsaken rock under the brutal sun, a being cut off from everyone else. He is isolated not only by the ocean but by eleven guards who surround him night and day, like a human wall. . . . The eternal silence, and the slow, protracted death suffered beneath the weight of a whole nation's execration!

Deriding the idea of a Jewish syndicate as obfuscatory nonsense, Zola called for the creation of a virtuous syndicate, "a syndicate to shape opinion and cure it of the madness fostered by the gutter press. . . . A syndicate to repeat each morning . . . that the honor of the army is not threatened, that only individual parties can be compromised. . . . A syndicate to campaign until the truth has been established, until justice has been restored, however great the obstacles, however long the struggle." To this syndicate he, Zola, belonged, and to it, he hoped, "all the decent people of France" would flock in their thousands.

Threatened then with mass desertion by its conservative readership, *Le Figaro* reluctantly allowed Zola to fire one last salvo, and the campaigner held nothing back, lamenting in his most pugnacious style the spectacle of virtue jeered and vice acclaimed. "We have witnessed a base exploitation of patriotism, the bogeyman 'foreigner' trotted forth in an affair of honor that concerns only our French family. The worst revolutionaries make all kinds of noise about the army and its leaders being insulted, when the effort has been, on the contrary, to place them very high, above reproach." The curtain had fallen on the first act of a frightening drama, he concluded. "Let us hope that tomorrow's action will restore us our courage and console us."

Zola could not yet have known how labyrinthine the drama really was, or how far the conspirators had already gone to strengthen their case against Dreyfus. Alarmed by reports of Scheurer-Kestner visiting high officials and conferring with Picquart's lawyer, they decided that the secret file needed more bulk. Accordingly, Gonse and Henry prevailed upon Captain Lebrun-Renault, the officer who had been responsible for guarding Dreyfus at the École Militaire on January 5, 1895, to swear that his prisoner had made a clean breast of things just before the public degradation. Further, Henry, who could still draw upon Schwartzkoppen's wastepaper basket for raw material, produced a slew of forged or falsified documents, with encouragement from above. "Set your mind at rest," he assured Maurice Paléologue of the ministry of foreign affairs on November 3. "Dreyfus was rightly condemned. While he was shark fishing on his island, we were uncovering proofs that damn him outright. I have a closetful."

It hadn't taken long for perjured testimony and forged documents to lead the plotters down the slippery slope to outright collusion with the actual traitor. It had begun on October 16, when Generals de Boisdeffre and Gonse discussed the danger of Esterhazy carelessly exposing himself. Could they afford the risk? If their elaborate construction fell apart, would they not perish in the ruins? Increasingly detached from reality, Dreyfus's guilt had become a dogma to be preserved by any means, and so it happened that on the evening of October 22 Henry and du Paty de Clam—the latter wearing a false beard—met Esterhazy at the Vanne reservoir, near the Parc Montsouris. They told him that he had stalwart champions but that he would have to obey all their instructions. There would be daily contact. Reassured, Esterhazy bade farewell to Schwartzkoppen in a tête-à-tête at the German embassy.

Daily contact did indeed occur as they all set about persuading high government officials that Lieutenant Colonel Picquart was the agent or pawn of a Jewish syndicate determined to substitute innocent Esterhazy for guilty Dreyfus. In letters dictated by Henry and addressed to President Faure, Esterhazy claimed that an anonymous benefactress—a "veiled lady"—had warned him about a plot and had furnished evidence, smuggled out of some "foreign legation," of Dreyfus's "baseness." By turns pathetic and brazen, he implored Faure to rescue him and threatened, if he were not rescued, to publish a document that might provoke war. The accuser should have been jailed without delay, but instead the accused officer in Tunisia was questioned at length. Esterhazy, who felt invulnerable, carried his offensive further still. Ignoring instructions, he bearded Picquart directly, in a letter written on November 6 or 7.

I have received these last days a letter in which you are formally accused of having fomented against me the most abominable machination to substitute me for Dreyfus. In that letter it is said, among other things, that you have bribed noncommissioned officers in order to have specimens of my handwriting, a fact pathetic and brazen, which is true, since I have verified it. It is also said that you have diverted from the ministry of war documents entrusted to your honor in order to compose a clandestine file that you have delivered to friends of the traitor. The matter of the clandestine file is factual, since I have in my possession today items that were taken from the file.

In the face of such a monstrous accusation and in spite of the proof that has been given me, I hesitate to believe that a superior officer of the French army could have been trading in the secrets of his service in order to attempt to substitute one of his comrades for the wretch the proof of whose crime he has evidence of. It is unthinkable that you evade a clear and frank explanation.

Meanwhile, Henry sent Picquart several bogus telegrams signed "Speranza" and "Blanche," one of which suggested quite pointedly that Picquart himself had fabricated the *petit-bleu.* Intercepted by the post office at Henry's behest, and photographed before leaving Paris, they were thrust, with feigned outrage, upon Minister Billot.

Henry and Esterhazy might have gone on fabricating evidence unperturbed had not two events combined to open their secret world a crack. On November 15, as we have seen, Mathieu Dreyfus made public his denunciation of Esterhazy. On that same day Picquart, in high dudgeon, filed an official military complaint against Esterhazy, "who, having been informed, I know not by whom, of the probe I conducted in the exercise of my office, has attacked me slanderously, first in a private letter, then in telegrams." The battle was joined at last, though not on level ground. Confronted with Mathieu Dreyfus's charge, Billot ordered General Georges de Pellieux, commandant of the Department of the Seine, to conduct an investigation. After only three days, Pellieux, to whom Boisdeffre showed the "coded" telegrams from "Speranza," declared Picquart more suspect than Esterhazy. Billot's fellow ministers then recommended another, fuller investigation, which lasted two weeks. Led by the same general, who had grown quite fond of Esterhazy, it produced the same verdict, with independent-minded witnesses never having been questioned and the conspirators' crudely forged evidence never having been subjected to handwriting analysis. Pellieux's report described Esterhazy as an innocent victim, Picquart as the "unwitting agent" of someone who had almost brought dishonor upon him, and the *petit-bleu* as a document without authenticity or plausibility.

But even then the matter was not yet resolved once for all. Would Pellieux's report, if accepted, not compel the military men to press charges against Mathieu Dreyfus in criminal court, before a jury beyond their control and a judge invoking hallowed rules of evidence?* Lest the Dreyfus trial take place all over again, this time out in the open, Generals Billot, Boisdeffre, Saussier, and Pellieux agreed that Esterhazy should beseech them to reject the report and give him the opportunity to exonerate himself at a court-martial. With some trepidation, Esterhazy played along. "I believe that you have in your hands all the evidence of the infamous plot hatched to ruin me," he wrote on December 1 to Pellieux (who corrected the letter in draft). "Only a decision reached [in a court-martial] will be able to demolish . . . this most cowardly slanderer." Many papers praised his élan.

No more rational than the press was the National Assembly, where, following Pellieux's report, deputies rallied around the flag in a tumultuous display of anti-Semitism orchestrated by Count Albert de Mun, Catholicism's most articulate legislator, who vilified the alleged syndicate. "We must know whether it is true that there is in this country a mysterious and hidden power strong enough to be able

---

*Attempts were made in the fanatically anti-Dreyfusard press to undermine Mathieu's credibility by suggesting that he, too, was a spy. In December 1897, *La Libre parole* published a letter from an officer garrisoned at Belfort, near the German border. It gave remarkably specific information about a villa Mathieu had built on the outskirts, calling attention to one feature, a turret, from which, the officer declared, Dreyfus could transmit military information to the enemy with simple optical instruments. The turret thus became the focus of the same paranoid fantasies that shrouded the Eiffel Tower. *La Croix* also published the letter.

to cast suspicion at will on those who command our army, on those who, come the day of reckoning, will dutifully lead our army against the enemy," he exclaimed on December 4. "We must know whether such a hidden power is strong enough to overwhelm the entire country, as it has done for more than a fortnight." These sowers of doubt were all foreigners, he declared, even if nominally French, whereas the elected representatives were, with some few exceptions, "Frenchmen concerned to preserve intact what remains, in the midst of our partisan spats, the common domain of our invincible hopes: the honor of the army." Amid the furor that de Mun's speech excited, Joseph Reinach, Baron Jacques de Reinach's nephew, who sat as a deputy from Digne, could feel "the hatred of three hundred hypnotized individuals" surge over his head. In this revivalist commotion left-wingers participated as stridently as those of the Right. The socialist leader Alexandre Millerand lambasted the government for even allowing an inquiry. Why didn't Reinach do something about rehabilitating his own tainted family instead of playing Voltaire and trumping up a new Calas Affair, he wondered—to the general acclaim of fellow legislators. Hadn't Jewish financiers enriched themselves in one scheme or conspiracy after another, always at France's expense?

By a substantial majority, the Chamber of Deputies declared itself "respectful" of Pellieux's verdict. It endorsed General Billot's "homage to the army." It denounced "leaders of the invidious campaign undertaken to trouble the public conscience." It buried the Dreyfus Affair.

Undaunted, Zola continued his personal campaign with a pamphlet scolding students who had demonstrated against Dreyfus in raucous marches through the Latin Quarter. "So there exist fresh young brains and souls that this idiotic poison has already deranged? How very sad, and how ominous for the coming twentieth century!" Three weeks later he addressed the whole nation in a pamphlet titled *Lettre à la France,* which the publisher Fasquelle brought out on January 6, 1898, just before Esterhazy's court-martial. Here Zola sounded a graver note, warning his compatriots against their penchant for military rule and declaring them to be infected still with the virus of Boulangism. "Republican blood does not yet run through your veins," he wrote. "Plumed helmets are what make your heart beat faster, and a king can't come to town without your falling in love with him." Right behind the scepter marched the cross. To bargain for one was to invite the other and thus revive a past of intolerance and theocracy.

> Today the tactic of anti-Semitism is quite simple. Catholicism tried in vain to gain sway over the populace by creating workers' circles and multiplying pilgrimages. . . . Churches remained deserted, the people no longer believed in God. But here an opportunity presents itself to stir up those common people, to poison them with this species of fanaticism, to have them march through the streets shouting: "Down with the Jews!" "Death to the Jews!" What a victory it would be if a religious war could be unleashed! . . . When Frenchmen have been turned into fanatics and executioners, when their love for the rights of man has been torn from their hearts . . . God will undoubtedly do the rest.

Zola implored France to come to her senses, calling the liberal bourgeoisie and emancipated working class "dupes" who would not have sided against Dreyfus, he felt quite sure, had they recognized the machinations of the army and the Church.

Duped himself, Zola interpreted the decision to prosecute Esterhazy as a sign of truth gaining the upper hand over villainy. It soon became clear, however, that Esterhazy's court-martial, which lasted only two days, January 11 and 12, was ritual theater. Everything had been arranged beforehand. Not Esterhazy but Picquart emerged as the real defendant, and while the former answered questions in a public session, playing the part of slandered warrior to applause from fellow officers, Picquart suffered rude treatment in a session held behind closed doors on the grounds that information aired during it might compromise national security. No sooner had he mentioned Billot, Boisdeffre, and Mercier than General de Pellieux, flouting legal procedure, forbade him to "implicate such glorious names." The presiding magistrate, General de Luxer, would not let Picquart finish his sentences until another judge, Commandant Rivals, who apparently had not attended rehearsals, asked that he be permitted to offer explanations essential to his defense. And the general staff—Gonse, Henry, et al.—testified against him, with tales of files rifled or of collusion over-heard. It all worked out as planned. Esterhazy's lawyer, though he knew exactly what outcome to expect, delivered a five-hour plea. The judges then acquitted the defendant after a three-minute conference. Inside the Cherche-Midi Prison, where Picquart and Mathieu Dreyfus found themselves insulted and threatened, this verdict provoked shouts of "Long live the army!" "Long live France!" "Death to the Jews!" "Death to the syndicate!" Outside, some fifteen hundred people cheered Esterhazy, with one stentorian voice proclaiming "Hats off to the martyr of the Jews!"

Seven weeks earlier, at the beginning of his article on Scheurer-Kestner, Zola had declared that his intention was not yet to discuss the affair in detail. "If circumstances have permitted me to study it and to reach a settled opinion," he wrote, "I am mindful of the fact that an inquest has been launched, that judicial procedures have begun, that common decency requires me to wait." But now the self-imposed stricture no longer applied. Justice had miscarried once again, uniformed magistrates had convicted Alfred Dreyfus for the second time, and Zola made up his mind to expose the plot. What came of this resolve was his *Lettre au Président de la République,* better known as *J'accuse.* Published on the front page of a new daily paper, *L'Aurore,* it owed its more famous title to *L'Aurore's* codirector Georges Clemenceau, who extracted it from the litany of indictments with which Zola's philippic concludes.

I ACCUSE Lieutenant Colonel du Paty de Clam of having been the diabolic agent of the judicial error . . . and of having for three years bolstered his dastardly deed with the strangest, most culpable machinations.

I ACCUSE General Mercier of having become an accomplice, at the very least out of weakness, in one of the century's most iniquitous plots.

I ACCUSE General Billot of having held in his hands the proof of Dreyfus's innocence and suppressing it, of having rendered himself guilty of this crime against justice and humanity for political reasons, to save the compromised general staff.

I ACCUSE Generals de Boisdeffre and Gonse of having helped commit this same crime, the one out of Catholic fervor, no doubt, the other in a spirit of solidarity that portrays the war ministry as the unassailable holy of holies.

I ACCUSE General de Pellieux and Commandant Ravary of having led a vile—that is, a monstrously biased—investigation, the report of which constitutes an imperishable monument of naïve audacity.

I ACCUSE the three expert graphologists—Messrs. Belhomme, Varinard, and Couard—of having prepared fraudulent and deceitful analyses, unless a medical examination should prove them to be afflicted with impaired vision and judgment.

I ACCUSE the war ministry of having used the press—particularly *L'Éclair* and *L'Écho de Paris*—to lead opinion astray and cover up its mischief.

FINALLY, I ACCUSE the first court-martial of having flouted the law by convicting the defendant with a document introduced secretly, and I accuse the second court-martial of having papered over this illegal maneuver by . . . deliberately acquitting a guilty man, on orders from above. . . .

As for the people I accuse, I do not know them, I have never seen them, I entertain neither rancor nor hatred. For me they are mere entities, spirits of social maleficence. And the act I accomplish here is but a revolutionary means of hastening the explosion of truth and justice.

EXAGGERATING THE BETTER to impress and relying upon his intuitive power where he lacked certain knowledge, Zola captured in these incantatory phrases the essence of what had transpired behind closed doors. On January 13, 1898, several hundred news criers recruited for the day by *L'Aurore* fanned out over Paris to hawk a special edition of the paper. Three hundred thousand copies had been printed, with the front page entirely taken up by *J'accuse.*

It electrified France. Around this manifesto gathered the disparate energies that became a coherent Dreyfusist movement. "The party of justice had been born," declared Joseph Reinach. "Dreyfusism was reinvigorated. . . . We could feel the confidence boil and rise with us," wrote Léon Blum, who called *J'accuse* a polemical text of "imperishable beauty." High-minded youths—students at the École Normale Supérieure, young writers associated with the avant-garde literary magazine *La Revue blanche,* young socialists alienated by official party doctrine—sprang forward as if awaiting some such clarion call and marshaled signatures for a protest.

Thenceforth, readers of *L'Aurore* seldom opened the paper without encountering protests or collective tributes. On February 2 a group of writers, artists, and scientists lauded Zola's "noble, militant attitude" even as they promised support "in the name of justice and truth." On February 6 support came from attorneys who offered him heartfelt thanks "for service rendered to the cause of Law, which touches all civilized nations." Every day brought more encouragement, and on his editorial rostrum Clemenceau described the supporters as a vanguard of "intellectuals," giving that nineteenth-century term its full, modern sense for the first time. "The syndicate—ours—grows apace," he exclaimed. "It redounds to the honor of thinking men that they have bestirred themselves before everyone else. Not a negligible thing. In the great movements of public opinion, one doesn't often see men of pure intellectual labor occupy the front rank."

In the civil war that had already divided friends all over France, *J'accuse* excited as much wrath as adulation, and letters of praise were matched by stacks of hate mail. Not without reason would the Vatican daily, *L'Osservatore romano,* exult: "Masonry and Judaism, sprung up together to combat and to destroy Christianity in the world, must now together defend themselves against the Christian awakening and against the people's wrath." It was incumbent upon

Émile Zola's open letter to Félix Faure, president of the Republic, January 13, 1898.

all good Catholics, declared a well-known anti-Dreyfusard, to join the Catholic Union Nationale's annual parade in honor of Joan of Arc and thus "protest against this Jewish campaign besmirching France." A Catholic National Congress urged the faithful to boycott all Jewish businesses. Had it been polled, a majority might have cheered the Jesuit journal *Civiltà cattolica* for asserting that the real mistake was not the "judicial error" trumped up by Dreyfus's coreligionists but the granting of the rights of citizenship to Jews during the eighteenth-century Revolution. Among his most fervent admirers, Édouard Drumont counted many parish priests. "France for the French" became a ubiquitous slogan, as anti-Semitism, ignoring party lines, raged across the country in brawls and in rallies organized by the Anti-Semitic League. *La Croix* (whose front-page device was Christ crucified) called for the expulsion of Jews from France. Was the Jew not "the enemy within, inassimilable, irreducibly opposed to our traditions, our way of life, our mentality and our interests?" Merchants on the rue des Juifs in Paris, claiming that their address hurt business, appealed successfully for a change of name. On January 15, 1898, in a meeting at Rivoli Hall, the anarchist Louise Michel denounced anti-Semitism as "a pretext by means of which monarchist Catholics might put the Republic in mortal danger if too many people fell for their cunning diversion," but even as she spoke hundreds of law students were swarming around a bonfire on the place de la Sorbonne chanting "Out with Zola! Down with the Jews! Death to the kikes [*youtres*]!"* During legislative elections in May 1898, *La Libre parole* advertised its candidate, Édouard Drumont, on an illuminated sign outside its offices, with the battle cry *"Mort aux Juifs."* Drumont was elected deputy from Algeria, where the previous year French residents demanding that the citizenship of Algerian Jews be revoked had launched a bloody pogrom.

To nationalists who opposed review or "revision" of Dreyfus's sentence, *J'accuse* was a pernicious document undermining institutions that mattered more than the guilt or innocence of one man. How

---

*They were a chorus of the Paris bar and law school faculty, whose members were in the main anti-Dreyfusard, according to one close study.

light, after all, was Alfred Dreyfus when weighed against *la grande armée*! If the latter, to prosper, required the former to serve out his life on Devil's Island, so be it, declared antirevisionists like Maurice Barrès, who may be said to have anticipated the totalitarian concept of an "objective crime." If France, to survive in its "organic" wholeness, required the French to sacrifice an exemplary alien, why hesitate? "At the end of the nineteenth century, in one sector of public opinion, a fortress-France nationalism asserted itself whose mission was to defend the cohesive social organism against modernity," writes the historian Michel Winock. This nationalism, for which Germany was a convenient enemy—fostering intellectual and moral reform by threatening invasion at the border—thus went far beyond revanchism.

> It oriented itself toward the interior, toward the past. . . . It directed its antagonism first and foremost against the democratic and liberal regime, the "Jewish, Masonic Republic," but beneath the political agenda one observed a spiritual reaction against decadence by people who understood the defense of French interests to be that of a completed civilization at war with the new mobility of things and beings. . . . Anti-Dreyfusards banked on two institutions: the Church and the army. Organized in accordance with principles of unity and hierarchy, these served, by their very nature, to strengthen the social fabric.

From this vantage point, Zola had already committed more sins than one man could ever expiate. After novels such as *La Conquête de Plassans* and *La Débâcle* and *Lourdes,* where ecclesiastics and military brass are portrayed in a harsh light, *J'accuse* did not surprise anti-Dreyfusards. It was, rather, the polemical epilogue to books listed high on their index, the final flourish of a subversive career, the work of a foreigner. "Just who is this Monsieur Zola?" asked Barrès. "The man is not French. . . . Émile Zola thinks quite naturally with the mind of an uprooted Venetian."[*] Did he also think with the mind

---

[*]Zola's father, a Venetian, had immigrated to France in 1830, ten years before Émile Zola's birth.

of an "intellectual"? In Barrès's estimation, that made him doubly foreign, the intellectual being an individual "who persuades himself that society must be founded on logic and who fails to understand that in fact it is based upon prior necessities, which may be foreign to individual reason."

Zola had invited prosecution, and in the National Assembly, where many legislators shouted approval when Albert de Mun called *J'accuse* "a bloody outrage," radicals as well as conservatives saw to it that his challenge was met. Under intense pressure from them, the cabinet drafted a charge on January 18. Making no mention of the Dreyfus case lest doing so provide grounds for retrial, it limited its subject to the phrase in which Zola accused the second court-martial of having "deliberately" acquitted a guilty man "on orders from above." Its strategy was supported only reluctantly by Esterhazy, among others, who feared that testimony would spill beyond this one grievance. However, Prime Minister Jules Méline, with his government's honor at stake, could not avoid litigation. To fortify itself, the general staff sought to discredit the principal witness for the defense by having an investigatory board recommend, on February 1, that Billot retire Picquart because of "grave misdeeds committed while in service."

Zola's trial opened at the Assize Court on February 7 and lasted more than two weeks, affording those who thronged the Palais de Justice—Marcel Proust among them—a spectacle fraught with dramatic incident. Led by Fernand Labori, behind whom Zola effaced himself, the defense team summoned nearly two hundred witnesses, from Mercier to Esterhazy, from chiefs of the general staff to members of the intelligence service, from the graphologists consulted during Dreyfus's trial to the judges who presided over Esterhazy's court-martial. At first all went better than expected as Labori obstinately challenged the absurd order that Dreyfus's trial be considered a res judicata, or a case adjudicated with no further appeal—that jurors might hear testimony arguing against Esterhazy's innocence but not evidence casting doubt upon Dreyfus's guilt. Transgression by transgression, the great lawyer built a case for retrial, and one by one the men who had convicted Dreyfus helped exculpate him despite themselves. The pseudoscientific humbug of Alphonse Bertillon's handwriting analysis provoked laughter even among the generals. Henry (now a lieutenant colonel) remained mute on the witness stand, claiming to be in a stupor induced by insomnia and illness. Commandant du Paty de Clam, whom Maurice Paléologue of the foreign affairs ministry described as a weird mixture of fanaticism, extravagance, and foolishness, played du Paty de Clam. "Buttoned tight at the waist in his finest uniform, a monocle riveted to his eye, he crossed the courtroom with the cadenced step of a Prussian military parade, stopped like a robot two feet from the stand, heels together, knees braced, back arched, saluted the Court and the jury in military fashion, and waited, stiffly" is how one account pictures him. "Once the oath had been taken, he refused to answer most of the questions. He then saluted the Court and the jury, pivoted, and left the room."

Beside these asinine figures, Picquart in his sky-blue, gold-braided jacket looked like Apollo. Though usually reserved, on this occasion the tall, thin colonel delivered a passionate tirade against those who had sought to dishonor him—"artisans of the other affair," as he called them—and, even with a dishonorable discharge pending, undoubtedly swayed the jury. By February 16, Zola's prosecutors felt deep concern. The war ministry received police reports that jurors felt inclined to acquit him.

At this juncture, General de Pellieux, an officer capable of real eloquence when arguing his convictions, joined the fray, to decisive effect. First he stated that Esterhazy could not have obtained the documents listed in the bordereau; then, with rhetorical bravado, he pronounced the whole issue of handwriting irrelevant and asked the jury:

> What do you want this army to become on the day of danger, which may be closer than you think? What do you want the poor soldiers to do, who will be led into battle by leaders discredited in their eyes? It is to the slaughterhouse that your sons would be led, gentlemen of the jury! But Zola would have won a new battle; he would write a new *Débâcle;* he would carry the French language everywhere in a Europe from which France would have been expunged.

It was a virtuoso performance, but Pellieux outdid himself one day later, after Picquart had explained at length how Esterhazy could easily have obtained documents listed in the bordereau. Because Labori had broken the "pact of silence" about Dreyfus's court-martial, Pellieux now took the witness stand again and declared:

> I will repeat the characteristically blunt words of Colonel Henry. You want the truth? Well, here it is! [In November 1896] there occurred an event that I would like to bring to your attention. We had at the ministry of war absolute proof of Dreyfus's guilt! And that proof I saw. At that time the ministry received a paper whose origin cannot be contested and which says—I will tell you what it contains: "There is going to be an interpellation concerning the Dreyfus affair. Never disclose the relations we had with the Jew."

No sooner had Labori requested that Pellieux produce this document than Gonse, who knew it to be Henry's crude forgery, intervened, claiming that national security or *raison d'état* superseded rules of evidence. In a final bit of theater, Pellieux then ordered an aide-de-camp to fetch General de Boisdeffre. Was not Chief of Staff Raoul Le Mouton de Boisdeffre's word better than any document? Was it not as good as gospel? So he implied, without contradiction from the presiding magistrate. And on February 18 Boisdeffre played his part impeccably. "I will be brief," he testified. "I confirm on all points General Pellieux's deposition as being exact and authentic. I have not a single word more to say; I don't have the right to; I repeat, gentlemen, I don't have the right to." Answerable to a higher authority than the Court of Appeals, this custodian of sacred intelligence warned the nation against itself. "You are the jury, you are the nation. If the nation does not have confidence in the leaders of the army, in those who bear the responsibility for national defense, they are ready to surrender that onerous task to others. You have only to speak. I will not say another word."

The verdict could have been returned then and there. Three days later, Zola made his own direct plea to the jury, in a tremulous voice often drowned out by hoots and insults. But neither his prepared speech nor Labori's exhaustive summary succeeded in working the jurors free from Boisdeffre's spell. On February 23 it took them only thirty-five minutes to find Zola guilty and to recommend the maximum punishment of one year in prison.

This was followed by a session of the Assize Court in which the eighty-year-old public prosecutor, Jean-Pierre Manau, denounced anti-Semitism and proclaimed that revisionists were "the honor of the country" rather than "traitors" or "sellouts." On April 2, it quashed Zola's conviction on technical grounds. But rejoicing was brief. Despite advice to the contrary from Prime Minister Méline, the military judges who had found Esterhazy innocent filed a slander suit against Zola based upon one sentence in *J'accuse:* "A court-martial has just dared to acquit Esterhazy by order, a supreme offense to all truth and all justice." Eschewing Paris as the venue of this second trial, the government chose Versailles, which swarmed with military personnel all year round, and scheduled it for late May. Nationalist zealots who spent the next six weeks anticipating a bloody showdown were to be bitterly disappointed. No sooner had order been called on May 23 than Labori questioned the competence of the Seine-et-Oise court to deliberate on misdemeanors that had taken place outside its jurisdiction. The presiding magistrate, a M. Périvier, who had made no effort to conceal his bias against Zola, rejected this point out of hand, whereupon Labori filed an appeal. Périvier was compelled to suspend proceedings, which he did with the irate observation that "nothing is above the law, nothing, nothing, not even M. Zola," and after only one hour, Zola departed Versailles.

Zola's second trial in the Court of Appeals at Versailles took place on July 18. It lasted somewhat longer than the first. As soon as proceedings began, Labori argued that members of a court-martial could not sue his client since they enjoyed no "civil status." Judge Périvier gruffly ruled against him, whereupon Labori stated that he could represent Zola properly only if debate were allowed to extend beyond the one sentence cited in the writ. Once again Périvier ruled against him, which prompted the attorney general to accuse Zola of seeking refuge in "the brambles of legal procedure." Labori then lodged an appeal, and when Périvier declared that the trial would continue nonetheless, Labori walked out, with Zola in tow. As Dreyfusards battled anti-Dreyfusards outside, Zola—who heard shouts of "Back to Venice!" "Go back to the Jews!" "Coward!"—was escorted through the crowd by dragoons.

That same evening, he crossed the Channel to England. He would remain self-exiled for almost a year.

SIX MONTHS AFTER the publication of *J'accuse,* xenophobia still held sway. When, on July 7, the new minister of war, Godefroy Cavaignac, who had been shown Henry's forged letters, quoted them in a speech denouncing Dreyfus—a speech loudly applauded by the Chamber, then posted in France's thirty-six thousand town halls—anti-Dreyfusards might never have felt more confident. But two days later the edifice of lies constructed since 1894 developed another serious crack. Paul Bertulus, a magistrate investigating Picquart's charge that the "Speranza" and "Blanche" telegrams were fraudulent, received dramatic testimony on July 9 after months of thankless research. It came from Esterhazy's young cousin Christian, who had often carried secret messages between Esterhazy and du Paty de Clam. Upon discovering that his dissolute cousin had stolen money from him, Christian sought out Fernand Labori and gave him not only his remarkable story but documents to prove it. Labori notified Bertulus through an intermediary, and on July 12 Esterhazy was incarcerated at La Santé. This turn of events infuriated Cavaignac, who arranged to have Picquart locked up—also at La Santé—on a charge of criminal indiscretion (three general staff officers having alleged that he had shown classified material to his lawyer, Leblois). At the general staff shock waves were felt. Boisdeffre and Gonse fell ill. Henry, his nerves frayed, sank into despair. "Save us; save us. . . . You must save the army's honor!" he begged Bertulus during a tearful interview.

During the month of August 1898, startling developments rekindled hope in the Dreyfus camp. This new chapter began with the war minister deciding to have documents in the so-called secret file closely examined. A man stubborn for good and ill, Cavaignac determined that rumors about forgery, which were growing louder every day, should be disproved without further delay. Quite the opposite happened. On August 13, a staff officer assigned to the investigation, Captain Louis Cuignet, discovered under lamplight that the famous Panizzardi letter quoted by Cavaignac himself before the Chamber and posted in town halls all over France had been spliced together from two different kinds of ruled paper. Once informed of this, Cavaignac did not approach the general staff right away. What he did instead was appoint a board to question Commandant Esterhazy, for whom he had as little use as for Captain Dreyfus. Panic-stricken, Esterhazy turned against his former protectors and, after claiming that the "Jewish syndicate" would have given him six hundred thousand francs to declare himself the author of the bordereau, swore, with evidence in hand, that du Paty de Clam had dictated his every move. Du Paty de Clam hemmed and hawed, whereupon the investigatory board judged Esterhazy to have violated neither honor nor discipline. Cavaignac discharged him anyway and went after Hubert Henry, like a hunter crushing a slug underfoot while stalking his real prey.

On August 30, Cavaignac himself interrogated Henry in the presence of Generals de Boisdeffre and Gonse, who remained silent throughout. The minister gave the unhinged colonel no quarter. Henry's indignant denials became weak equivocations as Cavaignac challenged him mercilessly. Point by point the truth was extracted and when at length Cavaignac asked, "In 1896, you received an envelope with a letter inside, an insignificant letter; you suppressed the letter and fabricated another one?" Henry surrendered. Arrangements were immediately made to have him placed under fortress arrest just outside Paris, at Mont-Valérien, where he spent the night in a room occupied seven months earlier by Georges Picquart. On August 31, Colonel Henry nerved himself with rum, assured his wife in a farewell note that the forged letter "merely confirmed" information conveyed to him orally, and, having told one last lie, slit his throat.

Those who believed that a triumphant dénouement lay at hand did not reckon seriously enough with anti-Dreyfusism. Reason was not

what had sent Alfred Dreyfus to Devil's Island in 1895, and the ideological fortifications that kept him there proved stronger than the bar-
rage of evidence arguing his innocence. Henry had no sooner been
buried than zealous nationalists made him a whited sepulchre. The
counterfeit documents for which Cavaignac had imprisoned him were
said to be "patriotic" forgeries, or lies that told the truth. "We were
not able to give you the great funeral that your martyrdom deserved,"
Charles Maurras wrote in the royalist paper *La Gazette de France.*

> We should have waved your bloody tunic and the sullied blades
> down the boulevards; marched the coffin, hoisted the mortuary
> banner like a black flag. . . . But the national sentiment will
> awaken to triumph and avenge you. From the country's soil . . .
> there will soon rise monuments to expiate our cowardice. . . . In
> life as in death, you marched forward. Your unhappy forgery
> will be regarded as one of your best martial deeds.

Maurras was quoted by *La Libre parole,* by *Le Petit journal,* by
L'Éclair. Their exculpatory crusade rested upon the argument that
Henry had acted as he did to thwart Picquart, and that his forgery had
foiled a treasonous plot. Cavaignac resigned from the war ministry on
September 5 rather than accept the conclusion of Henri Brisson, who
had succeeded Méline as prime minister, that revision was inevitable.
Cavaignac's successor, General Émile Zurlinden, followed suit twelve
days later, when Brisson refused to let him initiate legal proceedings
against Picquart. A third war minister, General Charles Chanoine,
then appointed General Zurlinden military governor of Paris, and in
that capacity the implacable Alsatian ordered Picquart court-
martialed on charges of having forged the *petit-bleu.* Just three weeks
after Henry killed himself, guards escorted Picquart from La Santé, a
civilian prison, to the Cherche-Midi military compound, where it had
all begun.

For its contention that the retrial of Alfred Dreyfus would leave
France defenseless, that the blood shed by Colonel Hubert Henry was
patriotic gore and his suicide an act of martyrdom, the military estab-

lishment received blessings from the clergy. To be sure, most bishops, being salaried by the State, kept their own counsel. No doubt the Vatican spoke for many of them when it observed that

> the Jewish race, the deicide people, wandering throughout the world, brings with it everywhere the pestiferous breath of treason. And so too in the Dreyfus case . . . it is hardly surprising if we again find the Jew in the front ranks, or if we find that the betrayal of one's country has been Jewishly conspired and Jewishly executed.*

But some churchmen had much to say on their own. Monsignor Mathieu, archbishop of Toulouse, declared to his parishioners, "You are still upset, are you not, by the deadly campaign being waged against our military chiefs, by this insurrection against justice, by this attempt to rehabilitate a traitor and by these efforts to incriminate an innocent man; you have protested against this crime of *lèse*-fatherland and shared the indignation it has prompted throughout the country."† And lower clergy spoke their minds as uninhibitedly as he. In December 1898, *La Libre parole* started a fund to help Colonel Henry's widow defray the cost of suing Joseph Reinach (he had called her deceased husband an accomplice of Esterhazy). Three hundred priests mailed in donations, many accompanied by anti-Semitic rants.†† Monks took it upon themselves to consecrate the skullduggery of the military elite. In July 1898, Father Henri-Martin

---

*The role of traitor was a God-given one in the divine scheme of things. "The Jew was created by God to serve as a spy wherever treason is afoot," declared *Civiltà cattolica* during Zola's trial.

†A kindred spirit, and possibly a relative of the archbishop, Rear Admiral Mathieu, who ran for office in the legislative elections of May 1898, declared during his candidacy, "Citizens, these are difficult times. The motto must be: France for the true Frenchmen and not for those foreigners naturalized yesterday who have no patriotic feelings in their hearts and became French only out of self-interest. Let us therefore be true Frenchmen. Our people will return to Christ, who is life."

††The fantasy of a certain Abbé Cros, for example, was to place his feet every morning and evening on a bedside rug made from the skin of "kikes."

Didon, a Dominican preacher whose sermons were oratorical events, sanctified France's beleaguered army during a commencement ceremony at the Collège d'Arcueil, where he served as director. "We must equip ourselves with coercive powers, we must not hold back, we must brandish the sword, smite, terrorize, cut off heads, impose justice," he insisted in the presence of the guest of honor, General Jamont, vice-chairman of the Supreme War Council. "Armed force thus employed is no longer brute strength but sainted energy put to beneficent use." It would have been naïve to imagine that Didon the disciplinarian had only permissive teachers in mind when he upbraided "intellectuals" for rejecting force, despite the excesses fostered by "a senseless freedom." Everyone understood, most especially General Jamont, an old warhorse alarmed by the threat, under a republican merit system, of brainy Polytechnicians such as Alfred Dreyfus displacing scions of a military caste in the École de Guerre.

Anti-Semitism was in full froth. Another priest, Father Vincent de Paul Bailly, who had launched thirty different publications since 1880 and edited the widely read Assumptionist daily *La Croix,* went even further than Didon in his tirades. After *L'Aurore* published *J'accuse,* hardly a day passed that Bailly did not find kindling to fuel his rage against Jews and Dreyfusards. "Free thought, standing in the dock with Zola, acts as an attorney for Jews, for Protestants, for all enemies of the Church, and the army must, despite itself, fire away," he wrote. "On all sides, people clamor for a strongman who would risk his life to tear France from the clutches of traitors, from the sectarians and imbeciles who are handing them over to the foreigner.... Ah! Who will deliver us from this pack of brigands?" In September 1899 the pope, fearful by then of a republican backlash, urged him "to stop shouting Dreyfus, Dreyfus" and to temper his relentless denunciations of the president.* But Bailly had nothing of temperance in his

---

*The Vatican trimmed its sails to the prevailing wind. Shortly after Dreyfus's second trial, when well-founded rumor had it that he would be pardoned if convicted again, the *Osservatore romano* ran an article titled "the Oppressors of the Jews," invoking the proclamation of a twelfth-century pope, Innocent III, that Jews are "the living witnesses of the true faith" and that Christians were not permitted to exterminate them. The popes, it went on to declare, had always treated Jews with "charity, tolerance, and

nature. He was all spleen, and, with notable exceptions, French clergy shared his humour.* How perilous it was to dissent may be judged by this letter of resignation from a priest named Georges Russacq to his bishop.

> When I took my vows, no one warned me that along with dogmatic orthodoxy the Catholic church imposed an orthodoxy of politics. During the Dreyfus affair, I chose not to be drafted into the ranks of nationalism. I would not follow the clergy who, faced with a matter of conscience, neglected an innocent man's rights and dwelled upon his Jewishness to gain an advantage in clerical polemics. At the most recent elections, I declined all overtures from candidates and all propaganda proposals by committees. Resolved as I was not to compromise the ministry with politics, I even abstained from voting. It turns out that all these things were unpardonable wrongs. My brethren exhale defiance and hostility and make life impossible. I therefore have the honor of tendering my resignation as the curate of Bou [a village near Orléans]. . . . I retire . . . only after much shedding of tears. But I am pledged to my conscience as I am to my peace of mind.

The letter was written in 1902, three years after Dreyfus's second trial, and three years before a radical republican legislature mindful of diatribes in *La Croix* and kindred publications (collectively christened "*la bonne Presse*") voted the separation of Church and State.

---

love." Three days later, it reported that the corpse of a Christian boy, his body drained of blood by Jews, had been discovered in a Hungarian village.

L'Univers lost many of its subscribers in the 1890s, when it endorsed Leo XIII's policy of reconciliation with the Republic. They defected to *La Libre parole* and *La Vérité* as well as to *La Croix*. After the publication of *La France juive*, Edmond de Goncourt reported the following dinner conversation with Édouard Drumont: "Drumont . . . informs us that he is giving anti-Semitic lectures [here and there], having been encouraged to do so by ecclesiastics who told him that the Holy Ghost would bring him the gift of public speech."

. . .

ON FEBRUARY 16, 1899, Félix Faure, France's dapper president, who, having made up his mind that the Affair was a res judicata, and who couldn't forgive Zola the famous indictment addressed to him in Clemenceau's paper thirteen months earlier, died of a stroke while entertaining his young mistress in the Élysée Palace. This bolt from the blue augured well for revisionists, who immediately nominated one of their own to be Faure's successor—Émile Loubet, the president of the Senate. Elected on February 18 by the bicameral legislature meeting in plenary session at Versailles, Loubet boarded a train for Paris, where crowds shouting *"L'élu de la synagogue!"* ("The synagogue's choice!") and *"Victoire de la trahison juive!"* ("Victory of Jewish treason!") filled the Gare Saint-Lazare. The Ligue Antisémitique* had recruited a great many demonstrators from among the capital's vagrant population, and these ran riot through the streets as Loubet proceeded to the Élysée, then to the ministry of foreign affairs. "All along his route, he was pursued by the whistles, hoots, vociferations of the patriotic and anti-Semitic leagues," Maurice Paléologue observed. "When at last the cortege halted in front of the ministry on the quai d'Orsay, the din was so formidable that I and my colleagues couldn't hear a single note of the 'Marseillaise,' which a military band was playing twenty steps away." Another mob swarmed up the rue de Rivoli to the place des Pyramides, where, leaning against the statue of Joan of Arc, Paul Déroulède (who had never recovered from Boulanger's fall) declared, "Today's election is an insult. . . . It is up to the people to choose the president of the Republic. . . . Let us not do anything right now, for in the Élysée lies a man whom I loved. . . . Come Thursday, I shall do my duty."†

---

*The adjective *"antisémitique"* would later be replaced by *"antisémite."* The term "anti-Semitism" was coined in 1879 in Germany by Wilhelm Marr, founder of the League for Anti-Semitism, and soon thereafter adopted in France.

†It was a year for leaning on Joan of Arc. In November, at the Hôtel des Sociétés Savantes, a Madame Marthe delivered a "philosophical and patriotic lecture" in honor of Joan of Arc. "The lecturer," according to a police report, "read a study of

Five days later, during the state funeral for Faure, Déroulède made good his threat. Joined by fellow members of the Ligue des Patriotes at the place de la Nation, he intercepted an infantry regiment returning from Père Lachaise Cemetery and, resplendent in the deputy's sash, twice exhorted the commander, General Gaudérique Roget, to lead a coup d'état, proclaiming: "Save France and the Republic! To the Élysée, General!" He was placed under arrest instead. The government did not treat the aborted coup as a naively quixotic gesture. Déroulède was tried for treason by the Senate (enough of whose members sympathized with the Ligue des Patriotes to acquit him, however).

Thereafter, events favored the revisionist cause, and men of stature—Jean Jaurès, René Waldeck-Rousseau, Anatole France—championed it eloquently. First, in March, the High Court of Appeals ruled that the charges preferred against Georges Piquart by General Zurlinden fell under common law rather than military jurisdiction; Picquart thus escaped a court-martial, much to the dismay of anti-Dreyfusards, who alleged in *La Libre parole* that the Jewish syndicate had obviously bribed key magistrates. Then, in May, the High Court ended its seven-month inquiry with a decision—rendered in solemn conclave on June 3, 1899—to annul the verdict of 1894 and summon Alfred Dreyfus before another court-martial. Attorney General Manau reported:

> The Court admits the new facts and new documents, etc., as being of a nature to establish the innocence of Dreyfus, Declares admissible and legally justifiable the demand for a revision of the judgment passed by the court-martial of December 22, 1894; SETS ASIDE and ANNULS the said judgment and dismisses the case and orders that Dreyfus present himself as the accused before another court-martial that it will designate in due course.

today's intellectuals, who do not measure up, in her opinion, to those of the Middle Ages. She evokes the philosophical ideas of Fénelon, Bossuet, Charles de Rémusat, and states that these philosophers always advocated healthy ideas that redounded to the glory of the nation."

On that same day, *Le Matin* published an interview with Esterhazy in which the psychopathic ex-major, while portraying himself as a mere pawn, admitted having written the bordereau. "This unexpected declaration left me flabbergasted," the interviewer confessed. "I cried out: 'What? It was you!' He said: 'Yes, I wrote the bordereau in the year 1894 on orders from Colonel Sandherr, my immediate superior. There was on the general staff an officer who committed treason. That officer was named Dreyfus. He had to be caught. And that is why I wrote the bordereau. As for the real reasons, I shall reveal them later.'" The collaborators were, in other words, serving justice by manufacturing the evidence they lacked against the man they "knew" to be a traitor. Like Henry's patriotic forgeries, theirs was a virtuous expedient.

More good news followed in the *mensis mirabilis* of June. On the tenth, former minister of justice Ludovic Trarieux hosted a large, celebratory dinner for Georges Picquart, against whom all charges were soon to be dismissed. On Sunday, the eleventh, thousands of republicans marched toward Longchamp singing the "Marseillaise." On the twelfth, the Chamber of Deputies, which passed a motion "to support only governments bent on vigorously defending the Republic's institutions," ousted Prime Minister Charles Dupuy after about eight months in office. He had been more than tolerant of nationalist hooliganism. And ten days later, René Waldeck-Rousseau, president of the Senate, formed a new government with ministers known mainly for their devotion to him and their sympathy for Dreyfus. "Waldeck, lawyer to Eiffel and Dreyfus, is presiding over the Witches' Sabbath, just to save an ignoble Jew," fumed *L'Intransigeant*. In *Le Gaulois*, the poet François Coppée wondered when the new Terror would begin.

Taken aboard a cruiser that slowly sailed across the Atlantic, Captain Dreyfus, feverish and bruised from clambering down ships' ladders, set foot on French soil at Port-Haliguen during the early hours of July 1, 1899. No one spoke. By lantern light a carriage drove the pariah between rows of soldiers to Quiberon, where gendarmes put him on a special train bound for the city in which his second court-martial would unfold: Rennes. At 6 a.m., Dreyfus entered yet another military prison. Finding himself ostracized shocked him. "The succession of emotions to which I was prey may be imagined," he later wrote.

> Bewilderment, surprise, sadness, bitter pain at a return to my country of that kind. Where I had expected to find men united in common love of truth and justice, eager to make amends for a frightful judicial error, I found only anxious faces, petty precautions, a wild disembarkation on a stormy sea in the middle of the night, with physical sufferings added to the trouble of my mind. Happily, during the long, sad months of my captivity I had been able to steel my will and nerves and body to an infinite capacity for resistance.

Edgar Demange and Fernand Labori gave him a detailed chronological account of what had happened since 1895. At that point, few people knew less about the Dreyfus Affair than Alfred Dreyfus, but trial transcripts and investigatory reports supplied by his two lawyers helped him catch up. He studied them with horrified fascination. When word spread of Dreyfus's landing in Brittany, people from all over France, Europe, and beyond extended fraternal greetings, Zola among them. Letters by the armful were delivered to his prison cell.

Even before Dreyfus's second court-martial began, there was drama to occupy the newspaper correspondents who gathered in Rennes. On Dreyfus's side, Demange and Labori clashed over legal strategy, with Labori wanting unconditional warfare and Demange favoring the government's proposal that Dreyfus accept a minority acquittal in exchange for a polite defense. On the other side, notable anti-Dreyfusards promised marvels and horrors, like barkers outside a carnival booth. General Mercier let it be known that the original bordereau, of which he possessed a photographic copy, had marginal notes in Emperor Wilhelm's own hand. Quesnay de Beaurepaire, the High Court of Appeals magistrate turned hatemonger, announced that the prosecution would conjure up a witness with categorical proof of Dreyfus's guilt. François Coppée declared that if war resulted from the publication of new documents revealing Dreyfus's servitude to Germany, then so be it: war might excite France's "rebirth and salvation." And for Maurice Barrès, who was interested less in justice than in the mythic underpinnings of a national identity, the trial at Rennes loomed as the battle at Armageddon. "The choice is clear," he wrote in *Le Journal.* "Dreyfus or our principal leaders. . . . Insult everything dear to us, the nation, the army. . . . Their plot is dividing and disarming France, and they are delighted by it." On this ultimate field of honor, "Aryans" who were pledged to save France from Mammon would confront the faithless, cosmopolitan Jew.

Dreyfus was brought before his seven military judges early in the morning of August 7, with spectators jamming a makeshift courtroom at the Rennes lycée. Fortified by stimulants, he walked stiffly to the witness box, like a toy soldier wound up for the occasion. "There was in everybody's eyes an amazement that reflected the difficulty they had in believing that this was really Dreyfus," Paléologue observed.

> From afar, from the mystery of his infernal island, this man, around whose head so much hatred and pity have gathered in the past five years, seemed, indeed, a symbol, an abstraction. For some he was a Judas, the personification of disloyalty; for others he was the personification of innocence immolated in the interests of a caste, the victim of a new Calvary, of the most monstrous crime ever committed against justice and truth. Now here he was, in flesh and blood, wearing a uniform, with gold braid on his sleeves, booted and spurred . . . but how worn and emaciated he was, to what a wreck of a human being he had been reduced! His arms were withered, his knees so thin that they seemed to pierce the cloth of his trousers.

Even Maurice Barrès felt twinges of compassion, but compassion did not visit the presiding judge, Colonel Albert Jouaust, who drove the white-haired, cadaverous thirty-nine-year-old defendant through a gantlet. The questioning was harsh in tone. Rebuked when he tried to explain himself, Dreyfus, always the self-disciplined soldier, most often gave terse replies—"No, my colonel," "Never, my colonel"— and left the impression with many sympathizers that he hadn't risen to the challenge, that, being incommensurate with his tragedy, he needed the buskins and mask of an ancient Greek for his star turn. One such sympathizer was Paléologue, who felt that Dreyfus's protestations of innocence somehow didn't ring true. "I recognized these pathetic phrases, having heard them on the sinister morning of the degradation," he wrote. "Then they had given me the inner certainty that Dreyfus was lying. Why, now that I *knew* that they were true, did they still sound so false to my ear? Why is this man incapable of putting any warmth into his words? Why in his most vigorous protestations can nothing of his soul pass through his strangled throat? There is something incomprehensible and doomed about him." "Incomprehensible" is a word that also appears in Maurice Barrès's caricature of the accused. "Sir Thomas Browne, the distinguished Englishman, often said that he would like to have known Judas Iscariot," he wrote, sounding very much like Proust's Baron de Charlus.

I have spent a month in Rennes and I know Dreyfus only as an enigma. In the Middle Ages, people evoked the deep mysteries of the unknown Southern sea by calling it "the Tenebrous Sea." That is what Dreyfus's soul is, a tenebrous sea. . . . Lord, scatter the shadows of this perfidious Jew so that I may see clearly. But wait! Is it not childish to speak of mystery when a foreigner does not react to events as one of us would? We are asking this child of Shem to display the handsome features of the Indo-European race. He is impervious to all the sensations excited in us by our soil, our ancestors, our flag, the word "honor."

Barrès's predilection for scientific ornament led him to draw a parallel between Dreyfus's dullness and the condition of "optical aphasia," which renders people incapable of seeing or understanding graphic signs. Like his cosmopolitan soul, the Jew's brain was un-French.

Yet another reporter observed that the accused should have been an actor playing Alfred Dreyfus—the Dreyfus aggrandized by national controversy. But when General Mercier mounted the witness stand in closed session several days later, it became clear that soldiers could in fact make accomplished thespians. With no new evidence to present, he spoke for four and a half hours, fluently recalling a mass of precise detail the better to validate dubious insinuations. Throughout this well-rehearsed speech he ignored Dreyfus, who sat nearby, and deigned to look at him only during his peroration.

> I have not reached my age without having discovered by sad experience that everything human is fallible. Consequently I have followed with keen anxiety all the arguments of the revisionist campaign. If the slightest doubt had crossed my mind, gentlemen, I should be the first to tell you so, for I am an honest man, and the son of an honest man. I should come before you to say to Captain Dreyfus: "I erred in good faith."

The last phrase sparked a moment of high drama, for no sooner had it been uttered than Dreyfus leaped to his feet like a galvanized corpse, shouting, "That is just what you should do! . . . It is your duty!" Momentarily taken aback, Mercier waited until the courtroom officer sat Dreyfus down, then said in conclusion: "But no! The certainty I have felt since 1894 has not undergone the slightest change; it has, on the contrary, been deepened by a more complete study of the case; and finally it has been strengthened by the futility of the efforts made to prove the innocence of the convict, despite the enormous sums squandered to that end!"

After a week, observers of every persuasion concurred that Dreyfusards enjoyed the advantage, Dreyfus notwithstanding. There were several reasons for this. Mercier's empty boast about absolute proof had detracted from his otherwise splendid performance. The very day he gave testimony, fifteen nationalists were arrested in Paris for plotting to overthrow the Republic. And on August 14, Rennes was shaken by the announcement that an attempt had been made upon Fernand Labori's life: someone (whom the police never identified) had shot him in the back as he made his way to court early that morning with Georges Picquart. Labori, who found the prospect of surrendering center stage more painful than the bullet near his spine, immediately declared that one week would suffice for convalescence. Sentiment went against nationalist fanaticism, and the lawyer received messages of encouragement. "Ah! My dear, my great and valiant friend," Zola wrote, "what joy when we learned this morning that you are out of danger. . . . We sat on pins and needles . . . fearing for your dear life but also for the cause of truth and justice, whose indispensable soldier you are. With you absent, all our worst premonitions sprang up again."

Those premonitions were richly justified. When Dreyfus's court-martial resumed in Labori's absence, Dreyfus himself became a supernumerary. The big lie gained credence, as general after general and minister after minister stepped forward, like undying spirits of vengeance, to reaffirm their belief that justice had been served five years earlier. Cavaignac lorded it over the courtroom. Wraithlike, with glaucous skin and eyes glistening inside deep sockets, he presented a brilliant summary of the general staff's case. "His imperious mask, his dogmatic self-assurance, the severity of his demeanor, gave him the air of an inquisitor addressing the Holy Office *de pravitate judaica*," Paléologue noted. "The members of the court listened in fascination; I could feel his indictment biting into their minds like acid eating into a copper plate." Equally effective was Cavaignac's former principal private secretary, General Gaudérique Roget, who argued that Dreyfus and Esterhazy had in all likelihood been collaborators. "With his very first words he established an ascendancy over the court," wrote Paléologue. "His martial figure, his crisp phrases, his loud voice, quickly put them all under his thumb; he might have been ordering them to carry out a maneuver."

On August 17 and 18, Georges Picquart spoke at length, but his elaborate testimony landed a glancing blow, and his appearance in civilian dress seemed to rob him of authority. Lesser military figures then paraded through the witness box with stories orchestrated by General Mercier, whose quarters in Rennes had become an anti-Dreyfusard salon. Where the Dreyfus camp featured quarreling coteries, anti-Dreyfusards marched as one and their monolithic organization trampled evidence underfoot. The return of Fernand Labori did not help. If one may believe Paléologue, who disliked him, his blustery, histrionic style of litigation made potential witnesses run for cover, even as it grated on the jury.

By August 24, Dreyfus's counselors were agreed that the verdict would go against him unless Germany could somehow be induced to betray Esterhazy and surrender the handwritten notes that had accompanied his bordereau. Soon thereafter, Waldeck-Rousseau himself solicited this material, but the effort failed. Fürst von Bülow, the German secretary of state for foreign affairs, explained that although "the current French government" was obviously "motivated by the proper point of view," German foreign policy had to consider the mutually hostile forces tearing France asunder. "The treatment Germany and specifically her monarch have received from the press is such that the imperial government feels compelled to avoid, insofar as possible, any further involvement of Germany and her emperor in [the Dreyfus Affair]. After all that has happened, we cannot expect that any fact or person thrown into the debate by Germany will be evaluated objectively."

On September 9, Edgar Demange delivered a poignant, well-wrought summation in which, after five hours of analysis, he entreated the judges to base their verdict on reasonable doubt. By way of rebuttal, the prosecutor, Carrière, urged them to heed their inner conviction, even if available evidence did not fully support it, saying: "The law does not ask jurors to explain how they have reached their beliefs. It does not prescribe rules to which they are obliged to submit their sense of the sufficiency of evidence. It asks them only one question, which comprises the full measure of their duty: are you deeply convinced?" In a final statement, Dreyfus protested his innocence once again. The judges deliberated for one and a half hours. At 4:45 p.m., with gendarmes having cordoned off the podium, Colonel Jouaust announced that a majority of five found the accused guilty, that it recognized "extenuating circumstances," and that the court-martial sentenced him to ten years in prison. While Demange wept, Dreyfus tried, as always, to remain impassive. Instantly, telegraph lines all over Europe and America were abuzz with news of the unspeakable outrage. Maurice Barrès was jubilant. "Public morality and national salvation wanted the condemnation of a traitor who was exploited by a faction," he wrote, regretting only that the "intellectuals," the "metaphysicians of sociology" most responsible for the

Affair would not be Dreyfus's fellow inmates. "If there are abuses and weaknesses in our general staff, if parts of our society have gone bad, if prejudices inhabit our national traditions, the remedial work must be undertaken with love, in the spirit of a paterfamilias managing the interests of his brood, and not with the audacity of these Neronian pedants and artists who cry: 'May a social order that will not bend to the ideal I have contrived for myself perish!' "

Two days after the sentence had been read, Joseph Reinach proposed in *Le Siècle* that the government grant Dreyfus an immediate pardon, "shredding a military judgment even before the ink has dried." A pardon, as he saw it, would be a first step toward full exoneration, and the idea took hold. With Mathieu Dreyfus's encouragement, Reinach approached Waldeck-Rousseau, who lost no time gathering support from his multifarious circle. It was difficult work, for at first conservative allies found the idea as objectionable as allies on the Left. General de Galliffet, who knew all about civil war from his experience of "bloody week," feared the predictable wrath of army brass and the Catholic bourgeoisie, while Clemenceau, noting that Dreyfus could be pardoned only if he withdrew his appeal, bridled at an implicit admission of guilt. But compassion prevailed, and on September 12, Mathieu carried the following text, which had been drafted by Jean Jaurès, to his brother in the Rennes military prison for him to sign:

> The government of the Republic grants me my freedom. It means nothing to me without my honor. Beginning today, I shall persist in working toward a reparation of the frightful judicial error whose victim I continue to be. I want all of France to know through a definitive judgment that I am innocent. My heart will be at rest only when there is not a single Frenchman who imputes to me the crime committed by another.

Everything—everything save the stubborn pride that had carried him through hell on earth—told Dreyfus to sign this defiant letter of submission: his broken health, his horror of a second ritual degradation, his yearning for family and freedom. So he signed it that day. It was made public one week later, after President Émile Loubet officially pardoned him at Galliffet's request.

IN JANUARY 1900 General Mercier ran for a seat in the Senate from Nantes, where one of five openly anti-Semitic newspapers, *L'Espérance du peuple,* asserted that conscionable Catholics should make it a point of honor to vote for him. He was elected.

Esterhazy was never condemned. He died in 1923 after spending most of the last two decades of his life in England writing articles for reactionary papers: first *La Libre parole,* then (anonymously) *L'Éclair.*

In 1906 the High Court of Appeals annulled the verdict of Dreyfus's court-martial at Rennes and restored him to the rank of captain, with seventeen years' seniority.

Émile Zola died in 1902. On June 4, 1908, his remains were transferred from the Montmartre Cemetery to the Panthéon. As ministers, generals, diplomats, magistrates, the president of the Republic, and the whole Dreyfus clan took seats around the catafalque, an orchestra played the funeral march from Beethoven's Third Symphony. Only one eulogy was delivered, in which Gaston Doumergue, minister of public instruction and fine arts, praised Zola for the exceptional courage he had displayed during the Dreyfus Affair. When President Fallières left to review a procession of republican guard, two shots rang out from within the group still seated. Horrified witnesses immediately realized that Alfred Dreyfus had been targeted. "[The president and official cortege] had just reached the entrance when I heard a muffled blast," Albert Clemenceau, Georges's brother, told *Le Figaro.* "I stepped over the bench that separated me from Mathieu Dreyfus and his neighbor. . . . Mathieu Dreyfus was holding the right hand of the man with a pistol, who had dropped his weapon but continued to fight furiously." Gendarmes arrested the would-be assassin, Louis Grégori, an editor at *Le Gaulois* and *La Presse militaire.* Dreyfus was found to have a bullet lodged in his forearm.

At his trial three months later, Grégori declared, "I appear before you because at my own risk I made a personal protest against the impudence of Dreyfus in glorifying the author of *La Débâcle* at the Panthéon and against the humiliation inflicted upon the army by being obliged to parade before a man who has twice been convicted by court-martial." He was acquitted by the jury.

CHAPTER VIII

THE BURNING OF THE CHARITY BAZAAR

I N MAY 1898, law students inspired by the Feast of Fools in Victor Hugo's *Notre-Dame de Paris* held a street fair to benefit the poor. On the boulevard Saint-Michel, where several hundred of them had rioted against Zola, Dreyfus, and Jews four months earlier, hundreds more marched behind blaring trumpets. The place de la Sorbonne replaced Hugo's place du Palais de Justice as a setting for the event. Parchment makers, public scriveners, silversmiths, pewterers, glass-blowers, barber-surgeons, and fortune-tellers plied their trades in stalls round about, making a medieval theme park of the Latin Quarter. At improvised theaters, mystery plays and farces were the bill of fare. If one found the Middle Ages enchanting, a reporter from *Le Temps* observed, the neighborhood had been transformed to one's taste.

Nostalgia for the city to which Baron Haussmann had laid waste extended well beyond the Latin Quarter. What remained of it became consecrated ground for Édouard Drumont, who in his first book, *Mon vieux Paris: Hommes et choses,* had led fellow Parisians as disgruntled as he was with foreigners thronging Paris for the Universal Exposition of 1878 on a tour of the city's time-worn neighborhoods.

The Carnavalet, a museum devoted to the history of the city, opened in 1880, when historical societies and journals were burgeoning. It's as if Haussmann the leveler had fathered a brood of antiquaries, many of whom would see their dreams come true at yet another Universal Exposition, in 1900. This one featured not only the grand Palace of Electricity but a miniature fifteenth-century Paris built on a long platform over the Seine, with half-timbered houses, turrets, a church demolished during the Revolution (Saint-Julien-des-Ménestriers), and taverns cluttering six thousand square meters between the Alma Bridge and the Eiffel Tower.* Employees in period costume mingled with visitors under a round tower forty meters high modeled after the medieval Louvre's fortifications, and a replica of Paris's first town hall, the Maison aux Piliers. Billed as Paris en 1400, the panorama was designed by the artist and scholar Albert Robida, who wrote an illustrated guidebook explaining the aesthetic or historical raison d'être of each structure.

Paris en 1400 was already a work in progress in May 1898, but people attending the law students' fair were less mindful of what Robida would unveil at the Universal Exposition than of another benefit with medieval décor that had taken place one year earlier, in May of 1897, and ended tragically: the Bazar de la Charité.

The bazaar was an annual event held under the auspices of Catholic high society. Two dozen charitable causes would unite for a week and be given booths staffed by fashionable ladies selling donated wares. Baron de Mackau, the royalist who had courted Georges Boulanger, served as chairman. In former years the bazaar had taken place on the rue La Boétie, near Saint-Philippe du Roule,

---

*On April 10, 1790, the Revolutionary assembly decreed the following: "Aside from Versailles, which must be preserved, other royal châteaux are now nothing more than gothic monuments, deteriorating and too costly to maintain. Perfect examples are the châteaux of Madrid, La Muette, Vincennes. As for Vincennes, . . . it behooves us, given the odious use to which arbitrary power put this ancient residence of our kings, to have it destroyed." The decree resulted as well in the demolition of some hundred churches, including Saint-Julien-des-Ménestriers, founded in the fourteenth century by the Brotherhood of Minstrels.

where much of *tout Paris* worshipped, but in 1897 it accepted a benefactor's offer of rent-free premises on a large triangular lot bounded
by the rue Jean Goujon and the Cours la Reine, a short walk from the
Rond-Point des Champs-Élysées. Construction began during the winter. The bazaar's organizers, who were quintessential products of their
age and class—steeped in the theater of salons, in opera, in the osten-
tation of liveried equipages, in the pomp of Catholic ritual—did not
countenance half measures. A pavilion eighty meters by twenty was
built to enclose the stage set of a medieval street. Wood-framed
cardboard-and-canvas inns with antiquarian signs hanging over the
entrance lined the pavilion's pitch-pine walls. Inside each one, count-
esses and marquises would, when the bazaar finally opened, flog their
virtuous merchandise for Catholic orphans, for the blind girls of
Saint-Paul, for parochial schools in the parish of Saint-Louis-en-l'Isle,
for Catholic workers' circles—for twenty-two *"oeuvres"* all told.
Sheltered by an immense canopy, visitors would bustle in their silk
and feathers from the "Gold Lion" to the "White Pelican" and "Spin-
ning Sow." They would refresh themselves at a buffet whose windows
faced the rear of a grand hotel on the Seine, the Hôtel du Palais. If
they sought entertainment, they would find it in a small, dark room
where M. Normandin, proprietor of a new contraption called the
"cinematograph," planned to have his projectionist, a man named
Bellac, show film of, among other unmedieval phenomena, an auto-
mobile race.

Completed six weeks early, the pavilion was put to holy use during
the Lenten season by the curate of Notre-Dame-des-Champs, who had
electric lights installed and staged mystery plays after dark. It opened
for business on May 3. Parish priests blessed it, as they did every year,
and ladies entered with purses at the ready (ladies greatly outnumber-
ing gentlemen on a Monday morning). The day's receipts, forty thousand francs, augured well for Catholic charities. On May 4, Monsignor
Cari, the papal nuncio, officially inaugurated the bazaar, thanking
its *"dames patronesses"* and visiting a booth at which the Duchesse
d'Alençon—a Bavarian princess whose sisters included Elisabeth,
Empress of Austria, and Marie-Sophie, Queen of the Two Sicilies—

held court. The crowd was such that most people were unaware of Monsignor Cari's brief visit. He had no sooner departed, shortly after 4 p.m., than disaster struck. By one account, Normandin's assistant, M. Bellac, came rushing out of the cinema, found Baron de Mackau, and told him frantically that the movie projector had burst into flames. Mackau begged him to keep quiet. He himself would somehow alert the more than sixteen hundred people present without causing panic. By all accounts, the baron did not immediately summon the fire brigade.

An investigation later determined that a match struck to light the projectionist's lamp had caused the fire, but Bellac may have failed to take an important precaution when operating the cinematograph, in which the intense glow produced by a controlled explosion of oxygen and ether inside an iron box containing chalk was focused through a lens at gelatin or celluloid film. Like solar rays passing through a magnifying glass, the process generated as much heat as light, making it necessary to introduce a coolant between the lens and the highly flammable film.* Some surmised that Bellac had forgotten that indispensable item.

Whether because celluloid flew in the air like bits of burning guncotton or because a match ignited etheric fumes, the silk canopy overhead caught fire. Moviegoers with clothes ablaze fled to the buffet and into the enclosed backyard, where hotel workers next door tore a window grille from its hinges and helped them inside. Fire spread from the projection room across the pavilion, trapping dozens at one end behind a curtain of flames. Pandemonium reigned. Visible from the rue Jean Goujon, between the pavilion's warped planks, were women inside scurrying madly to and fro as fire raced toward them feeding on the canvas, cardboard, wood, and silk. It consumed the entire bazaar in less than half an hour, time enough to yield material for innumerable stories recounted by the press. Cabbies rammed the wall with carriage poles. Typesetters at *La Croix,* which had its plant on the Cours la Reine, brought ladders. On the street side, rescuers

*The Lumière brothers had invented the movie camera two years earlier.

grabbed arms and legs poking through a space at ground level like limbs of the damned already halfway to hell. Some escapees found succor across the rue Jean Goujon, where Théodore Porgès, a banker whose wife would perish, had his town house and Alphonse de Rothschild his stable. General Munier, who looked like a human torch (and later died), plunged into the horse trough. Others did the same, or fell into the arms of stableboys who fetched blankets, sponges, and basins of water. Remarkably, at least sixteen hundred people came out alive. One hundred and seventeen, almost all of them women, did not. Their remains were found in culs-de-sac at either end of the pavilion and piled up behind bodies that lay in a cramped vestibule between two doorways set at right angles, blocking the exit. The dead, most of whom could be identified only by their teeth or by jewelry salvaged from the pavilion and displayed in an adjacent building, included the Comtesse de La Blotterie, the Comtesse d'Hunolstein, the Comtesse de Mimeral, the Vicomtesse de Saint-Périer, the Marquise de Bouthillier-Chavigny, Mlle Yvonne de Mandat-Grancey, Mme Albert de Vatimesnil, the Vicomtesse Maurice de Beauchamps, the Vicomtesse de Damas, the Vicomtesse Fernand de Bonneval, Vicomtesse d'Isoard de Vauvenarges, and the Duchesse d'Alençon. They were young mothers, dowagers, unmarried daughters. On May 5, *Le Figaro* described a hideous scene. "Impossible to determine, even on close inspection, whether this frightful debris belonged to men or women," wrote the reporter. "The guts of most bodies had spilled out. Some seem to have been decapitated . . . [I saw] a girl of ten whose entire upper torso was charred, the lower part almost intact; she was shod in very fine little boots and wore a collar the medallions of which bore the initials D.G. . . . Arms and legs contorted in one last, supreme paroxysm show how the unfortunate must have suffered, for they were not asphyxiated, as in other fires. They were literally burned alive." An older colleague assured him that the hecatomb was worse than anything he had seen during the Franco-Prussian War (having presumably missed the slaughter of Communards).

By the ninth, black crepe had been draped over Saint-Clotilde, Saint-Philippe-du-Roule, Saint-Thomas-d'Aquin, the Madeleine. Paris, where, day after day, hearses displaying coats of arms proceeded to Père Lachaise Cemetery and railroad stations, was a scene of funereal glamour. Reporters spread across the city to cover requiem masses at all the *hauts lieux* of aristocratic worship. And while these solemnities were taking place, people thronged to the rue Jean Goujon. The lot, around which a wooden palisade had been erected, became a pilgrimage site. *Le Gaulois* also noted that it had become a draw for tourists of American and English nationality. Carriages clogged every avenue leading off the Champs-Élysées and place de la Concorde.

During acrimonious times, in a capital perched on the edge of what would amount to civil war, the disaster, whose gruesomeness had been borne home in the brutally clinical reportage of several dozen journalists, occasioned a fortnight of shared grief. Due credit was given by *La Libre parole* to rich Jews—Alphonse de Rothschild and Théodore Porgès—for improvising hospital wards. At the metropolitan synagogue near the place des Victoires, the Consistoire Central Israélite de France commemorated all victims, not only Porgès's wife,

The smoldering ruins of the Charity Bazaar, 1897.

Photographs, May 1897, from the Charity Bazaar, printed in La Chronique Universelle. *One photograph is of the catastrophe's most illustrious victim, the Duchesse d'Alençon; another is of the window in the Hôtel du Palais behind the doomed pavilion, from which a grate was torn to rescue some hundred and fifty scorched escapees.*

Mathilde, in a memorial service conducted by France's chief rabbi, Zadoc Kahn. His sermon impressed one reporter as a "masterpiece of sober and deeply felt eloquence." The watchword in newspapers was "solidarity." It behooved wolves and lambs, kids and leopards to lie down with one another. "Some of our confrères allege that houses situated opposite the Bazar de la Charité kept their doors shut," wrote the right-wing Catholic *Éclair.* "We are happy to report that there is incontestable evidence of the opposite, that everyone showed admirable devotion, ineffective though it all too often proved to be, alas." Elsewhere, a socialist, M. Bourceret, insisted upon his compassion for the "100 families belonging to the class conventionally called the aristocracy." Etched in his mind was the horrifying sight of corpses laid out in rows at the Palace of Industry.* Only someone devoid of humanity could not grieve over "the shapeless, charred mass that, an hour earlier, had been flesh and bone belonging to amiable, sentient creatures who epitomized the felicities of a carefree, gilded life." He knew no proletarian visited by "evil thoughts of satisfied vengeance or egotistical indifference." One newspaper, *Le Jour,* organized a banquet to honor thirty-two Parisians who had risked their lives rescuing people from the blaze. A gymnasium on the rue Huyghens in Montparnasse was transformed into a banquet hall, with bunting, pennants, musicians, floral bouquets, and a six-course meal fully itemized on the paper's front page. Journalists of every persuasion joined politicians representing every party at the table of honor. "Social solidarity is certainly not an idle term," declared *Le Jour*'s editor in chief, André Vervoort. "Our unforgettable gala proved it. From all over Paris, from all classes, men and women, the rich and the humble, answered our summons, sensing that their presence would add to the luster of this celebration: just recompense for the courage and self-sacrifice exhibited on the rue Jean Goujon." The government awarded a knighthood in the Legion of Honor to a heroic cabdriver so badly burned that he couldn't eat or shake hands, who wore his work clothes to the banquet.

Peace was a mayfly. By mid-month, all the familiar antagonisms had been released from their tacit vow of solidarity, and shouted louder than ever. Bourceret the socialist, for example, couldn't contain himself. The magnanimous impulses he ascribed to proletarians only framed his contention that upper-class folk were, unlike the com-

---

*Situated where the Grand and Petit Palais now stand, this enormous structure survived from the Exposition of 1855. It was to be demolished soon afterward.

mon man, hard-hearted. "[We] did not, in this sad circumstance, follow the example always given by Catholics and conservatives whenever some misfortune afflicts republicans or free-thinkers, who offer ridiculous and ungracious interpretations, and, far from mourning with us, indulge in sarcasm on the fallacious pretext that our relatives or friends were the object of the well-merited wrath of divine justice." Articles in the conservative press describing the dead as having died "on the field of honor" and having been "heroines," or "victims of duty," irritated him. The "millionaire wives of nobility or of high finance" should receive due credit for their charitable activity and patronage of good works, he declared. "But how can you ask anyone to believe that in the ordinary course of things they place themselves in danger by going to some pavilion or art gallery and selling trinkets behind a counter." Those who placed themselves in danger were the firemen, the cabdrivers, the grooms, the typesetters, the nuns, the hotel workers, who came to their rescue.

Before long, rumors began to circulate, and gain credence, that the virtual absence of male victims told a scandalous story, that gentlemen at the bazaar, far from helping women, had trampled them underfoot in their own frantic attempts to escape. *La Libre parole*, whose editorial slant was populist rather than royalist, ran with the story.* One of its writers, Gaston Méry, attacked rich aristocrats collectively. "What did they do, these clubmen, these connoisseurs of horseflesh and frequenters of vernissages . . . who dined all year round in dinner jackets or waltzed in red dress coats with their incinerated partners? . . . The stories being told in salons around town are abominable. One would like to name names, but the right moment for that has not yet come. Let us merely cite the facts. A woman who tried to open a window was violently thrust aside and thrown to the

---

*It will be remembered that Drumont severely reprimanded inhabitants of the Faubourg Saint-Germain for continuing to socialize with the Rothschilds after the crash of the Union Générale. In 1896, at a "Christian Democratic Congress" organized by Catholic activists eager to build popular support for the Church (and counter socialism) with a program that emphasized economic justice, Drumont chaired the "anti-Semitic" section. He styled himself a "Catholic socialist."

ground, while fourteen men climbed through the window before her. A nun who had fallen near the cinema turnstile, after losing her wimple, was trampled by a herd of frenzied gentlemen. Wherever one looked, one saw men swiping their canes to clear a path for themselves." *Le Jour* elaborated upon this theme. Other papers followed suit. Thus did the aristocratic poltroon become a subject of popular verse—set to music, printed on broadsides, and sold in working-class neighborhoods for a penny or two. Typical was "Les Chevaliers de la Frousse" (The Knights of Cold Feet), subtitled "Conspuez les Snobs" (Jeer the Snobs).* Baron de Mackau, for one, would never lose the stigma of having survived. Held responsible for lax security, he was brought to trial in August, along with Bellac the projectionist.

While Théodore Porgès and Alphonse de Rothschild were given due credit after the conflagration, in subsequent weeks no good deed by a rich Jew went unpunished. Young Henri de Rothschild, who had reached the scene soon after fire broke out and noted the tardy arrival of medical assistance, proposed to organize an emergency ambulance service for the Champs-Élysées district under the auspices of *Le Figaro*. Himself a medical student, he would help finance the project. *La Libre parole,* claiming that a year earlier gamekeepers had killed a "French peasant" trespassing on Rothschild property and been rewarded for it, heaped scorn on him. "I knew perfectly well that Henri de Rothschild, grandson of the usurer peddler from Frankfurt-am-Mein, was given to occasional displays of black humor, but I did not think that he had been reduced to this degree of wretched insensitivity," wrote Raphael Viau.† A more remarkable outburst of anti-

---

*One of its stanzas went: *"D'ces joyeux fêtards / De notre aristocratie, / De ces joyeux fêtards / En vrais chevaliers fuyards / Se sont éclipsés / Frappant comme à l'écurie, / Se sont éclipsés / En piétinant les blessés."* ("These joyous merrymakers of our aristocracy, these joyous merrymakers, scampering horsemen, flicked out of sight, lashing out like horsemen in a stable, flicked out of sight, and trampling over the wounded.")

†Henri de Rothschild later practiced pediatric medicine, wrote prolifically, founded a famous children's hospital at Berck-sur-Mer, donated a large library of incunabula to the French nation, financed the research of Pierre and Marie Curie, and amassed the world's greatest private collection of Chardin paintings.

Semitism followed the announcement in *Le Figaro,* which had launched a public subscription to collect as much money for Catholic charities as might have been raised at the bazaar, that the Baroness Clara de Hirsch, widow of Maurice, had contributed, in her husband's memory, the staggering sum of 937,438 francs. The journalist Paul de Cassagnac greeted this news in his paper *L'Autorité* with an article titled "Trop, trop de juifs!" (Too many, far too many Jews!)* He thought it impertinent that a Jewess should have donated more money than all Catholic donors combined. And that *Le Figaro* praised "Israelites" as "the most generous, the most zealous" subscribers made him the more irate. Jews were not more generous or zealous, only richer. Had *Le Figaro* become the official organ of "cosmopolitan Jewry"? Did it not understand that the Jews' very virtues raised a presumption of guilt? Clara de Hirsch's gift was bad enough, but with the Baroness James de Rothschild joining fifteen "Christian women" on a committee appointed to divvy up the subscription fund, would Christians be expected to reciprocate? And how? By promoting Judaism? Did this promiscuity augur an entente cordiale between "Christ's faithful and descendents of the people who preferred Barabbas?" He found it all "much too fin-de-siècle," presumably meaning by "fin-de-siècle" a spirit subversive of all the discriminations on which a stalwart Frenchman (and Bonapartist) predicated his honor.

The most clamorous dispute broke out less than a week after the catastrophe. What provoked it was a memorial service at Notre-Dame cathedral on Sunday, May 9, attended by high government officials. *Le Temps* reported that it had the odor and all the accoutrements of a state ceremony. Paris itself, where sabbatical services did

---

*Among other hysterical evocations of Jewish ubiquity was Léon Chaine's in *Vers l'Avenir* (1896): "[One must not] close one's eyes to the existence of a Jewish Question, to a Jewish peril, to the fact that there are too many Hebrews, far too many Hebrews in circulation. The Jew is everywhere, he has invaded everything." According to the consistorial census of 1897, there were seventy-two thousand Jews in all of France—forty-five thousand residing in greater Paris, where the total population exceeded 2.5 million.

not usually inhibit commerce, closed down.* Over the portal of Notre-Dame hung a black pall with the silver initials "R.F." (République Française). To the right, near the equestrian statue of Charlemagne, stood a catafalque festooned with wreaths commemorating "the martyrs of charity." Members of the diplomatic corps, together with French officialdom, and relatives of the dead who did not object to pomp sat up front in Notre-Dame's crowded nave. Prince Radziwill, wearing the uniform of a Prussian general, represented the emperor of Germany, and Prince Galitzin the emperor of Russia. The bewigged lord mayor of London, carrying a huge mace, entered shortly before noon, preceded by two ushers in cocked hats and followed by English officers in fancy dress uniform. The presidential escort arrived soon afterward. Monsignor Richard, archbishop of Paris, welcomed Félix Faure, president of the Republic, and led him to a seat behind the balustrade of the choir. When the service concluded, Father Ollivier, a Dominican monk who often preached at Notre-Dame, entered the pulpit and delivered a sermon worthy of Joseph de Maistre, the early nineteenth-century fugleman of counterrevolution. *La Libre parole* printed it the next day.

Gentlemen,

Death is terrifying, even when it comes belatedly and cuts down lives that have long since ceased to flower. How much more terrifying is it when it reaps lives in full bloom, ripe with expectations of happiness, lives that have barely begun to enjoy the fruit of their labors.

But what can one say about these catastrophes the mystery of which vexes even the sturdiest spirits and breaks the best-tempered hearts? Just when joy is most legitimate, most pure for being born of charity, most vital because it is above all the joy of youth; when smiles are to be seen everywhere—in heaven, in nature, in hearts and on lips; amidst this bounty of hope, death bursts on the scene and with one swipe, the most horrible imag-

---

*A law making "Sabbath rest" obligatory had been repealed in 1880.

inable, lays waste to all this youth, all this beauty, all this strength, all this happiness! Its passage is so swift that one might doubt it ever came were it not for the ruin in its wake. . . .

Why did it happen? What design does such horror serve? Are we then in the hands of a blind power that smites without awareness of its blows, a power one can neither question nor curse to any purpose because it cannot hear and would not deign to reply?

Ah! God of Catholic France, God whom we call our Father, in whose tenderness we believe as much as in your justice, you are not capable of such wild rage. . . . Your hand strikes us for reasons we are allowed to understand so that we may freely subscribe to your design and make our tears the price exacted for your mercy.

O sovereign master of men and societies, no doubt you sought to teach this brazen century, in which man speaks incessantly of his victories over you, a terrible lesson. You turned against him the conquests of his science, showing it to be vain when divorced from yours. And you made of the torch he claims to have torn from your hands, like Prometheus, an instrument of reprisal. What created an illusion of life produced the horrible reality of death, and in the mournful silence that has enveloped Paris and France during the past four days, one hears an echo of the biblical admonition: "By the dead on your path shall ye know that I am the Lord."

But God does not take satisfaction in sterile vengeance. When he flagellates he means to save, thus allying the requirements of his glory and the imperatives of mercy. Mercy above all, for he is, above all, Eternal Love.

Having preferences is in the nature of love, and peoples are as much the objects of it as individuals. This has been made known to France by all the predilections that have marked her history and have made her misfortunes no less than her glorious successes palpable proofs of divine love. Eldest daughter of the Church of Christ, she follows the same path as her Mother and participates in the Church's ordeals. She is paid usuriously for the services she renders but is chastised without delay for her desertions or revolts, and all the more severely for having become so crucial to the accomplishment of the divine plan governing the conduct of peoples. Her place is at the head of humanity and not in its wake. It leads as the standard of Christ. . . .

Alas, in our times France, by deserting its traditions yet again, has deserved this punishment. Instead of marching at the head of Christian civilization, she has consented to follow as a servant or slave of doctrines as foreign to her genius as to her baptism. She has conformed to mores that reflect nothing of her proud and generous nature, and her name has become synonymous with folly and ingratitude to God. Synonymous as well, therefore, with misfortune, for God, not wanting to abandon her, could not but subject her to expiation [italics added].

Barely twenty-six years ago—and witnesses to your vengeance have not had time to forget it—you delivered a blow to France's head by demanding as victims of expiation and propitiation men of every rank and age, and you laid on the battlefield of a double war soldiers and priests, financiers and men of letters, artisans and magistrates, sailors and laborers. Certainly these were great and noble victims, whose sacrifice constituted the best claim to your justice and mercy—that of free consent, or even joyous acceptance, for all went to their deaths in a manner befitting this old nation, where the sword always evokes the Cross.

Therefore, when under the vaults of this basilica, which have long resounded to our cries of sorrow or enthusiasm, we deposited the bloody remains of all these venerable dead, around the coffin in which the martyred archbishop sleeps, we had every right to hope that your justice was satisfied and that your mercy opened doors to the future!*

---

*The martyred archbishop was Georges Darboy, archbishop of Paris, killed by the Communards. The "double war" was a reference to the Franco-Prussian War and the civil war that ensued.

Oh, God of our fathers, bless you for not having rejected their children and having believed them capable of paying the ransom of their fathers' faults. . . .

And yet, the expiation was not sufficient, and the holocaust lacked its purest victims! No doubt, they suffered cruelly, these proud, sweet women whose fathers, whose sons, whose husbands, whose brothers had shed their blood for the fatherland. They suffered all the more because they had hidden their tears at the hour of separation so as not to soften the warriors' mettle . . . but it seems that God did them wrong by requiring only tears, prayers, lessons, examples. In our country, from time immemorial, women have had virile hearts, and in the matter of sacrifice, their role has been as beautiful as that of their sons or spouses. It was therefore necessary that they add some of their own blood to the cup.

No doubt, many of the mourners who had served during the Franco-Prussian War, or lived through it, and had made the pilgrimage to Chartres in 1873, heard Monsignor Pie's sermon echoed in Father Ollivier's. Indeed, "twenty-six years ago" sounded very like something Pie had said—that "eighty years" of sinfulness required "honorable amends." The numbers were different, but they formed a symbolic equation condemning secular government and modernity. In 1793, the first Republic executed Louis XVI, piled aristocrats into tumbrels for conveyance to the guillotine, and devised a new calendar relegating the past to an "ancien régime." In 1871, when the Third Republic began its slow gestation, France again turned away from throne and altar. Aristocrats were martyred at the Charity Bazaar as they had been during the Terror, and "old France," in the form of a medieval stage set, burned to the ground.

Although *Le Temps* called Father Ollivier's sermon "unexpected," the paper should have known better, for a day after the fire *La Croix* admonished its readers, "We can only bend our heads beneath the hand of God whose will we must always bless. This immense hecatomb is a pure sacrifice expiating many faults." The anticlerical press was less timorous than *Le Temps*. One commentator observed that Father Ollivier bore a strong family resemblance to such ideological terrorists as Ravachol, Auguste Vaillant, and Émile Henry, all of whom had killed in the name of anarchism. Like these bombers, the Dominican held present-day society to be criminal, and, invoking a higher law, demanded that it burn for its crimes.

What exercised the Left even more than Ollivier's exploitation of grief to further the political and doctrinal ends of the Church was the fact that "R.F." hung over Notre-Dame's portal, that a Catholic service bore the imprimatur of the Republic. André Vervoort, who would hail the official separation of Church and State eight years later, conceded in *Le Jour* that it made great theater. "Catholic ceremonies are decorative beyond compare. When it comes to striking the imagination, stirring hearts, commanding respect, there are few stage directors the equal of priests wearing richly embroidered sacerdotal garments and singing, amidst intoxicating scents, the lugubrious *De profundis* and the stately *Magnificat* in candle-lit crypts." But why, he wondered, should Félix Faure, a professed Freemason, have lent himself to a demonstration of Catholic "mummery"? Was it not true that with few exceptions the bereaved, having already buried their dead, stayed away? Another paper, *Le Radical,* agreed. Details of Félix Faure's hour or two at Notre-Dame would astonish readers, wrote one editor, beginning with the sign of the cross made over him when he entered the cathedral.

Readers might not have been all that astonished. In any case, other news soon supplanted commentary on the fire. Summer came and went. In August 1897, a lower court found Armand de Mackau guilty of criminal negligence for not having summoned the fire brigade expeditiously and not acquainting the one employee hired to stand guard at the bazaar with the location of fire extinguishers. It fined him five hundred francs. In December, the fine was upheld on appeal. Despite the cloud hanging over his head, he continued to serve in the legislature as a deputy from the Orne district of Normandy.

The same tribunal sentenced Bellac the projectionist to a year in prison, and his assistant, who lit the fatal match, to eight months.

·   ·   ·

TIME AFTER TIME in fin-de-siècle Paris, the celebration of martyrs proved to be as much a virtuous cover for intolerance as the enthronement of Pity had been under Robespierre. Martyrs crowded the pages of *La Libre parole* and *La Croix,* where xenophobic nationalism and religious bigotry joined in decrying a Republic whose hospitality to foreigners, above all Jews fleeing Russian pogroms, betrayed the fatherland. (Most Catholic papers were prodigal of praise for *La Libre parole.*) Everyone agreed that France faced a demographic crisis. Its falling birthrate and multitude of foundlings dying in infancy caused widespread alarm. But of equal concern to Drumont, Father Bailly, and Barrès was the country's identity crisis. Might the Joans of Arc who perished at the Charity Bazaar have died in vain? Was Frenchness itself a potential martyr, and France—*"la vraie France"*— bound for extinction?* Jews, Freemasons, socialists, and anarchists were all to be combated "for the defense of civil society, of the fatherland and of the cross of Jesus Christ," declared Henri Delassus, a canon specially honored by the pope, in his diocesan weekly, *La Semaine religieuse.* "Anti-Semitism must be part and parcel of Catholicism." On December 11, 1897, *La Libre parole* announced that a deputy named Beauregard would soon submit a bill "vital to national interest and social security." Like Father Ollivier, M. de Beauregard portrayed postwar France ("the previous twenty-seven years") as a country increasingly alienated from itself. Those three decades had seen "Jewry, the cosmopolitan Element," pervade French officialdom. Should this rampant infiltration by agents of foreign powers continue, France, he warned, would "inevitably be erased from the map of Europe before the end of the twentieth century."†

---

*So thought the Union Nationale, an overtly anti-Semitic Catholic confederation. It declared in an electoral manifesto that France's social "demoralization," symptoms of which were the increase in crime, divorce, and unemployment, presaged doomsday.

†Earlier in the century, conservatives often vested their paranoid fantasies of invasion and alienation in foreign women entering Paris on the new railroad lines. The railroad was seen as the preeminent instrument of an erotic force that would, unless stringent

Legal barriers were needed against "those who dream of making France a second Poland" and establishing "a preponderance of the Israelite race." His bill would therefore forbid every individual of Jewish origin to occupy a post in any branch of French government. It also stipulated that any Frenchman born of foreign parents not be permitted, until the second generation, to exercise a function involving state control. *La Libre parole* declared it would not comment on legislation whose desirability was self-evident. Undermining a "completed civilization," the new mobility of things and people, whose perfect embodiment was the Jew, called for moats, for fences, for the consecration of a national taxonomy. Two years earlier, in 1895, when a deputy, M. Baudry d'Asson, demanded the annulment of the 1791 law that granted civil equality to Jews, the Chamber rejected his proposal by a mere 93 votes, 299 to 206.

THE FLOOD OF foreigners, the unproductiveness of wombs, the immolation of aristocrats, the triumph of secularism, the shaming of the army, all figured as portents of decadence in radical right-wing lamentation. How could a country sapped from within and deficient in numbers wage war, win back its lost provinces, and bulk larger among nations? To unreconstructed anti-Dreyfusards that was the question, and the future might never have looked bleaker to them than on August 30, 1898, when Colonel Hubert Henry killed himself after confessing that he had fabricated the documents used to incriminate Dreyfus. But, as we have seen, belief trumped evidence. The suicide soon inspired a fable according to which Colonel Henry, far from soiling his uniform, had, almost alone, braved a Jewish world con-

---

measures were taken, destroy the French family and substitute for France itself a mongrel pornocracy governed by queens all in the image of Manet's *Olympia*. Alexandre Dumas fils arraigned the railroad network in his play *Francillon*, where one character blames society's ills on "the invasion of women from abroad, the glorification of courtesans, the daily trainload of exotic mores that enter the city on every line, hastening local degenerations," and he reiterated this diagnosis in his preface to *La Dame aux camélias*. It was with deliberate irony that Marcel Proust placed words sympathetic to Dreyfus's cause in the mouth of a courtesan, Robert de Saint Loup's mistress Rachel.

spiracy.* Here was a would-be savior out of whose mortal wound flowed blood for a ritual of tribal self-affirmation, wrote Charles Maurras. "Every sacred drop . . . still runs warm wherever the heart of the nation beats." Like another Savior's blood, it gave life to the communicant, and communicants came forward in strength when funds—glorified as the "Henry Monument"—were solicited for Mme Henry's slander suit against Joseph Reinach.† Their names ran down long columns in *La Libre parole*. They were dukes, counts, and marquesses; senators and deputies; cooks and maids; shopkeepers and millers; tailors and clothiers; lawyers and doctors; priests in their hundreds and officers in their thousands. They were young Paul Valéry and Maurice Barrès.‡ "[He] didn't get the funeral his martyrdom deserved," Maurras declared. "Exponents of individual morality will call him 'senseless.' We call him heroic! Having taken seriously the

---

*This explanation was concocted the day after his death, in *La Libre parole*. "We shall not allow ourselves to be bothered by the Jewish press, which is doing its scalp dance. This brave officer, a simple soul and passionately devoted to the uniform, was crazed by the Jewish campaign. He thought he was doing a good deed in giving to his superiors the means of answering the furious attacks of the Syndicate, without leaking any documents injurious to national defense or compromising the intelligence service."

†The notice for a public subscription was titled "Colonel Henry's Devotion to his Country" and read: "When an officer is reduced to committing an alleged forgery in order to restore peace to his country and rid it of a traitor, that soldier is to be mourned. If he pays for his attempt with his life, he is a martyr. If he voluntarily takes his life, HE IS A HERO."

‡In 1899 a journalist named Pierre Quillard published a volume almost seven hundred pages long containing the names and comments of contributors. Here are examples: "From an antisemitic merchant in Boulogne-sur-Mer who hopes that the Hebes are blown away, above all Joseph Reinach, that unspeakable son-in-law and nephew of the Panama swindler one of whose victims I am." "From a cook who would rejoice in roasting Yids in her oven." "Long live Christ! Love live France! Long live the Army! A curate from a little very antisemitic village." "One franc to pay for the cord that hangs Reinach." "Joan of Arc, help us banish the new English." "Two francs to buy a round of drinks for the troopers who will shoot Dreyfus, Reinach, and all the traitors." A resident of Baccarat wanted "all the kikes" in the region—men, women, and children—thrown into the immense ovens of the famous crystal factory. Another contributor longed, prophetically, for the day that a "liberating boot" would appear over the horizon.

idea of national salvation . . . he believed at first that others thought as he did. Instead, he crashed against a wall of silence. His impromptu judges, who have the mental scope of process servers, reckoned that legality and private morality govern everything, oblivious as they are of the fact that for [the elect] whose consciences are burdened with certain very broad obligations, there exist . . . 'unwritten laws,' a higher, more rigorous, more extensive sphere of morality." Maurras's language was not fundamentally different from that of Joseph de Maistre. A hundred years earlier—long before "collective uncon-scious" became a convenient term for it—de Maistre enunciated the precept that "nations have a general overriding *soul* or character and a true moral unity which makes them what they are." Their happiness and power, in his view, hinged on the stifling of "individual reason" and the vesting of absolute authority in "national dogmas, that is to say, useful prejudices."*

*In February 1899, Count Édouard de Lur-Saluces, a confidant of the Duc d'Orléans, advised him to embrace anti-Semitism as a useful means of broadening support for the royalist cause. "One cannot deny that today anti-Semitism is becoming ever more popular. . . . We should turn to our advantage a movement gathering strength day by day. The king should march ahead of the crowd, boldly and resolutely [articulating] its sentiments." Four years later, the Duke, and Boulanger's former patroness the Duchesse d'Uzès, helped to finance the launching of a radical right-wing workers' fed-eration called les Jaunes, which, like Boulangism, eventually collaped under the weight of multiple allegiances.

CHAPTER IX

Two Banquets

Nothing collapses more quickly than civilization during crises like this one [1848]; lost in three weeks is the accomplishment of centuries. Civilization, life itself, is something learned and invented. Bear this truth well in mind: Inventas aut qui vitam excoluere per artes. *After several years of peace men forget it all too easily. They come to believe that culture is innate, that it is identical with nature. But savagery is always lurking two steps away, and it regains a foothold as soon as one stumbles.*

—Sainte-Beuve, quoted by George Eliot in
Impressions of Theophrastus Such.

Ernest Renan wrote "L'Avenir de la science" during the 1848 revolution but did not publish it until 1890, two years before his death, when it ripened into a document of greater relevance than he could have foreseen. A feeling that the book's youthful fervor might compensate for its flaws and serve an embattled cause persuaded him to rescue it from oblivion. "I thought that it might provide consolation and support to a few young souls enamored of truth and beauty, struggling, as all distinguished minds must struggle, to discover the ideals by which they will live," he wrote in a prefatory letter. "I also wanted to profess my profound faith in reason and the modern mind at a time when so many depressed souls are collapsing into the arms of those who revile critics and wish that the world were more ignorant."

One notable fugitive from modernity was the novelist Joris-Karl Huysmans, who had begun literary life as Émile Zola's sword bearer only to renounce the scientific aspirations of the naturalist movement and seek richer pasture for the soul in religious mysticism. Huysmans followed a well-trodden path. While priests tended increasingly meager flocks, charismatic priests who specialized in the conversion of "distinguished minds" flourished. To Zola's way of thinking, these conversions suggested a revival of the Romantic *mal du siècle*. "Pessimism twists people's guts, mysticism fogs their brains. The ghosts we routed with shafts of light have returned, the supernatural has armed itself again, the spirit of legends sees an opportunity for conquest in our weariness and anguish."

The charge of "bankruptcy" or "decadence" was commonplace among writers disposed to portray science as a small, desert kingdom bordering the wide, lush expanse of the "unknowable." Science had spent itself, they cried. It didn't support life. Baffled by man's origins and ends, incapable of providing the basis for a moral doctrine and the remedy for social ills, it had nothing to offer but trivial tokens of well-being. Paul Bourget, the author of a thesis-novel called *Le Disciple* (which struck a discordant note during the Exposition summer of 1889), exhorted French youth to respect the enormous *part de Dieu* in human affairs. "Even Littré,"—positivist though he was—"spoke . . . of the ocean of mystery beating against our shore. . . . If you are told that behind it lies emptiness, abysmal darkness and death, have the courage to retort: 'You do not know.' "

A more persistant advocate of the unknowable was Ferdinand Brunetière, who held forth from his director's lectern at *La Revue des deux mondes*. "Not all that long ago, erudite incredulity was generally taken to be a mark, or proof, of superior intelligence and strength of mind," he wrote in 1895, in "Après une visite au Vatican," an article auguring his conversion. "The non-believer didn't doubt the importance of 'religions' in history, nor, above all, the importance of 'religion' or of 'religious feeling' in the development of humanity. . . . But, along with Auguste Comte, he nonetheless regarded 'the theological state' . . . as an infantile phase in the life of the mind. 'Religions,' according to a recently published book, 'are the purified residue of superstitions. The value of a civilization is in inverse proportion to its religious fervor.' "

What entitled science to this pride? Brunetière asked. "In fact, the physical or natural sciences had promised us that they would banish 'mystery.' Not only have they not banished it, but we clearly see today that they never will. They are unable properly to pose the only questions that matter: those that bear upon the origin of man, the law of his conduct and his destiny. The unknowable surrounds us, it envelops us, it clasps us."* Hence, man's "need to believe," the most cogent proof of which, he asserted, lay in the fervor of modern nonbelievers. "Whoever has shaken off the authority of legitimate belief has become not an unbeliever . . . but a fanatic. And every single doctrine of our day has triumphed over religion only by assuming the guise of one. Examples are legion, for what have men not made idols of in this waning century? They have idolized Science, and Progress."† During the

---

*Brunetière was prominent among conservatives repelled by the sordidness, pessimism, and scientific pretentions of Zola's hugely influential *Rougon-Macquart* who found an antidote to French naturalism in the Russian novel. Between 1883 and 1885 *La Revue des deux mondes* published articles on Turgenev, Tolstoy, Dostoyevsky, and Gogol by Melchior de Vogüé. They appeared as a volume, *Le Roman russe,* in 1886 and make much of the primitive Christianity that humanizes Russian realism with a "breath of pity." This "breath," wrote de Vogüé, "is the spirit, the certain and impenetrable element that moves and envelops us, that *disconcerts all our explanations. . . .* Clay is what belongs to the realm of positivist [scientific] knowledge; it is what we learn about man in a clinic or a laboratory. It will take us quite far, but so long as one doesn't infuse that breath, one hasn't created a living soul: *the point at which we cease to understand is the point at which life begins*" [italics added].

†Brunetière might have made a more provocative case for the resemblance of cultural foes by quoting on the one hand Joseph de Maistre, a deep-dyed Catholic, and on the other Hippolyte Taine, an exponent of scientific positivism. Taine, who maintained that nations have an essential character or soul shaped by three forces—"*race,*

past twenty-five or thirty years, a doctrine "passing for a religion of matter" had reigned supreme as "positivism" in philosophy and as "realism" or "naturalism" in art and literature. "It descends directly from the eighteenth century—the 'great century,' according to some, but certainly the least Christian, the least French in our history." If he read the omens right, its day was done. France, Brunetière prophesied, would experience a rebirth of "idealism."

Had Renan still been alive, he might have challenged "Après une visite au Vatican." The response to it came instead from his lifelong friend Marcelin Berthelot, a chemist of great distinction and a political figure of note. Napoléon III's government had created a chair for him at the Collège de France. Some years later he became permanent secretary of the Academy of Sciences, succeeding Louis Pasteur. The great tide of republican sentiment during the early 1880s swept him into the Senate, where prime ministers sought him out for their cabinets, first in education, then in foreign affairs.* Berthelot, who during the 1860s had often dined at Magny's restaurant with Sainte-Beuve, Flaubert, Renan, George Sand, and Hippolyte Taine, did not suffer Ferdinand Brunetière gladly. The critic's argument that science had never fulfilled its metaphysical promises was dismissed as humbug. Had any promises made since the seventeenth and eighteenth centuries by a natural philosopher in the name of science not been kept? To be sure, mankind continued to eat the bread of affliction, but, unlike Scripture, which counseled resignation, science had reduced the sum of the world's misery and injustice by arming sighted mortals against blind fate. One could not shape one's course in life by points as far outside the human compass as "origins" and "ends." While science acknowledged these problems, it went no further. Barring no

---

moment, milieu" (race, the historical moment, the material environment)—would not have taken exception to de Maistre's dictum, "The answer to all questions about the *nature* of man resides in history; the philosopher who would demonstrate what man must be by a priori arguments, does not deserve consideration." This dictum also chimed with a basic postulate of doctrinaire nationalists.

*In the Third Republic, members of the lower house, the Chamber of Deputies, elected a certain proportion of the Senate to life terms. Such was the case with Berthelot.

horizon, it did not pretend to have penetrated the essence of things. Quite the contrary—it willingly admitted the growing incertitude of its ideal constructions.

No one was surprised to hear Berthelot enumerate the intellectual and material benefits of science. Where he belled the cat was in arguing for secular morality, maintaining that mankind had betrayed itself by conferring transcendent authority upon laws of its own creation. To "objectify" those laws, it had deified them. And deification promoted a spirit of intolerance nicely summarized in the maxim "Truth on this side of the Pyrenees, error on the other." The "man of our times," he declared, "finds deep within his own conscience the notion of good and evil, and the feeling of duty that Kant called the categorical imperative." Kant, the pillar of lycée philosophy courses under the Republic, was singularly loathed by men who saw little good flowing from the Enlightenment—by Brunetière, Barrès, and others sworn to a closed world in which selfhood was collective, the collective soul was inalienably French, and salvation superseded inquiry.* "Both history and mental pathology," he warned, "show that nations and individuals who have adopted mystery and divine inspiration as fundamental guides have soon found themselves cast into material, intellectual, and moral ruin."

Berthelot's essay "La Science et la morale" appeared in the *Revue de Paris* magazine on February 1, 1895. Later that month, an organization called the Union of Republican Youth made plans for a "Banquet of Science" honoring Berthelot. It took place on April 4 in a restaurant near the Porte de Vincennes large enough to accommodate the eight hundred sixty people whose presence was recorded by the Grand Orient of Freemasons.

---

*In an article titled "Enemies of the French Soul," Brunetière wrote, "How shall we defend our patrimony of power and glory, with what arms, if we begin by fighting amongst ourselves? If we work with our own hands to . . . destroy this hereditary communion of feelings and ideas that is the 'French soul'?" The most dangerous enemies, he went on to say, were the "enemies within"—intellectuals, individualists, "internationalists," and freethinkers who "in a desperate assault upon all our traditions" confuse "freedom of mind and independence of heart."

Everything about the banquet was large. Fifty-eight men (fin-de-siècle banquets were almost always exclusively masculine affairs) made up the honorary committee. They included eminent scientists and physicians, historians, sculptors and painters, politicians, writers, jurists, anthropologists. Raymond Poincaré, the minister of education, sat with Auguste Rodin, Émile Zola, and Henri Brisson, the president of the Chamber of Deputies. Eleven honored guests spoke. Having sounded the keynote in "La Science et la morale" (reprints of which were on sale for five centimes), Berthelot heard them all proclaim the need to inculcate moral values based not upon dogma but upon a reasoned, humane understanding of society. Science was the guiding light; religious fanaticism was the torch that had set fires under Michel Servet and Giordano Bruno. In his own speech, which *Le Temps* printed on its front page, Berthelot honored eighteenth-century philosophers responsible for freeing thought from the "oppressive yoke" of theocracy, monarchy, and feudalism. "[Out of their writings] came the French Revolution," he declared. "Allow me, gentlemen, to insist upon the fundamental character of that Revolution. Many revolutions have occurred in the last few centuries, but none . . . proclaimed, in the acts that constituted them, their independence from religious ideas of every kind. Not one proclaimed its desire to seat human societies on the solid, definitive foundation of science and reason." Normally reserved, Berthelot held nothing back, as if determined on this very public stage to slay once and for all the dragon in clerical black.* And Zola, when his turn came, lent Berthelot a vigorous hand, inveighing in particular against the *Index librorum prohibitorum,* the papal index on which most of his own works had been placed. This list was, he declared, an infallible guide "to everything new, bold, and generous" engendered by the human spirit. "Ah! Little men, cramped brains, politicians armed with paltry expedients, dogmatists at bay, authoritarians reheating old, unreal-

---

*But on more than one occasion, Berthelot defended the practice and principle of religious tolerance in the secular state. "One must guard against the exclusion of religious practices degenerating into provocation or the persecution of sincere feelings whose genuineness and moral stature cannot be doubted."

ized dreams, science will pass through and blow you away like dry leaves."

A PHOTOGRAPH OF Zola taken five years later, at the Universal Exposition of 1900, shows him with a cane tucked jauntily under his arm and his top hat brushed to a sheen, looking like a vindicated impresario. His exile was over, Dreyfus was free, republicans were firmly in power. Catholic teaching orders knew that if the Left had its way, they would face expulsion sooner rather than later. For French who set store by Gambetta's admonition *"Le cléricalisme, voilà l'ennemi!,"* prospects of a divorce between Church and State signaled the dawn of an enlightened era. And at the Exposition, enlightenment had its shrine in the Palace of Electricity. As spectacular as the fireworks Mark Twain admired during the Exposition of 1867 were the electric lights playing over Paris that summer. Searchlights illuminated the Champ de Mars. They turned the Seine violet, pearl gray, blood-red. "Electricity was gathered, condensed, transformed, bottled, spooled out like thread," wrote the novelist Paul Morand. "It was discharged into water and onto fountains, let loose onto roofs and into trees. . . . It was the religion of 1900." It became a servant of art as well, coloring the silk veils Loie Fuller swirled around herself at the Folies Bergère.

Unreconstructed anti-Dreyfusards who used "internationalist" as a slur treated this World's Fair no less rudely than they had its immediate predecessors, and perhaps more so, for Germany, excluded from two postwar fairs, made its presence felt at this one in exhibitions of industrial might and scientific prowess. On display were its optics, its chemistry, its fabrics, its shipbuilding. While the main German pavilion looked innocuously rustic, German dynamos and cranes scaled to a race of Brobdingnagians dwarfed everything around them at the Galerie des Machines. As a courtesy—but in effect adding insult to injury—Emperor Wilhelm lent three of his favorite Watteaus to the exposition's salon: *L'Embarquement pour l'île de Cythère, L'Enseigne de Gersaint,* and *Les Comédiens.*

The centerpiece of the Exposition Universelle of 1900, the Palace of Electricity, surmounted by a statue of "the Genius of Electricity," 265 feet above the Champ de Mars. It was described as "Louis XV" in style.

Despite his umbrageous view of anything international on French soil, Charles Maurras arranged a dinner honoring Maurice Barrès at the Restaurant International du Trocadéro in July. Arrangements would have been more elaborate if Barrès hadn't felt that a full-blown banquet lacked the gravitas appropriate to dire times. Three years earlier, he had published two volumes of his trilogy *Le Roman de l'énergie nationale*—*Les Déracinées,* which describes the undoing of several young lycée graduates misguided by their Kantian professor of philosophy, and its sequel, *L'Appel au soldat* ("The Soldier Summoned"), which unfolds within the larger narrative of General Georges Boulanger's meteoric rise and fall. Maurras therefore called this event "The first dinner of the *Appel au soldat,*" and may have had in mind Boulanger's conquest of Kabylian redoubts when he chose to meet near the Trocadéro—a neighborhood transformed into an Arab village for the Exposition. "*L'Action française* believes in the virtue of iron," he wrote. "It has never ceased to urge upon contemporary

France the necessity for energetic 'intervention.' When the first orga-
nizer of nationalist doctrines established this obvious necessity in a
true masterpiece, we could not but wish to thank him." Paul Bourget,
a member of the Académie Française, toasted Barrès as follows:

> Flaubert used to say, during the anguished aftermath of the war
> of 1870: "We are all suffering the sickness of France." You said
> the same thing to yourself when at age twenty you endured the
> crises which you evoke so movingly in *Sous l'oeil des barbares*
> and in the first few chapters of *Les Déracinés*. You understood
> that your malaise was not a purely personal matter, that the
> country was sick *in* you, as it is in all of us, and with marvelous
> lucidity you pinpointed, if not all the causes of this malady, at
> least the most immediate and powerful.

The most immediate and powerful cause of France's decline, he went
on to say, was the 1789 Revolution, which enshrined an ideology that
separated the French from their dead.

> For a century now France has disregarded the great law of con-
> tinuity that expects each generation to consider itself the
> usufructuary of a treasure acquired through the good will of
> ancestors and to leave its heirs more than it received. Once per-
> suaded of this truth, you sought to comprehend yourself, in your
> own words, as "one instant of something immortal," to "root"
> yourself once again in your past, in your soil, in that Lorraine
> from which your family sprang.

Barrès then addressed his confrères, preaching a gospel of visceral
particularism reminiscent of the neo-Romantic mythology propagated by *völkisch* ideologues in Germany.*

---

*Barrès himself considered the Revolution the true progenitor of nationalism; abolish-
ing "historical contracts" and joining battle with the armies of Europe, it freed the
French to cohere as a Folk. Maurrasian royalism and Barresian proto-fascism found
common ground in their antipathy to everything that went by the name of cosmopolitan.

Certain words—*France, Patrie*—evoke in certain men, you and I among them, so many anciently connected ideas that they rustle in the mind like leaves in the forest. They cannot be heard by people lacking these associations. Intelligence has nothing to do with it: however swiftly their minds work, they cannot feel as we do. A single instinct, I would venture to say the same physiology, defines us. . . . How proud I am to receive the approbation of minds such as yours for the idea of "rootedness," for this cult of "earth" and of the "dead."

Last to speak was Henri Vaugeois, a cofounder of the *Action française* periodical, who contended even more emphatically than Maurras and Bourget that republicanism was the disease sapping France's vital spirit, and bloodshed was the cure. "All of us here agree, I hope, on the morality, the legitimacy of iron. We have no hypocritically puritanical objections to it, do we? It seems to us that one has the right to save one's country despite itself. It seems to us that there have always been instances of virtuous violence in history, and that beating a sick man bloody is better than letting him rot."

Vaugeois's brutal valediction echoes the commencement address given by Father Didon at the Collège d'Arcueil in July 1898: "We must equip ourselves with coercive powers, we must not hold back, we must brandish the sword, we must smite, terrorize, cut off heads, impose justice. Armed force thus employed is no longer brute strength but sainted energy put to beneficent use." In its oratory, militant Catholicism made common cause with revanchist nationalism. At Lourdes, before the legislative elections of 1901, pilgrims were exhorted by a Jesuit priest to "wield the sword, the electoral sword that separates the good and the wicked. . . . At the next elections there will be two candidates, Barabbas and Jesus Christ. . . . Will you vote for Barabbas?" And the pastoral letter issued by the archbishop of Paris asserted that voters had to choose between a society governed by the word of the Gospel and a society misled in the name of progress by "anti-Christian sects proclaiming the absolute independence of human reason."

Action française and the Church would eventually clash. But in

1900 it seemed obvious to many citizens who leaned toward Barabbas that nationalism was, as one prominent republican put it, "the mask of the eternal clerical enterprise." Articles in *Action française* and in *La Croix* bear him out. When in the spring of 1898, Joseph Valabrègue, a Provençal Jew tarred by the brush used against his brother-in-law Alfred Dreyfus, indignantly sent professions of patriotism to *La Croix,* the paper's official mouthpiece replied: "I am French, the son of a Frenchman; I shall live and die as such. But you, you are a Jew, the son of a Jew and you will die a Jew. . . . You know full well that all through history—from Judas, who sold his God, to Dreyfus, who sold France—your race has bred so much treason, iniquity, and rapacity that you must at all costs hide your name, as the escaped convict hides his red bonnet." In this ontological court, rules of evidence did not apply. Charles Maurras praised Roman Catholicism as a "temple of definitions" offering people blessed asylum from that bane of human consciousness—"uncertainty."

SEVEN MONTHS AFTER the Banquet of Science, Marcelin Berthelot was appointed minister of foreign affairs in the cabinet of Léon Bourgeois, a future Nobel laureate. He served for six months—long enough to observe European imbroglios from up close (and to put a naval squadron in Eastern European waters by way of protesting a Turkish massacre of Armenians) but not to implement the policies of peaceful arbitration with which Bourgeois's name became associated. In 1900, after receiving the Royal Society of London's highest scientific award, the Copley Medal, Berthelot was elected to the French Academy.

A greater source of satisfaction than the honors bestowed upon him was the Republic's final thrust toward separation of Church and State. It began in 1901 with measures against religious orders and conventual communities (*"congregations"*). For the second time since 1880—but in even greater earnest—the legislature required them to apply for residency permits, and ended up granting very few. Unlike the 1880 legislation, the 1901 law applied to men and women alike. There were over sixteen thousand schools run by religious orders.

Within a year thirteen thousand had been closed. Tens of thousands of monks and nuns left France, with Augustinians of the Assumption leading the exodus. Those who didn't were spared only on the condition that they no longer preached to laymen or taught children except within the strict confines of Bible class.

Prime Minister Émile Combes, a former seminarian—and physician—whose animus against the Church was deaf to diplomacy, justified this purge when he spoke at the unveiling of a statue of Ernest Renan in Renan's hometown of Tréguier. Six thousand troops (two for every resident) had been sent to preserve order if devout Bretons should threaten to riot. The prime minister's fellow speakers were Marcelin Berthelot and Anatole France. "We freethinkers who regard Renan as an example," Combes declared, "do not take shelter from the doubts raised by our intellect behind dogma. The light of reason is our beacon. But neither—unlike the Catholic priest anathematizing dissent from his bully pulpit—do we impose upon others our rule of conduct and way of thinking." His quarrel, he insisted, was not with religion so much as with its ministry. He had no intention of trespassing upon the private world of heart and conscience in which religion made its rightful home. On the contrary, he would, if need be, defend it against intruders. "All we ask of religion—because we are entitled to do so—is that it keep within its temples, that it limit its instruction to the faithful, and that it refrain from unwarrantable interference in the civil and political domain." It was clerics who had brought the mailed fist of the Republic down upon themselves by attempting to influence "the direction" of society during the Dreyfus Affair and since the captain's pardon. "Nothing stops their encroachments: neither old laws nor new ones." A *New York Times* correspondent reported that Berthelot and Anatole France were greeted with hostile cries, "the last named also with shouts of '*À bas Dreyfus!*' "*

---

*The *Times* correspondent also had this to say: "[Renan's] famous 'Prayer upon the Acropolis' is the most exquisite piece of pagan psalmody in modern prose. It was recited on the occasion of the unveiling of his statue at Tréguier, and the fact of its being a prayer created a little confusion in the perfervid mentality of the Breton bigots."

One year later, at Auxerre in Burgundy, Combes announced that his government would bend all its energies toward separating Church and State. It was not enough to have expelled religious orders from France and removed crucifixes from courtrooms, to have forbidden soldiers from associating in religious circles and priests from taking the competitive examination (or *"agrégation"*) for posts on the faculty of lycées and universities. Napoléon's treaty with the Church, the Concordat, had finally to be dissolved. "The Republic of 1870 rid France of the last remnants of monarchy; now we must free her once for all from bonds that still tie her to organized religion," Combes declared.

> Because our administration has obstinately pursued this goal, it has been hounded by partisans of every reactionary color: by royalists whose representative [Philippe d'Orléans] whiles away the time in impotent intrigues abroad; by Bonapartists lying in wait behind some barrack house for the chance to pull off a *coup de force;* by nationalists, who should be ashamed, but are not, of prostituting patriotism to one-man rule; by clerics, the most insidious and redoubtable of all, for linking the other three.*

Combes had long since fallen from power when, on December 9, 1905, after months of heated debate, the Assembly passed a Law of Separation. Catholicism—"the religion of most French," as the Concordat styled it—no longer had any official status. It lost its emoluments but gained the freedom to serve a more congenial master. Where Paris had held sway over the French episcopate, Rome was now empowered to do and deny.

As for Marcelin Berthelot, science fully occupied him until his health began to fail. He died on March 18, 1907, and was interred in

---

*The memoirs of Alphonse Daudet's militant right-wing son Léon illustrate the easy alliance—and common anti-intellectualism—of reactionary modes. "I was not yet a royalist in 1897. *L'Action française* was yet to be founded. But I was already nationalist and clerical, thanks to my good old Nîmois blood, which proved stronger than the adulterated instruction [I received in public schools] and the influence of the literary and political milieux."

the Panthéon, a year before the State transferred Émile Zola's remains from Montmartre Cemetery.

LITERATURE OF A later period, notably Roger Martin du Gard's *Jean Barois* (1913) and *Les Thibault* (1922–40), in which families split apart over Dreyfus and religion, belie the notion that secularism held absolute sway after 1905. No victory was definitive. The battle raged wherever Catholicism and antirepublicanism had strong constituencies. In *La Grande pitié des églises de France,* Maurice Barrès chronicled his efforts to rescue village churches orphaned by the Law of Separation. Dilapidated houses of worship were doomed (largely because Pope Pius X, in rejecting the law outright, denied the Church recourse to an arrangement that would have protected its material estate). Art and liturgical objects would be destroyed, auctioned by municipalities, or, if judged to be of museum quality, confiscated by the State. "This noble debris would not arrest people's attention in a Paris museum, while here its value is inestimable," Barrès wrote of a little church in Lorraine unremarkable except for some sixteenth-century stained glass, four exuberantly sculpted Renaissance columns, and bas-reliefs that pictured scenes of the Passion. "Its value resides in its linking the mystical and the classical. It was born of this canton's marriage to Catholicity." The *enracinés,* the "rooted," lived under laws imposed by a secular republic, but their inner and *inborn* government could not be separated from "Catholicity." "The laws of our mind won't comply with the whims of legislators. We Lorrainers have been set upon by two hostile bands: Prussians who are destroying our language, and sectarians [the government in power] who would destroy our religion, that is, the language of our sensibility." Neither one of the aliens would ultimately prevail, he asserted. "When the steeples have collapsed and the holy statues been relegated to the company of Gallo-Roman Dianas and Mercuries in the dusty halls of our departmental museums, a new generation will come forth, who will want to resurrect the temples of the soul in our French hamlets."

Barrès's more primitive fantasy was that the new generation would insist upon slaking the thirst of the dead with libations of blood.

Blood was needed to reconsecrate France, to *regenerate* it, to liberate the energy held in thrall by arid rationalists. When France declared war against Germany on August 4, 1914, Barrès rejoiced. The bell had tolled for individualism. On that day, he noted in a war chronicle, quarrelsome parliamentarians spoke as one, with uncommon eloquence. It was a "sacred" day—a day on which true Frenchmen, practicing Catholics and lapsed alike, could not tell God's blessing from the warm sun. "Even if it involves the awful lessons of battle, I've wanted nothing more than for Frenchmen to unite around the great ideas of our race. So they have. Blood has not yet rained upon our nation and war has already made us [at the Assembly] feel its regenerative powers. It is a resurrection."

The army—whose prestige, Barrès and others felt, ought to have taken precedence over considerations of justice for one wretched soul—had been grievously insulted; but war would set France straight. The celebrants prophesied in chorus that a decadent nation would regain its health once released from the *horrible quotidien* of peacetime. Fire, mortal danger, and the common enemy would enforce a collective truth. At the Front, disparate elements would fuse into the "organic" society so loathsome to Kant-besotted intellectuals for whom France's honor had depended upon the exculpation of Dreyfus. Men suddenly plucked out of civilian life and thrown together in their hundred thousands would not suffer from anomie. On the contrary, the battlefield would seat them in their Frenchness. Those who fell would fall as martyrs to the cause of national rebirth.

Almost everywhere, religious fervor sounded the call to arms along with bellicose patriotism, ignoring Pope Benedict XV's determined effort to reconcile the warring parties. Church joined State in what came to be known as "the sacred union." And that union, the sacredness of which rested upon the moral certainty that France stood for civilization and Germany for barbarism, engaged men of every faith. Indeed, Jews professed their love of country as ardently as Catholics, Alfred Dreyfus himself being a conspicuous example. Retired from the army, Dreyfus, who was destined posthumously to be incriminated a second time under Vichy, volunteered for service, and in 1917 held commands in Paris and at the Front as a lieutenant colonel.

ACKNOWLEDGMENTS

For their invaluable help I wish to thank the staffs of the Paris Police Archives and of the Cabinet des Estampes of the Bibliothèque Nationale; and Donna Sammis of the Frank Melville Memorial Library at the State University of New York, Stony Brook.

I wish to thank as well *The Hudson Review* and *The New England Review* for publishing adaptations of two chapters.

For their encouragement and staunch friendship, I am deeply grateful to: Andrea Bayer, Christian Beels, Carol Blum, Paula Deitz, Paul Dolan, Stephen Donadio, Benita and Colin Eisler, Andrea Fedi, Joseph Frank, Perry Goldstein, B. Bernie Herron, Phyllis Johnson, Marlo Johnston, Jacqueline Simon, Patricia Strachan, and Brenda Wineapple.

A most generous friend and reader is Ruth Kozodoy, who gave the manuscript the benefit of her fine ear and devotion to clarity.

It is my good fortune to have the most genial of agents in Georges Borchardt and a wonderful editor in Victoria Wilson, whose faith and patience made this book possible. Her editorial assistant, Carmen Johnson, has been impeccable from first to last.

NOTES

PREFACE

xxiv "Germanic science": *Questions contemporaines,* Ernest Renan. Paris: Michel Lévy, 1868, p. V.

xxv "The qualities I love": *Mes Cahiers,* vol. XI, Maurice Barrès. Quoted by Michel Winock in *Nationalisme, antisémitisme, et fascisme en France.* Paris: Seuil, 1982, p. 105.

CHAPTER I: FROM *The Life of Jesus* TO THE SACRÉ-COEUR

3 "Study and dramatize": *Zola et son temps: Lourdes, Rome, Paris,* René Ternois. Paris: Les Belles-Lettres, 1961, p. 149.

5 "How indispensable it is": *Histoire religieuse de la France contemporaine,* Adrien Dansette. Paris: Flammarion, 1965, p. 185.

5 "All told, the clergy": Dansette, p. 189.

6 "Only two things, God and Liberty": *Histoire du Catholicisme libéral en France, 1828–1908,* Georges Weill. Paris: Félix Alcan, 1909, p. 31.

7 "[We cannot] predict": *Mirari vos,* Gregory XVI. Papal Encyclicals Online.

7 "must expect marked unpopularity": Article on Montalembert in *The Catholic Encyclopedia.*

8 "an era of civilization": Dansette, p. 263.

9 "a saint the likes": Ibid., p. 264.

9 "The principles whose triumph": *L'Église de France dans la Révolution de 1848,* Paul Christophe. Paris: Éditions du Cerf, 1998, p. 26.

9 "Christian courage": Ibid., p. 21.

9 "There are two forces": Dansette, p. 273.

10 "All my political beliefs": Ibid., p. 57.

10 "the genius of strength and order": Christophe, p. 89.

11 "For me it was like the discovery": *Recollections,* Alexis de Tocqueville. New York: Doubleday, 1970, p. 102.

12 "the barbarization": *Fin-de-Siècle Vienna,* Carl Schorske. New York: Vintage, 1981, p. 144.

12 "What now remains of those barriers": *Democracy in America,* Alexis de Tocqueville. New York: Knopf, 1963, I, p. 327.

12 "Do you not see that your doctrine": *Oeuvres complètes,* Alexis de Tocqueville. Paris: Gallimard, 1959, IX, pp. 203–04.

14 "I took the measure": *Souvenirs d'enfance et de jeunesse,* Ernest Renan. Paris: Éditions Garnier-Flammarion, 1973, p. 180.

15 "The science of the human mind": Renan, *Souvenirs,* p. 5.

16 "No one present": preface to *La Vie de Jésus,* Ernest Renan. Paris: Gallimard, Éditions Folio, 1974, p. 5 (from *Cahiers de jeunesse* in *Oeuvres complètes,* vol. 9, pp. 245ff).

16 "[Jesus] called such showy architecture": Renan, *La Vie de Jésus,* p. 136.

17 "We see him trampling": Ibid., p. 138.

17 "During the heroic ages": Ibid., p. 139.

18 "Let's accept the plain truth": Ibid., p. 533.

18 "You great imposter": *Renan d'après lui-même,* Henriette Psichari. Paris: Plon, 1937, pp. 230–31.

18 "the corruption flowing": Ibid., p. 232.

18 "Poor errant soul": Ibid., p. 237.

19 "Long live Mary": from "Le Culte des saints et le culte marial en France au XIXe siècle" by Dominique Javel, in *Mouvements religieux et culturels en France de 1800 à 1914,* ed. Christian Amalvi. Paris: Sedes, 2001, p. 119.

19 "depraved fictions": *The Papal Encyclicals,* Ed. Anne Freemantle. New York: Putnam, 1956, p. 139.

19 "the Roman Pontiff": Ibid., p. 152.

19 "At this time there are found": Ibid., p. 137.

20 "The prophecies and miracles": Ibid., p. 144.

20 "Your emperor is a deceitful": Dansette, p. 304.

21 "In his experience": *Pio Nono,* E. E. Y. Hales. London: Eyre & Spottiswoode, 1954, pp. 271–72.

21 "The history of the Church presents": Dansette, p. 322.

22 "We must no longer dream": To George Sand, July 5, 1869, in *Correspondance Flaubert/Sand,* ed. Alphonse Jacobs. Paris: Flammarion, 1981, pp. 235–36.

25 "Today a tragic session": *Choses vues: 1870–1885,* Victor Hugo. Paris: Gallimard, Éditions Folio, 1972, p. 148.

27 "Meeting follows meeting": "Chroniques et polémiques," Émile Zola, in *Oeuvres complètes,* ed. Henri Hitterand. Paris: Cercle du Livre Précieux, 1970, vol. XIII, p. 445.

27 "The communal revolution": *La Commune de 1871: Le Journal officiel avec ses décrets, affiches, et proclamations.* Paris: Éditions de Delphes, 1965, p. 159.

28 "Liturgical objects": Ibid., p. 78.

29 "We all know it": *Paris pendant les deux sièges,* Louis Veuillot. Paris: Librairies de Victor Palmé, 1871, vol. II, p. 272.

29 "[I saw] a thin column": *Oeuvres en prose complètes,* Paul Verlaine. Paris: Gallimard (Pléiade), 1972, p. 547.

31 "The cross, banished": Veuillot, vol. II, p. 450.

31 "Above the bloody scenes": *Histoire du Cardinal Pie,* Monsignor Baunard. Poitiers: H. Oudin, 1886, p. 429. See also, "The Conflict in

French Politics: Bishop Pie's Campaign Against the Nineteenth Century," Austin Gough, in *Conflicts in French Society,* ed. Theodore Zeldin. London: Allen and Unwin, 1970.

33 "the traditions of chivalric devotion": *Lourdes: Body and Spirit in the Secular Age,* Ruth Harris. London and New York: Penguin Books, 1999, p. 259.

33 "To what state of prostration": Ibid., p. 498.

33 "We go in circles": Baunard, p. 499.

34 "Long have we been oblivious": Dansette, p. 340.

35 "It was from France": *France and the Cult of the Sacred Heart,* Raymond Jonas. Berkeley: University of California Press, 2000, p. 198.

35 "a lightning-rod": Ibid., p. 217.

35 "But our committee": *L'Univers,* July 24, 1873.

37 "What I object to": *L'Univers,* July 24, 1873.

37 "A monument of provocation": in *La République anticléricale, xix–xx$_e$ siécles,* Jacqueline Lalouette. Paris: Seuil, 2002, pp. 185–86.

CHAPTER II: BIRTH PANGS OF A SECULAR REPUBLIC

39 "Only when one begins to see Humanity": Dansette, p. 363.

40 "I have brought piety down": *Le Nationalisme français: 1871–1914,* ed. Raoul Girardet. Paris: Armand Colin, 1970, pp. 187–88.

40 "Time in his forward flood": *Eumenides,* Aeschylus, Richmond Lattimore translation. Lines 852–53.

40 "What I fear": Dansette, p. 322.

41 "The Right, on hearing": Zola, *Oeuvres complètes,* vol. XIII, p. 591.

41 "Have we not seen": *La Vie politique en France,* René Rémond. Paris: Armand Colin, 1969, vol. II, p. 309.

42 "[That flag] has always": *France Under the Republic,* D. W. Brogan. New York: Harper & Brothers, 1940, p. 83.

43 "[A republic) is": *The Third Republic of France,* Guy Chapman. London: Macmillan, 1962, p. 37.

43 "Society is dying": *Journal,* Edmond de Goncourt. Paris: Fasquelle et Flammarion, 1956, vol. II, pp. 827–28.

44 "new barbarians [who] threaten": *Les Débuts de la Troisième République,* Jean-Marie Mayeur. Paris: Seuil, 1973, p. 26.

44 "With God's help": Ibid., p. 27.

44 "The return of Henri V": *Correspondance,* Ernest Renan/Marcelin Berthelot. Paris: Calmann Lévy, 1929, pp. 435–36.

46 "all the blubber": Zola, *Oeuvres complètes,* vol. XIII, p. 714.

46 "legitimate king": Mayeur, p. 30.

46 "I've just left": Dansette, p. 389.

46 "There, deep down": *La Troisième République française,* Comte de Gobineau. Strassburg: Verlag Trübner, 1907, p. 41.

47   "The president of the Republic": Brogan, pp. 109–10.
48   "Fear! That is their political means": Rémond, pp. 311–12.
49   "Opposing us is only one enemy": *L'Anticléricalisme en France*, René Rémond. Paris: Fayard, 1976, p. 177.
49   "A league, an association": Rémond, *L'Anticléricalisme*, p. 182.
50   "You know full well": *L'Enfance de la Troisième République*, Jacques Chastenet. Paris: Hachette, 1952, p. 221.
51   "*Le cléricalisme, voilà*": Rémond, *L'Anticléricalisme*, p. 185.
52   "Considering that the government": Rémond, *La Vie politique*, p. 356.
53   "For me, the idolatry": Goncourt, vol. II, p. 1199.
53   "We must": Rémond, *La Vie politique*, pp. 358–59.
53   "no imprudence": Chastenet, p. 255.
54   "I believe in the lay State": *Jules Ferry*, Jean-Michel Gaillard. Paris: Fayard, 1989, p. 181.
55   "Instruction and education": Gaillard, pp. 185–86.
55   "Bishops know perfectly well": Gaillard, p. 187.
55   "He insisted that I use": Rémond, *L'Anticléricalisme*, pp. 195–96.
56   "More than ever": *L'Univers*, September 18, 1878.
57   "You must close the book": *Histoire de la Troisième République*, ed. Jean Héritier. Paris: Librairie de France, 1932–33, vol. I, p. 113.

CHAPTER III: THE CRASH OF THE UNION GÉNÉRALE
60   "I was surrounded": Goncourt, vol. II, p. 782.
60   "Every nation [wants]": *Le Temps*, May 1, 1878.
61   "consolidating the financial strength": *Le Krach de L'Union Générale*, Jean Bouvier. Paris: PUF, 1960, pp. 22–23.
63   "Something of a promoter": Ibid., p. 9.
64   "During the thirty years": Archives de la Préfecture de Police, Ba 967 (Bontoux file).
66   "In Italy, in Germany, in Austria": Bouvier, p. 23.
67   "Laissez-faire, devised": Schorske, pp. 117–18.
68   "the drawbacks of": Bouvier, p. 96.
68   "Gathering over centuries": Ibid., p. 100.
69   "Catholics are threatened": *L'Union Générale: Sa Vie, Sa Mort, Son Programme*, Eugène Bontoux. Paris: Albert Savine, 1888, p. 244.
70   "All of Lyon": Bouvier, p. 112.
71   "I departed for Vienna": Sûreté report in Archives de la Préfecture de Police, Ba 967.
71   "maneuvers of a group": Bouvier, p. 147.
71   "plot hatched by German": Ibid., p. 147.
72   "machine for speculating": *Le Voltaire*, February 3, 1882.
73   "the practice of law": Bontoux, p. 195.

74 "laborious and intelligent": Bouvier, p. 36.

74 "if all usury is condemned": quoted in *The Gift,* Lewis Hyde. New York: Vintage, 1983, p. 130.

75 "Today, the entire might": *La France juive devant l'opinion,* Edouard Drumont. Paris: Éditions du Trident, 1987, pp. 71–72.

75 "that would cause the ruin": Ibid., p. 91.

75 "Son of our innate enemy": Ibid., pp. 76–77.

76 "That is how the Rothschilds": Ibid., p. 77.

77 "If, instead of worshipping": Ibid., p. 91.

78 "Nothing softens": Ibid., p. 94.

79 "Amidst the enormous brouhaha": Archives de la Préfecture de Police, Ba 967 ("Le Krach de l'Union Générale," pamphlet published by *La Libre parole,* p. 2).

79 "wrapping the traitor": Bontoux, p. 4.

79 "We had laid the foundation": Ibid., p. 8.

80 "Because it had emerged": Ibid., p. 16.

CHAPTER IV: FRANCE ON HORSE

82 "Everyone had something to say": Archives de la Préfecture de Police de la Seine, Ba 460.

83 "This prohibition will enter": *L'Univers,* May 30, 1878.

83 "Better late than never": *La Lanterne,* May 29, 1878.

84 "Georges has always been": *The Astonishing Adventure of General Boulanger,* James Harding. New York: Charles Scribner's Sons, 1971, p. 7.

89 "His reputation in the garrison": Ibid., p. 44.

89 "It was beautiful": Ibid., p. 53.

91 "[Boulanger's] chief attribute": *Le Général Boulanger,* Jean Garrigues. Paris: Orban, 1991, p. 35.

92 "One of my choices": *Souvenirs: 1878–1893,* Charles de Freycinet. New York: Da Capo Press, 1973, p. 329.

93 "We questioned him": Ibid., p. 349.

94 "He seemed scarcely forty": Harding, p. 67.

94 "He came here to the barracks": Ibid., p. 68.

96 "The crowd feels instinctually": *Après le Procès: Réponse à quelques "intellectuels,"* Ferdinand Brunetière. Paris: Perrin et Cie., 1898.

96 "There's something about you": Harding, p. 66.

96 "General Boulanger . . . has become": Ibid., p. 81.

96 "We have to fear": Garrigues, p. 81.

98 *"Tu seras plus qu'un roi"*: Ibid., p. 85.

98 *"The Fatherland.* To serve one's country": Girardet. p. 77.

99 "Throughout the whole": Harding, p. 118.

99   "Boulangism was the collective yearning": *Ce que mes yeux ont vu,* Arthur Meyer. Paris: Plon, 1912, p. 63.

100   *"Boulanger! La France répète"*: Harding, p. 120.

101   "The renown he craves": Gaillard, pp. 623–24.

102   "Citizens! Your presence here": *Le Boulangisme,* Adrien Dansette. Paris: Fayard, 1946, p. 92.

102   "I absolutely blame": Ibid., p. 96.

103   "For some time": Gaillard, p. 628.

105   "[Dillon] told me": Meyer, p. 71.

106   "He has all that is needed": Dansette, *Le Boulangisme,* p. 121.

107   "I had and still have": Ibid., p. 123.

108   "You are called upon": Ibid., p. 132.

109   *"Le peuple entier"*: Harding, p. 156.

109   "Today, most great soul-conquerors": *La Psychologie des foules,* Gustave le Bon. Paris: Alcan, 1895, p. 63.

110   "inexplicable vertigo": Freycinet, p. 400.

111   "sound and fury": Ibid., p. 402.

111   "These discussions for which": Dansette, *Le Boulangisme,* p. 193.

111   "At your age": Garrigues, p. 172.

113   "The important thing about popular heroes": *Rural Society and French Politics,* Michael Burns. Princeton, N.J.: Princeton University Press, 1984, p. 79.

113   "I shall never, whatever the circumstances": Dansette, *Histoire religieuse,* p. 443.

113   "might have much to gain": Ibid., p. 262.

113   "The arithmetic of our defeat": Ibid., p. 212.

114   "We are devoted": *The Boulanger Affair,* Frederic Seager. Ithaca, N.Y.: Cornell University Press, 1969, p. 159.

115   "If I had voted": *Journal,* Edmond and Jules de Goncourt. Paris: Laffont, 1989, vol. III, January 27, 1889.

116   "January 27, 1889": Freycinet, p. 419.

116   "They clearly understand": Dansette, *Le Boulangisme,* p. 265.

119   "General Boulanger didn't deceive us": Meyer, p. 97.

119   "We must reconstitute": Dansette, *Le Boulangisme,* p. 343.

120   "I didn't believe": Ibid., p. 348.

120   "The horseman fell from his mount": Meyer, p. 97.

120   "It would be a cowardly act": Dansette, *Le Boulangisme,* p. 362.

120   "My obligation": Garrigues, p. 347.

120–21   "I'm weeping": Dansette, *Le Boulangisme,* p. 362.

122   "I am convinced": Ibid., p. 365.

122   "Intelligence, what a very small thing": *La Droite révolutionnaire,* Zeev Sternhell. Paris: Editions du Seuil, 1978, p.16.

123 "One cannot understand": in *Three Against the Third Republic,* Michael Curtis. Princeton, N.J.: Princeton University Press, 1959, pp. 33–34.

CHAPTER V: THE OGRE OF MODERNITY: EIFFEL'S TOWER
126 "The general impression": Gaillard, p. 621.
128 "[My parents] worked relentlessly": *Gustave Eiffel,* Daniel Bermond. Paris: Perrin, 2002, p. 27.
128 "I particularly remember": Ibid., p. 39.
130 "I'm at the office": Ibid., p. 86.
131 "The general aspect of the bridge": Ibid., p. 102.
132 "You can't imagine": Ibid., p. 139.
133 "After having seen the desert": *Eiffel,* Michel Carmona. Paris: Fayard, 2002, p. 83.
134 "We visited the Louvre": *The Innocents Abroad,* Mark Twain. New York: New American Library, 1966, p. 100.
136 "My dear Sir": *Imperial Masquerade: The Paris of Napoleon III,* S. C. Burchell. New York: Atheneum, 1973, p. 126.
136 "The two emperors, the king of Prussia": Bermond, pp. 148–49.
137 how different kinds of iron: Ibid., p. 153.
137 "This gives us a security": Ibid., p. 157.
138 "by the erection of a stupendous column": "Harbingers of Eiffel's Tower," Frank Jenkins, in *Journal of the Society of Architectural Historians,* vol. XVI, no. 4, December 1957, p. 22.
139 "Whenever men have become skilful architects": *Lectures on Architecture and Painting,* John Ruskin. New York, 1877, p. 37.
139 "As did the descendents of Noah": Jenkins, p. 26.
139 "a new scheme rendering it possible": Bermond, p. 247.
140 "The grandiose is called for": Ibid., p. 250.
140 "this Babel of modern industry": Bermond, p. 250.
140 "Before coming together": quoted online, the official site of the Eiffel Tower, www.tour-eiffel.fr/teiffel/uk/documentation/dossiers/index .html?id=4_12, accessed May 23, 2009. See *La Tour de 300 mètres,* Gustave Eiffel. Paris: Société des Imprimeries Lemercier, 1900.
141 "The fact is": Bermond, p. 263.
144 "A thick cloud of tar and coal": quoted online, the official site of the Eiffel Tower.
146 "Not only is it visible": quoted in *The Tallest Tower,* Joseph Harriss. New York: Houghton Mifflin, 1975, p. 22.
146 "Writers, painters, sculptors": in "Les Artistes contre la Tour Eiffel," *Le Temps,* February 14, 1887, and in *1889: La Tour Eiffel et l'Exposition Universelle.* Paris: Éditions de la Réunion des Musées Nationaux, 1989, p. 28.

149   "raising edifices": Arthur Lote in *L'Univers,* April 4, 1889.
151   "Official France prey to the enemies": V. de Marolles in *L'Univers,* April 19, 1889.
151   "Things down below, heavy things": *Remarques sur l'exposition du centenaire,* Melchior de Vogüé. Paris, 1889, pp. 25–26.
152   "I am dismayed, but hardly surprised": *La Question juive,* Jacques de Biez. Paris: Marpion et Flammarion, 1886, pp. 137ff.
152   "That station would be linked": Eiffel, p. 10.
152   "Thus, everything": de Biez, pp. 137ff.
152–53   "We sons of France": *La Fin d'un monde,* Édouard Drumont. Paris: Albert Savine, 1888, p. iv.
153   "With its instinctual hatred": Ibid., p. xvi.
153   "In reality, Jews": in *La Libre parole,* November 24, 1892.

CHAPTER VI: THE PANAMA SCANDAL
156   "If you have faith": Brogan, p. 269.
157   "The Panama Canal may thus be seen": *Les Deux scandales de Panama,* Jean Bouvier. Paris: Julliard, 1964, p. 61.
158   "During his recent voyage": Ibid., p. 69.
158   "Fevers prevalent": Ibid., p. 67.
160   "The confidence that you": Bermond, p. 281.
160   "You must opt": Bouvier, *Les Deux scandales,* p. 97.
161   "There is a whole clientele": Ibid.
161   "On June 18, conditions": Ibid., p. 96.
162   "I must conclude": Ibid., p. 102.
164   "I've never witnessed": Ibid., pp. 106–107.
165   "You have lent me": Ibid., p. 129.
165   "I request": Ibid.
165   "Your friend is trying": Ibid., p. 134.
168   "When offered arms": *Leurs figures,* Maurice Barrès. Paris: Émile-Paul Frères, 1917, p. 68.
170   "Cornelius Herz received notification": Archives de le Préfecture de Police [Panama file].
171   "It seems that all": *La Libre parole,* November 26, 1892.
172   "Those people [Jews] have differently": *La Libre parole,* November 24, 1892.
173   "We are being pillaged": "Un Prototype des scandales politico-financiers: Le Krach de l'Union Générale," J. Verdès-Leroux, in *Le Mouvement social,* January–March 1969, no. 66, p. 99.
173   "Hatred of the Republic": Ibid., p. 99.
174   "To think": Goncourt, vol. III, p. 798.
174   "The three had gone unpunished": *Regards sur l'Affaire Dreyfus,* Daniel Halévy. Paris: Éditions de Fallois, 1994, p. 86.

CHAPTER VII: THE DREYFUS AFFAIR

This chapter adapted from my account of the Dreyfus Affair in Zola: A Life.

175 "I have received no word": *L'Affaire*, Jean-Denis Bredin. Paris: Julliard, 1983, p. 65.

178 "From the very first day": *Histoire de l'Affaire Dreyfus*, Joseph Reinach. Paris: Fasquelle, 1929, vol. I, pp. 308ff.

178 "They put me in the strictest": *Five Years of My Life: The Diary of Captain Alfred Dreyfus*, Alfred Dreyfus. New York: The Peebles Press, 1977, p. 42.

179 "The individual arrested": *La Libre parole*, October 29, 1894.

179 "Whereas Judas": *La Croix*, November 2, 1894.

179 "Along with his extensive knowledge": Bredin, p. 89.

180 "The Dreyfus affair sticks": *L'Affaire telle que je l'ai vécue*, Mathieu Dreyfus. Paris: Grasset, 1978, p. 35.

180 "Someone in the ministry": Bredin, p. 93.

180 "the most urgent": see Reinach, vol. I, p. 276, and *L'Affaire sans Dreyfus*, Marcel Thomas. Paris: Fayard, 1961, p. 173.

181 "there are some secrets": Reinach, vol. I, p. 417.

182 "He has no relative": Bredin, p. 100.

182 "The country sees": Ibid., p. 476.

183 "When he advanced toward us": *Scènes et doctrines du nationalisme*, Maurice Barrès. Paris: Félix Juven, 1902, p. 135.

185 "Your brother's cause": Bredin, p. 133.

185 "Lazare lost no time": Ibid., p. 135.

185 "I know some who": *Les Juifs en France à l'époque de l'Affaire Dreyfus*, Michael Marrus. Paris: Calmann-Lévy, 1972, p. 212.

186 "ageless, his body stooped": Bredin, p. 160.

188 "It may be imagined": Ibid., pp. 161–62.

188 "I could not believe": Mathieu Dreyfus, p. 83.

189 "Our circle of action": Bredin, p. 170.

190 "[He] had serious financial problems": Ibid., p. 146.

191 "keep the two cases separate": Reinach, vol. II, p. 230.

191 "In my opinion": Bredin, p. 162.

191 "What do you care": Ibid., p. 163.

191 "The minister has just told me": Ibid., pp. 173–74.

192 "I have read that an elected deputy": Ibid., p. 167.

192 "Paris, Midnight 35": Thomas, p. 378.

194 "The sole basis": Bredin, p. 200.

195 "I see it as a monstrosity": Zola, vol. XIV, p. 779.

195 "Our factual accounts": *Émile Zola: Un Intellectuel dans l'Affaire Dreyfus*, ed. Alain Pagès. Paris: Librairie Séguier, 1991, p. 57.

196 "Captain Dreyfus was condemned": Zola, vol. XIV, p. 891.

197 "We have witnessed": Ibid., p. 901.

198   "Set your mind at rest": *Journal de l'affaire Dreyfus,* Maurice Paléologue. Paris: Plon, 1955, p. 58.

199   "I have received these last days": Bredin, p. 196.

199   "who, having been informed": Ibid., p. 200.

200   "I believe that you have": Ibid.

200   "We must know whether": Ibid., p. 215.

201   "Republican blood": Zola, vol. XIV, p. 915.

203   "If circumstances have permitted me": Ibid., p. 895.

203   "I accuse Lieutenant Colonel": Ibid., pp. 930–31.

205   "noble, militant attitude": Pagès, p. 130.

205   "The syndicate—ours—": Ibid., p. 129.

205   "Masonry and Judaism": *The Popes Against the Jews,* David Kertzer. New York: Vintage Books, 2002, p. 148.

208   "At the end of the nineteenth century": *Nationalisme, antisémitisme et fascisme en France,* Michel Winock. Paris: Éditions du Seuil, 1990, p. 164.

208   "Just who is": Barrès, *Scènes et doctrines,* p. 40.

209   "who persuades himself": Ibid., p. 45.

209   "grave misdeeds": Bredin, p. 239.

210   "Buttoned tight at the waist": Reinach, vol. III, p. 368.

210   "artisans of the other affair": Bredin, p. 245; verbatim transcript of the Zola trial, Paris: Librairie du Siècle, 1898.

210   "What do you want this army": Bredin, p. 248.

211   "I will repeat": Ibid., p. 249.

211   "I will be brief": Ibid., pp. 250–51.

212   "the honor of the country": Ibid., p. 280.

212   "A court-martial has just dared": Ibid., p. 281.

212   "nothing is above the law": Pagès, p. 222.

213   "Save us; save us": Reinach, vol. IV, p. 76.

214   "In 1896 you received": Bredin, p. 304.

215   "We were not able to give you": *Maurras,* Stéphane Gioconti. Paris: Flammarion, 2008, p. 165, and in *La Gazette de France,* September 6, 1898.

216   "the Jewish race, the deicide people": Kertzer, p. 184.

216   "The Jew was created": *Les Chrétiens et l'affaire Dreyfus,* Pierre Pierrard. Paris: Les éditions de l'Atelier, 1998, p. 130.

216   "You are still upset": Dansette, *Histoire religieuse,* p. 555.

216   "Citizens, these are difficult times": *The Anti-Semitic Moment,* Pierre Birnbaum. New York: Hill and Wang, 2003, p. 60.

217   "We must equip ourselves": Dansette, *Histoire religieuse,* pp. 555–56, and Pierrard, pp. 128–29.

217   "Free thought, standing in the dock": Dansette, *Histoire religieuse,* p. 556.

217   "to stop shouting": Dansette, *Histoire religieuse,* p. 556.

217   "the living witnesses": Kertzer, p. 183.

217   "charity, tolerance": Ibid., p. 185.

218   "Drumont . . . informs us": *Journal,* Goncourt. Paris: Laffont, 1989, vol. IV, p. 22.

218   "When I took my vows": Lalouette, pp. 102–103.

219   "All along his route": Paléologue, p. 173.

219   "Today's election": Bredin, p. 346.

219   "The lecturer read": Archives de la Préfecture de Police de la Seine, Ba 460.

220   "The Court admits the new facts": *The Dreyfus Case: A Documentary History,* ed. Louis L. Snyder. New Brunswick, N.J.: Rutgers University Press, 1973, p. 256.

221   "to support only governments": Bredin, p. 359.

221   "Waldeck, lawyer to Eiffel": Ibid., p. 363.

221–22   "The succession of emotions": Alfred Dreyfus, p. 238.

222–23   "rebirth and salvation": Bredin, p. 369.

223   "The choice is clear": Ibid., p. 370.

223   "There was in everybody's eyes": Paléologue, p. 194.

224   "I recognized these pathetic phrases": Ibid., pp. 195–96.

224   "Sir Thomas Browne": Barrès, *Scènes et doctrines,* p. 144.

225   "I have not reached my age": Bredin, p. 379.

225   "That is just what you should do": Ibid., p. 379.

226   "Ah! My dear, my great": Zola, vol. XIV, p. 1526.

226   "His imperious mask": Paléologue, p. 210.

226   "With his very first words": Ibid., pp. 215–16.

227   "the current French government": Bredin, p. 385.

227   "The law does not ask jurors": Ibid., p. 393.

227   "extenuating circumstances": Ibid., p. 394.

227   "Public morality and national salvation": Barrès, *Scènes et doctrines,* pp. 208–10.

228   "The government of the Republic": Alfred Dreyfus, p. 398.

229   "[The president and official cortege]": *Le Figaro,* June 4, 1908.

229   "I appear before you": *The New York Times,* October 27, 1910 (quoted in Grégori's obituary notice).

CHAPTER VIII: THE BURNING OF THE CHARITY BAZAAR

232   "Aside from Versailles": *Rapport des comités réunis des domaines, des finances, de l'aliénation des biens nationaux,* Bertrand Barrère. Paris: Imprimerie nationale, August 6, 1790.

232   Paris en 1400.: For a study of the project, see *Consuming the Past: The Medieval Revival in Fin-de-siècle France,* Elizabeth Emery and Laura Morowitz. Burlington, Vt.: Ashgate, 2003. Newspaper articles about the fire are drawn from three files in the Archives de la Préfecture de Police,

B1313–1315 ("L'Incendie du Bazar de la Charité"). Most of the articles on Ollivier's sermon appeared on the following day, May 10, 1897. It was published in its entirety by *La Libre parole* on May 9, 1897.

241   "[One must not] close": Pierrard, p. 33.

247   "Anti-Semitism must be": Ibid., p. 55.

249   "Every sacred drop": *La Gazette de France*, September 6, 1898.

249   "We shall not allow ourselves": *La Libre parole*, September 1, 1898.

249   "When an officer is reduced": in Snyder, p. 224.

249   "[He] didn't get the funeral": *La Gazette de France*, September 6, 1898. Partly quoted in Giocanti, pp. 164–65.

250   "nations have a general": from "Des souverainetés particulières et de nations," in *Oeuvres complètes*, Joseph de Maistre. Lyons: Vitte, 1884, vol. I, p. 325, quoted in *The Defeat of the Mind*, Alain Finkielkraut. New York: Columbia University Press, 1995, p. 16.

250   "national dogmas": de Maistre, vol. I, p. 365, and Finkielkraut, p. 21.

250   "One cannot deny": *The Boulanger Affair Reconsidered*, William D. Irvine. New York: Oxford, 1989, pp. 172ff.

CHAPTER IX: TWO BANQUETS

251   "Nothing collapses more quickly": *Impressions of Theophrastus Such*, George Eliot. New York: Belford, Clarke and Co., 1886, p. 144.

251   "I thought that it might provide": *L'Avenir de la science*, Ernest Renan. Paris: Calmann Lévy, 1890, p. 3.

252   "Pessimism twists": *L'Oeuvre,* Émile Zola. Paris: Garnier-Flammarion, 1974, pp. 417–18.

252   "Even Littré": *Le Disciple,* Paul Bourget. Paris: Plon-Nourrit, 1901, p. 14.

252   "Not all that long ago": "Après une visite au Vatican," in *Questions actuelles,* Paul Bourget. Paris: Perrin, 1907, pp. 3ff.

253   "is the spirit, the certain": *Le Roman russe,* Melchior de Vogüé. Paris: Plon, 1892, p. xxvi.

254   "The answer to all questions": de Maistre, vol. I, p. 316, and Finkielkraut, p. 27.

255   "man of our times": Ibid., p. 462.

255   "How shall we defend": *Discours de combat,* Ferdinand Brunetière. Paris: Perrin, 1900, vol. I, p. 163.

256   "[Out of their writings]": *Le Temps,* April 5, 1895.

256   "One must guard against": *Vie de Berthelot,* Léon Velluz. Paris: Plon, 1964, p. 234.

256   "Ah! Little men": Zola, *Oeuvres,* vol. XIV, p. 840.

257   "Electricity was gathered": *1900,* Paul Morand. Paris: Flammarion, 1958, pp. 68ff.

258   "*L'Action française* believes": in Barrès, *Scènes et doctrines,* pp. 112ff.

259   "Flaubert used to say": Ibid., p. 114.

260   "Certain words": Barrès, *Scènes et doctrines,* p. 116.

260   "All of us here agree": Ibid., p. 118.

260   "wield the sword": Dansette, *Histoire religieuse,* p. 573.

260   "anti-Christian sects": Ibid., p. 573.

261   "the mask": Ibid., p. 573.

261   "I am French": in Pierrard, p. 47.

261   "temple of definitions": in *Le Ralliement et l'action française,* Mermeix. Paris: Fayard, 1927, p. 313.

262   "We freethinkers": in *1905, La séparation des Églises et de l'État,* ed. Yves Bruley. Paris: Perrin, 2004, pp. 113–14.

262   "the last named": *The New York Times,* September 27, 1903.

263   "The Republic of 1870": Bruley, p. 158.

263   "I was not yet": *Souvenirs politiques,* Léon Daudet. Paris: Éditions Albatros, 1974, p. 42.

264   "This noble debris": *La Grande pitié des églises de France,* in *L'Oeuvre de Maurice Barrès.* Paris: Le Club de l'Honnête Homme, 1966, vol. VIII, pp. 12ff.

265   "Even if it involves": *Chronique de la grande guerre,* Maurice Barrès. Paris: Plon, 1968, pp. 123–24.

INDEX

Page numbers in *italics* refer to illustrations and captions

A Note on the Type

The text of this book was set in Sabon, a typeface designed by Jan Tschichold (1902–1974), the well-known German typographer. Based loosely on the original designs by Claude Garamond (c. 1480–1561), Sabon is unique in that it was explicitly designed for hotmetal composition on both the Monotype and Linotype machines as well as for filmsetting. Designed in 1966 in Frankfurt, Sabon was named for the famous Lyon punch cutter Jacques Sabon, who is thought to have brought some of Garamond's matrices to Frankfurt.

Composed by North Market Street Graphics,
Lancaster, Pennsylvania
Printed and bound by Berryville Graphics,
Berryville, Virginia
Designed by Maggie Hinders